D0192240

Japanese

lonely planet

phrasebooks
and
Yoshi Abe

Japanese phrasebook
5th edition –July 2008

Published by
Lonely Planet Publications Pty Ltd ABN 36 005 607 983
90 Maribyrnong St, Footscray, Victoria 3011, Australia

Lonely Planet Offices
Australia Locked Bag 1, Footscray, Victoria 3011
USA 150 Linden St, Oakland CA 94607
UK 2nd Floor, 186 City Rd, London EC1V 2NT

Cover illustration
All that gurittās by Daniel New

ISBN 978 1 74104 231 3

text © Lonely Planet Publications Pty Ltd 2008
cover illustration © Lonely Planet Publications Pty Ltd 2008

 10 9 8 7 6 5 4 3 2

Printed through The Bookmaker International Ltd.
Printed in China

acknowledgments

Thanks to the following people for their contributions to this phrasebook:

Yoshi Abe for supplying the translations and transliterations, and for lending his expert advise on aspects of Japanese linguistics and culture. Yoshi holds a Bachelor of Arts in Anthropology and Linguistics, and a Masters Degree in Anthropology. He also has ample experience as a Japanese teacher and translator, wrote the previous edition of this phrasebook and co-authored Lonely Planet's *World Food Japan*. Yoshi would like to thank Leonie Boxtel for her practical advice as an experienced expat living in Tokyo and for her invaluable support. He also wishes to thank Annelies Mertens at Lonely Planet for her precise work and patience as an editor.

Commissioning editors Karina Coates, Rachel Williams and Karin Vidstrup Monk for getting the ball rolling and seeing the project through until the end.

Publishing managers Peter D'Onghia and Ben Handicott for supporting this edition. Project manager Fabrice Rocher for assembling and tirelessly managing the project team.

Assisting editors Francesca Coles, Piers Kelly, Branislava Vladisavljevic and Laura Crawford for their contributions.

Layout designers Jacqui Saunders, David Kemp and Katherine Marsh for lending a hand with the finishing touches.

Series designer Yukiyoshi Kamimura for the book and cover designs, and inside illustrations. Daniel New for the cover illustration.

Thanks also to cartographic designer Wayne Murphy and managing cartographer Paul Piaia for the language map, Mark Germanchis and Ben Handicott for production support and LP's print production department for getting the book to the printer.

make the most of this phrasebook ...

Anyone can speak another language! It's all about confidence. Don't worry if you can't remember your school language lessons or if you've never learnt a language before. Even if you learn the very basics (on the inside covers of this book), your travel experience will be the better for it. You have nothing to lose and everything to gain when the locals hear you making an effort.

finding things in this book

For easy navigation, this book is in sections. The Tools chapters are the ones you'll thumb through time and again. The Practical section covers basic travel situations like catching transport and finding a bed. The Social section gives you conversational phrases, pick-up lines, the ability to express opinions – so you can get to know people. Food has a section all of its own: gourmets and vegetarians are covered and local dishes feature. Safe Travel equips you with health and police phrases, just in case. Sustainable Travel, finally, completes this book. Remember the colours of each section and you'll find everything easily; or use the comprehensive Index. Otherwise, check the two-way traveller's Dictionary for the word you need.

being understood

Throughout this book you'll see coloured phrases on each page. They're phonetic guides to help you pronounce the language. Start with them to get a feel for how the language sounds. The pronunciation chapter in Tools will explain more, but you can be confident that if you read the coloured phrase, you'll be understood. As you become familiar with the spoken language, move on to using the actual text in the language which will help you perfect your pronunciation.

communication tips

Body language, ways of doing things, sense of humour – all have a role to play in every culture. 'Local talk' boxes show you common ways of saying things, or everyday language to drop into conversation. 'Listen for ...' boxes supply the phrases you may hear. They start with the phonetic guide (because you'll hear it before you know what's being said) and then lead in to the language and the English translation.

introduction 8

tools 11

practical 45

japanese

China
Russia
Sakhalin (Russia)
Sea of Okhotsk
Kuril (Russ (Disput
Sapporo
HOKKAIDŌ
North Korea
Sea of Japan (East Sea)
Morioka
HONSHŪ
J A P A N
Sendai
South Korea
Nikkō
Nagano
☆**Tokyo**
Yokohama
Korea Strait
Hiroshima
Kōbe
Kyoto
Nagoya
SHIKOKU
Ōsaka
Kōchi
PACIFIC OCEAN
Kitakyūshū
Fukuoka
Nagasaki
KYŪSHŪ
East China Sea
Yakushima
see inset
Philippine Sea
Kagoshima-Ken (Japan)
0   200 k
0   100 mi

KYŪSHŪ
China
Yakushima
Okinawa
Naha
Nansei-Shotō Is. (Japan)
Taiwan

■ official/national language
▨ Ryūkyūan dialects

Japan
China
PACIFIC OCEAN
Philippines

Japanese – or ni·hon·go（日本語）– is spoken by over 125 million people. While it bears some resemblance to Altaic languages such as Mongolian and Turkish and shows strong grammatical similarities to Korean, linguistic researchers have not been able to prove its origins. Despite this absence of a clear link to related languages, there are noticeable influences from nonrelated languages. Chinese is not only responsible for the existence of many Sino-Japanese words in Japanese, but also for the use of the originally Chinese kanji writing characters which the Japanese use in combination with the indigenous hiragana and katakana scripts. Trade with several European countries from the 16th until the 19th century has led to the inclusion of some Portuguese and Dutch loanwords and since the end of WWII many loanwords have come from English.

Other languages spoken in Japan include Ainu and Ryūkyūan. Ainu is unrelated to Japanese, and was once spoken in northern Honshū and the islands of Hokkaidō and Sakhalin. Today it is sadly on its way to extinction. The Ryūkyūan language varieties are also quite different from but still

---

at a glance ...

language name: Japanese

name in language:
ni·hon·go（日本語）

language family:
unconfirmed

approximate number of speakers:
125 million

close relatives:
Ryūkyūan,
Korean (arguably)

donations to English:
aikido, bento box, bonzai, futon, geisha, harikiri, ikebana, judo, jujitsu, kamikaze, karaoke, karate, kendo, kimono, ninja, origami, sake, sashimi, sumo, sushi, tatami, tsunami, wasabi, yakuza

related to Japanese – some consider them to be dialects of Japanese. They are spoken by the older generations in Okinawa, but no longer by the younger people in this region.

The Japanese dialects spoken on the main islands can be roughly grouped as eastern and western dialects and, with Ryūkyūan, complete the picture of Japan's three groups of dialects. These dialects generally do not hinder communication throughout Japan – the language spoken in Tokyo serves as the lingua franca and is used in broadcasting and education. It's also the language used in this phrasebook, so you should have few problems making yourself understood just about anywhere in Japan.

Despite appearances, it's not that hard to get a basic grip on the language. Japanese pronunciation is fairly easy to master for English speakers – unlike some languages in the Asian region it does not have tones – and the grammar is fairly simple. Japanese uses an array of registers of speech to reflect social and contextual hierarchy, but these can be simplified to the form most appropriate for a wide range of social situations – which is exactly what we've done in this phrasebook. As it may take a long time to master written Japanese, this phrasebook focuses on the spoken language, although we've added the script everywhere alongside the pronunciation so you can use it to point out phrases.

We're confident that this phrasebook will be useful in Japan. It contains all the key words and phrases you'll need to get by, plus all the social lingo to open up a world of possibilities for social interaction and cultural exchange with the locals. By taking the time to acquaint yourself with Japan's language you'll also be accessing a vital part of a rich and ancient culture and a modern dynamic society. Your efforts to speak Japanese, no matter how modest, will guarantee you a warm welcome by the locals.

abbreviations used in this book

a	adjective	m	masculine	pol	polite
f	feminine	n	noun	sg	singular
lit	literal translation	pl	plural	v	verb

Japanese pronunciation is not considered difficult for English speakers. Unlike some other Asian languages, it has no tones and most of its sounds are also found in English.

vowel sounds

Vowels in Japanese can be either short or long. The long ones should be held twice as long as the short ones and are represented in our pronunciation guides with a horizontal line on top of them.

symbol	English	Japanese example
a	run	na·ka
ā	father	sak·kā
e	red	sa·ke
ē	reign	pē·ji
i	bit	ni·ji
ī	bee	shī·tsu
o	pot	mot·to
ō	paw	pas·pō·to
u	put	mu·ra
ū	moon	kū·ki

It's important to make the distinction between short and long vowels as vowel length can change the meaning of a word, as in these examples:

彼	ka·re	he
カレー	ka·rē	curry
おじさん	o·ji·san	uncle
おじいさん	o·jī·san	grandfather

All vowels in the table on the previous page are 'pure' meaning they're pronounced individually – they do not tend to run together to form vowel sound combinations (diphthongs). Pronounce them clearly and slowly to make yourself understood: eg, i·e (家), 'house' and ī·e (いいえ), 'no'.

There are a few vowel sound combinations, however, that roughly correspond to diphthongs in English:

symbol	English	Japanese example
ai	**ai**sle	d**ai**·ga·ku
air	p**air**	**air**·kon
ow	c**ow**	t**ow**·ru
oy	t**oy**	k**oy**

The vowel u is sometimes not pronounced in Japanese. This so-called 'reduced' vowel most often occurs between k and s and in verb endings like des (です) and ·mas (ます). As it's a silent vowel, we haven't included it in the coloured pronunciation guides.

consonant sounds

As the next table shows, most consonant sounds are pretty close to their English counterparts.

To make yourself understood clearly, it's important, however, to make the distinction between single and double consonants as this can produce a difference in meaning:

坂	sa·ka	slope
作家	sak·ka	writer
過去	ka·ko	past
かっこ	kak·ko	brackets

Pronounce the double consonants with a slight pause between them.

symbol	English	Japanese example
b	**b**ig	**b**a·sho
ch	**ch**ili	**ch**i·zu
d	**d**in	**d**ai·ga·ku
f	**f**un (almost like 'fw' with the lips in a rounded position, especially before 'u')	**f**u·ro
g	**g**o (always a hard sound as in 'go')	**g**ai·jin
h	**h**it	**h**i·to
j	**j**am	**j**ū·su
k	**k**ick	**k**an·ji
m	**m**an	**m**u·su·me
n	**n**o	**n**o·ri
p	**p**ig	**p**an·tsu
r	**r**un (halfway between 'l' and 'r')	**r**en·ji
s	**s**o	**s**a·ba·ku
sh	**sh**ow	**sh**i·ma
t	**t**in	**t**a·bi
ts	hi**ts**	**ts**u·na·mi
w	**w**in	**w**a·sa·bi
y	**y**es	**y**u·ki
z	is/**z**oo	**z**a·ru

word stress

Syllables are pronounced fairly evenly in Japanese, so there's no need to indicate stressed syllables.

reading & writing Japanese

Written Japanese is actually a combination of three different scripts. The first, kanji, consists of ideographic characters. The other two, hiragana and katakana, are 'syllabic' scripts – each character represents a syllable.

kanji

Kanji are ideographs (symbols that each represent a concept, idea or thing as well as pronunciation, rather than a word or set of words) borrowed from Chinese, eg 本 (hon) for 'book', 娘 (mu·su·me) for 'daughter' and 日本語 (ni·hon·go) for 'Japanese language'. Each kanji may be made up of anything from one to over 20 brush strokes written in a particular order. Some kanji characters have two or more ways of being pronounced depending on the context. Eg, the kanji 水 is pronounced mi·zu when it means 'water', but su·i when it's part of another word like 水筒 (pronounced su·i·tō) for 'water bottle'.

There are over 2000 kanji in use in modern Japanese, of which 1945 are considered essential for everyday use. Of these, the Ministry of Education has designated 1006 characters as basic – these are taught at primary school level.

hiragana

Hiragana is used to represent particles and grammatical endings particular to Japanese and are placed alongside the ideographic characters – one single Japanese word can contain both scripts. There are 46 basic hiragana characters each representing a particular syllable. They can be combined to represent over 100 different syllables (see the table on page 16).

Where's the market?
市場はどこですか?　　　　　i·chi·ba wa do·ko des ka

Note that in the phrase above the word for 'market' (i·chi·ba) is written in kanji (市場), but the rest (the particle wa (は), the question word do·ko (どこ), the verb des (です) and the interrogative particle ka (か)) in hiragana.

katakana

Each hiragana character also has a katakana equivalent (see the table on page 16). Katakana are used to represent recent borrowings from other languages, especially English. They're also used to write foreign names – you might want to figure out how to write your own name in Japanese.

credit card
クレジットカード　　　　　ku·re·jit·to·kā·do
My name is Anthony.
私の名前は　　　　　　　　wa·ta·shi no na·ma·e wa
アンソニーです。　　　　　an·so·ī des
I'm from Australia.
オーストラリアから来ました。ō·sto·ra·rya ka·ra ki·mash·ta

Note that the Japanese words for 'credit card', 'Anthony' and 'Australia' are all written in katakana.

The tables on the next page show the basic as well as some of the combined hiragana and katakana characters. For each syllable you'll find the pronunciation (in **red**) with its hiragana symbol above and katakana symbol below it.

hiragana & katakana script table

あ **a** ア	い **i** イ	う **u** ウ	え **e** エ	お **o** オ									
か **ka** カ	き **ki** キ	く **ku** ク	け **ke** ケ	こ **ko** コ	きゃ **kya** キャ	きゅ **kyu** キュ	きょ **kyo** キョ	が **ga** ガ	ぎ **gi** ギ	ぐ **gu** グ	げ **ge** ゲ	ご **go** ゴ
さ **sa** サ	し **shi** シ	す **su** ス	せ **se** セ	そ **so** ソ	しゃ **sha** シャ	しゅ **shu** シュ	しょ **sho** ショ	ざ **za** ザ	じ **ji** ジ	ず **zu** ズ	ぜ **ze** ゼ	ぞ **zo** ゾ
た **ta** タ	ち **chi** チ	つ **tsu** ツ	て **te** テ	と **to** ト	ちゃ **cha** チャ	ちゅ **chu** チュ	ちょ **cho** チョ	だ **da** ダ	ぢ **ji** ヂ	づ **zu** ヅ	で **de** デ	ど **do** ド
な **na** ナ	に **ni** ニ	ぬ **nu** ヌ	ね **ne** ネ	の **no** ノ	にゃ **nya** ニャ	にゅ **nyu** ニュ	にょ **nyo** ニョ					
は **ha** ハ	ひ **hi** ヒ	ふ **fu** フ	へ **he** ヘ	ほ **ho** ホ	ひゃ **hya** ヒャ	ひゅ **hyu** ヒュ	ひょ **hyo** ヒョ	ば **ba** バ	び **bi** ビ	ぶ **bu** ブ	べ **be** ベ	ぼ **bo** ボ
ま **ma** マ	み **mi** ミ	む **mu** ム	め **me** メ	も **mo** モ	みゃ **mya** ミャ	みゅ **myu** ミュ	みょ **myo** ミョ	ぱ **pa** パ	ぴ **pi** ピ	ぷ **pu** プ	ぺ **pe** ペ	ぽ **po** ポ
や **ya** ヤ		ゆ **yu** ユ		よ **yo** ヨ								
ら **ra** ラ	り **ri** リ	る **ru** ル	れ **re** レ	ろ **ro** ロ	りゃ **rya** リャ	りゅ **ryu** リュ	りょ **ryo** リョ					
わ **wa** ワ				を **o** ヲ	ぎゃ **gya** ギャ	ぎゅ **gyu** ギュ	ぎょ **gyo** ギョ	びゃ **bya** ビャ	びゅ **byu** ビュ	びょ **byo** ビョ		
ん **n** ン					じゃ **ja** ジャ	じゅ **ju** ジュ	じょ **jo** ジョ	ぴゃ **pya** ピャ	ぴゅ **pyu** ピュ	ぴょ **pyo** ピョ		

This chapter will help you make your own sentences. It's arranged alphabetically for ease of navigation. If you can't find the exact phrase in this book, remember that with just a little grammar, a few gestures, a couple of well-chosen words, you'll generally get the message across.

Note that we have added literal translations to every phrase to clarify Japanese sentence structures. The use of particles in Japanese – shown in red in the literal translations – has been explained in **particles** and **prepositions**.

a/an

Japanese does not have words equivalent to the English indefinite and definite articles 'a/an' and 'the':

It's a/the hotel.
　ho·te·ru des　　　　　　　　ホテルです。
　(lit: hotel is)

Words are used without articles and context will tell you whether 'a' or 'the' is meant. If you do want to point out a specific item (indicated by 'the' in English), you can use a demonstrative (see **this & that**).

adjectives & adverbs see describing things

articles see a/an

be

The word des (です) roughly corresponds to the English verb 'be' and like any verb in Japanese, it doesn't change according to who or what it refers to; des can mean 'I am' or 'she is' or 'we are' etc depending on the situation – there's one form only for all subjects. Japanese verbs do change their form however when they're expressing the past tense and/or negative. The table below shows how des changes in these cases:

present positive		present negative	
です	des	じゃありません	ja a·ri·ma·sen
past positive		**past negative**	
でした	desh·ta	じゃありませんでした	ja a·ri·ma·sen desh·ta

I'm Australian.
> wa·ta·shi wa ō·sto·ra·rya·jin des
> (lit: I wa Australian is)

私はオーストラリア人です。

I'm not a medical doctor.
> wa·ta·shi wa i·sha ja a·ri·ma·sen
> (lit: I wa doctor is-not)

私は医者じゃありません。

It was rainy yesterday.
> ki·nō wa a·me desh·ta
> (lit: yesterday wa rain was)

きのうは雨でした。

The person I met last night was not Mr Takagi.
> yū·be at·ta hi·to wa ta·ka·gi·san ja a·ri·ma·sen desh·ta
> (lit: yesterday met person wa Tagaki-Mister not-was)

ゆうべ会った人は高木さんじゃありませんでした。

Note that you drop the particle of the word that immediately precedes a form of the verb des (see **particles**).

counting things

For information on numbers and counters (or 'classifiers' as they're also called) see **numbers & amounts**, page 37.

describing things

As in English, adjectives come before the noun they describe. There are two types of adjectives: 'i adjectives' that end in a vowel or ·i (い) and 'na adjectives' that end in na (な).

We had a nice meal.
oy·shī sho·ku·ji o shi·mash·ta   おいしい食事をしました。
(lit: nice meal o did)

That is a beautiful building.
a·re wa ki·rē na ta·te·mo·no des あれはきれいな建物です。
(lit: that-over-there wa beautiful building is)

Adverbs, which describe a verb or an adjective, can be formed by replacing the ·i (い) ending of 'i adjectives' with the ending ·ku (く). The adjective ha·yai (速い), for example, becomes the adverb ha·ya·ku (速く).
   Many adverbs in Japanese, however, exist as a word in their own right. For example, to·te·mo (とても) 'very', yuk·ku·ri (ゆっくり) 'slowly' and kyō (今日) 'today', to name a few.

future

Future tense is expressed by using the same forms as for the present tense – in Japanese it's most often understood from context that the future is concerned. If you'd like to make it crystal clear that you're talking about the future, you can also use a word or expression of time such as a·shi·ta (明日) 'tomorrow', rai·ge·tsu (来月) 'next month' or su·gi ni (すぐに) 'soon' in your sentence.

have

Possession can be shown in various ways in Japanese. The easiest way is to use the possessive particle no (の) after the noun, pronoun or proper noun that indicates who or what possesses something:

my friend
wa·ta·shi no to·mo·da·chi   私の友達
(lit: I no friend)

It's hers.
ko·re wa ka·no·jo no des   これは彼女のです。
(lit: this wa she no is)

Takashi's hotel
ta·ka·shi no ho·te·ru   たかしのホテル
(lit: Takashi no hotel)

An alternative way of expressing possession is to use the verb mot·te i·mas (持っています) 'have', or the expression ga a·ri·mas (があります) 'there is something to me':

I have money.
(wa·ta·shi wa) o·ka·ne o   (私は)お金を
mot·te i·mas   持っています。
(lit: (I wa) honourable-money o have)

I have a car.
(wa·ta·shi wa) ji·dō·sha   (私は)自動車
ga a·ri·mas   があります。
(lit: (I wa) car there-is)

more than one

Japanese nouns are the same whether they refer to one or more persons, objects, places or concepts. If you want to count or express a particular number of items you'll have to add a classifier (also called counter) to the noun.

For more details, see **nouns** and **numbers & amounts**, page 37.

TOOLS

20

my & your

To indicate possession, use a pronoun (see **pronouns**), noun or proper noun followed by the particle no (の):

This is my book.
ko·re wa wa·ta·shi no hon des   これは私の本です。
(lit: this wa I no book is)

Mr Kamimura's suitcase
ka·mi·mu·ra·san no sūts·kēs   上村さんのスーツケース
(lit: Kamimura-Mister no suitcase)

schoolteacher
gak·kō no sen·sē   学校の先生
(lit: school no teacher)

Also see **have** and **particles**.

negative

To make a verb in the present tense negative, replace the ending ·mas (ます) with ·ma·sen (ません):

I smoke.
ta·ba·ko o su·i·mas   タバコを吸います。
(lit: cigarette o inhale)

I don't smoke.
ta·ba·ko o su·i·ma·sen   タバコを吸いません。
(lit: cigarette o inhale-not)

To make a verb in the past tense negative, replace ·mash·ta (ました) with ·ma·sen desh·ta (ませんでした):

I came by train.
den·sha de ki·mash·ta   電車で来ました。
(lit: train by did-come)

I did not come by train.
den·sha de ki·ma·sen desh·ta   電車で来ませんでした。
(lit: train by come did-not)

In Japanese, adjectives also have a negative form. For 'i adjectives' replace the ending ·i (い) with ·ku (く) and negate them by adding a·ri·ma·sen (ありません) or nai des (ないです):

新しい	a·ta·ra·shī	new	新しく	a·ta·ra·shi·ku	ku-form of 'new'
古い	fu·ru·i	old	古く	fu·ru·ku	ku-form of 'old'

For 'na adjectives', keep only the stems of the word (ie drop the ending na (な)), then negate them by adding ja a·ri·ma·sen (じゃありません) or ja nai des (じゃないです):

きれいな	ki·rē na	clean/beautiful	きれい	ki·rē	stem of 'clean/beautiful'
簡単な	kan·tan na	easy	簡単	kan·tan	stem of 'easy'

nouns

Japanese nouns have no gender (masculine or feminine) or plural forms: you always use the same form of the noun whether you're referring to a masculine or feminine person, object, place or concept, and whether it's singular or plural.

box/boxes	ha·ko	箱
person/people	hi·to	人
ticket/tickets	kip·pu	切符

Make sure you always use a particle after the nouns when using them in a phrase (see **particles**).

particles

A Japanese noun or pronoun is almost always followed by a particle. Particles are short words that display the function of the preceding word in the sentence. They show, for example, whether the preceding word is the subject (who or what is doing something) or the object (the person or thing that's affected by the action expressed by the verb) of the sentence. Sometimes particles act as prepositions, eg like the English 'to' or 'in'. You'll often come across the following particles in Japanese:

ga (が) **subject particle**
The particle ga (が) indicates the subject of the sentence when this is not omitted from the sentence as often happens in Japanese:

This is my address.
　ko·re ga wa·ta·shi no jū·sho des　これが私の住所です。
　(lit: this ga I no address is)

wa (は) **topic particle**
The particle wa (は) marks the topic or the focal point of the sentence. It's often used when clarifying or stressing a particular point.

I'm a teacher.
　wa·ta·shi wa kyō·shi des　　　私は教師です。
　(lit: I wa teacher is)

When the subject of the sentence is stressed or contrasted, it's also the topic of the sentence, in which case the form ga will appear.

o (を) **object particle**
The particle o (を) marks the object of the sentence.

I ate sushi.
　su·shi o ta·be·mash·ta　　　　すしを食べました。
　(lit: sushi o eat-did)

no (の) **possessive particle**
The particle no (の) shows that something belongs to someone/something (also see **have**):

Miyuki's house
mi·yu·ki·san no i·e みゆきさんの家
(lit: Miyuki-Miss no house)

ni (に) particle

The particle ni (に) can be used in four different ways:

day/month/year	on Monday	月曜日に	ge·tsu·yō·bi ni
time	at five o'clock	5時に	go·ji ni
location	in the shop	店に	mi·se ni
destination	to the station	駅に	e·ki ni

e (へ) particle (direction)

The particle e (へ) indicates direction and is very similar to the destination function of ni (see above).

I'm going to Ginza.
gin·za e i·ki·mas 銀座へ行きます。
(lit: Ginza e go)

de (で) particle

The de (で) particle indicates location – it has a similar function as the location function of ni (に). It can also express the means of doing something:

at the entrance
i·ri·gu·chi de 入口で
(lit: entrance de)

I'm going by train.
den·sha de i·ki·mas 電車で行きます。
(lit: train de go)

ka (か) interrogative particle

The particle ka (か) is added to the end of a statement to turn this into a question. Also see **questions**.

I speak English.
ē·go ga ha·na·se·mas 英語が話せます。
(lit: English ga speak)

Do you speak English?
ē·go ga ha·na·se·mas ka 英語が話せますか?
(lit: English ga speak ka)

past

There are only two basic tenses in Japanese: present tense, which is also used to express the future, and past tense. To form the past tense, simply replace the ending ·mas (します) (ie the polite verb ending used in this phrasebook) with the ending ·mash·ta (しました).

I study at university.
dai·ga·ku de ben·kyō shi·mas   大学で勉強します。
(lit: university de study do)

I've studied marketing.
mā·ke·tin·gu o   マーケティングを
ben·kyō shi·mash·ta   勉強しました。
(lit: marketing o study did)

As with the present tense, Japanese verbs in the past tense don't change according to the subject (ie whether the subject is I, you, he/she/it, we, you (pl) or they).

planning ahead see future

plural see more than one

polite forms

Japanese shows different forms of formality by choosing particular words and often changing the forms of the verbs. This phrasebook uses standard polite ·mas (ます) forms which will be suitable for most situations you encounter. To keep this safe middle ground, also avoid the use of second person pronouns, as they might sound too direct (see **pronouns**). You'll also notice that the Japanese often add the prefixes o· (お) and go· (ご) to certain nouns to indicate politeness or reverence:

sake   o·sa·ke   お酒
rice/meal   go·han   ごはん
I'll introduce you. go·shō·kai shi·mas ご紹介します。
                    (lit: honourable-introduction do)

Sometimes these prefixes mean 'your honourable ...'. Only use these when talking about or to others, never when talking about yourself or your situation.

your husband	go·shu·jin	ご主人
	(lit: your-honourable-husband)	
my husband	shu·jin	主人
	(lit: husband)	
How are you?	o·gen·ki des ka	お元気ですか?
	(lit: your-honourable-healthy is ka)	
I'm fine.	gen·ki des	元気です。
	(lit: healthy is)	

possession see have and my & your

prepositions

English prepositions are often rendered by particles such as ni (に), e (へ) and de (で) in Japanese. Also see **particles**.

above	上に	u·e ni	in (time)	なか	na·ka
across	横切って	yo·ko·git·te	in front of	前	ma·e
after	あと	a·to	near	近く	chi·ka·ku
at (time)	に	ni	on	となり	u·e ni
at (place)	で	de	over	むこうに	mu·kō ni
before (time)	前	ma·e	through	上に	tōt·te
during	あいだ	ai·da	to	へ	e
for	ため	ta·me	under	下に	shi·ta ni
from	から	ka·ra	with	いっしょに	is·sho ni
in (place)	に	ni	without	なしで	na·shi de

pronouns

Subject pronouns are often omitted in Japanese when the person is obvious from context. Japanese pronouns vary based on the level of formality – in this phrasebook we have used an appropriate pronoun for each phrase.

I/me	(polite)	私	wa·ta·shi
	(formal)	わたくし	wa·tak·shi
	(used by men only)	僕/おれ	bo·ku/o·re
you sg	(polite)	あなた	a·na·ta
	(used by men to subordinates)	きみ	ki·mi
she/her		彼女	ka·no·jo
he/him		彼	ka·re
we/us		私たち	wa·ta·shi ta·chi
you pl		あなたたち	a·na·ta ta·chi
they/them	m	彼ら	ka·re ra
	f	彼女たち	ka·no·jo ta·chi

Note that there are no different pronouns for subjects (eg I, she), objects (eg me, her) and possessives (eg my, her). The difference between these is indicated by the particle that follows the pronouns in the sentence: wa (は) for the topic, ga (が) for the subject, o (を) for the object and no (の) for the possessive (for more details see **particles**):

I saw her.
wa·ta·shi ga ka·no·jo o
mi·mash·ta
(lit: I ga she o see-did)

私が彼女を見ました。

She saw me.
ka·no·jo ga wa·ta·shi o
mi·mash·ta
(lit: she ga I o see-did)

彼女が私を見ました。

It's hers.
so·re wa ka·no·jo no des
(lit: that wa she no is)

それは彼女のです。

Note that often it's better to avoid using second person pronouns altogether, as this might seem to direct.

questions

To ask a yes/no question, just add ka (か) to the end of a statement and raise your intonation towards the end of the sentence as you would in English.

This is the tourist office.
ko·re wa kan·kō·an·nai·jo des これは観光案内所です。
(lit: this wa tourist-office is)

Is this the tourist office?
ko·re wa kan·kō·an·nai·jo des ka これは観光案内所ですか?
(lit: this wa tourist-office is ka)

To ask more specific questions, you can use the Japanese equivalents of 'who', 'where', 'what', 'how', 'why' etc. Note that often they tend to come towards the end of the sentence (see **question words**).

question words

who	だれ/どなた	da·re/do·na·ta pol
Who is it?	だれですか?	da·re des ka
what	何/なに	nan/na·ni
What is this? What are you doing?	これは何ですか? なにをしますか?	ko·re wa nan des ka na·ni o shi·mas ka
which	どちら	do·chi·ra
Which train goes to Ginza?	どちらの 電車が銀座 に行きますか?	do·chi·ra no den·sha ga gin·za ni i·ki·mas ka
when	いつ	i·tsu
When's the next bus?	次のバスは いつですか?	tsu·gi no bas wa i·tsu des ka

at what time	何時に	nan·ji ni
At what time does the boat leave?	船は何時に出ますか?	fu·ne wa nan·ji ni de·mas ka
where	どこ	do·ko
Where are the toilets?	トイレはどこですか?	toy·re wa do·ko des ka
how	どのように	do·no yō ni
How does this work?	どのようにしますか?	do·no yō ni shi·mas ka
how much/how many	どのくらい/いくつ	do·no·ku·rai/i·ku·tsu
How much do you want?	どのくらいほしいですか?	do·no·ku·rai ho·shī des ka
How many are there?	いくつありますか?	i·ku·tsu a·ri·mas ka
how much (money)	いくら	i·ku·ra
How much does it cost?	いくらですか?	i·ku·ra des ka
why	なぜ	na·ze
Why (is that so)?	なぜですか?	na·ze des ka

the see a/an

there is/are

There are two ways of expressing that something exists in Japanese. For animate objects (people and animals) the verb i·mas (います) is used. For inanimate objects (things) a·ri·mas (あります) is used.

There are many good restaurants in Tokyo.

tō·kyō ni wa ī res·to·ran   東京にはいいレストラン
ga ta·ku·san a·ri·mas   がたくさんあります。
(lit: Tokyo in wa good restaurant ga many there-are-*inanimate*)

There are four dogs in the garden.

ni·wa ni i·nu ga yon·hi·ki i·mas   庭に犬が4匹います。
(lit: garden in dog ga four there-are-*animate*)

this & that

To refer to or point out a person or object, use one of the words in the table below. Note that the element ko· (こ) refers to someone or something close to the speaker, so· (そ) to someone or something close to the listener and a· (あ) to something far from both the speaker and listener.

near speaker		near listener		far from both	
this	ko·re これ	that	so·re それ	that over there	a·re あれ
this (book)	ko·no (hon) この (本)	that (book)	so·no (hon) その (本)	that (book) over there	a·no (hon) あの (本)
here	ko·ko ここ	there	so·ko そこ	over there	a·so·ko あそこ
this way	ko·chi·ra こちら	that way	so·chi·ra そちら	that way over there	a·chi·ra あちら

How much does this cost?
   ko·re wa i·ku·ra des ka   これはいくらですか?
   (lit: this wa how-much is question)
That train is full.
   so·no den·sha wa man·in des   その電車は満員です。
   (lit: that train wa full is)

verbs

Verbs are pretty straightforward in Japanese. First of all, they don't change according to the person. The form shi·mas (します) can mean 'I do', 'you do', 'they do' etc. Secondly, Japanese only has two basic tenses, present and past. The present tense is also used to express the future (see **future**).
   In Japanese dictionaries, verbs will usually be listed in their 'plain form'. This form is not appropriate for most conversations though. In this phrasebook, we have chosen the polite ·mas (ます) form for most phrases, and for ease of use we have also listed the verbs in the dictionary in the ·mas (ます) form.

	·mas form		plain form	
eat	ta·be·mas	食べます	ta·be·ru	食べる
drink	no·mi·mas	飲みます	no·mu	飲む
do	shi·mas	します	su·ru	する
buy	kai·mas	買います	kau	買う
come	ki·mas	来ます	ku·ru	来る
go	i·ki·mas	行きます	i·ku	行く

There are some contexts, however, in which the verb forms change. This is the case, for example, in negative phrases (for more details on this, see **negatives**), when making a request, or when using the verbs with other verbs such as 'can' and 'must'. These more complex cases have not been included in this phrasebuilder, however, as you can make yourself easily understood without knowing the ins and outs of these constructions.

Remember that the verb goes at the end of the sentence.

word order

Unlike English where word order is typically subject–verb–object the order of a Japanese sentence is typically subject–object–verb. The subject is often omitted from the sentence if it's clear from context.

I bought a ticket to Hiroshima.
(wa·ta·shi wa) hi·ro·shi·ma ma·de　(私は)広島までの
no chi·ket·to o kai·mash·ta　　　チケットを買いました。
(lit: (I wa) Hiroshima to no ticket o bought)

When building Japanese phrases it's important to keep each particle (see **particles**) straight after the word it belongs to – no other element should come between a word and its particle. These 'building blocks' – ie words and their particles – can be moved around in a sentence, as long as the basic subject–object–verb order is respected and the verb goes at the end of the sentence. Compare the phrases on the next page in which the building blocks have been underlined.

I write a postcard in Japanese.
   (wa·ta·shi wa) ni·hon·go de ha·ga·ki o ka·ki·mas
   (私は) 日本語ではがきを書きます。
   (lit: (I wa) Japanese de postcard o write)
   (wa·ta·shi wa) ha·ga·ki o ni·hon·go de ka·ki·mas
   (私は) はがきを日本語で書きます。
   (lit: (I wa) postcard o Japanese de write)

yes/no

yes	hai	はい
no	ī·e	いいえ

Do you understand?
   wa·ka·ri·mash·ta ka   わかりましたか?
   (lit: understand-did ka)
Yes, I do (understand).
   hai wa·ka·ri·mash·ta   はい、わかりました。
   (lit: yes understand did)
No, I don't (understand).
   ī·e wa·ka·ri·ma·sen   いいえ、わかりません。
   (lit: no understand-did-not)

Note that the complete verb is often repeated after 'yes' or 'no' in Japanese.

yes/no questions see questions

language difficulties
言葉の問題

Do you speak English?
英語が話せますか？　　　　　　ē·go ga ha·na·se·mas ka

Does anyone speak English?
どなたか英語を　　　　　　　　do·na·ta ka ē·go o
話せますか？　　　　　　　　　ha·na·se·mas ka

Do you understand?
わかりましたか？　　　　　　　wa·ka·ri·mash·ta ka

Yes, I do understand.
はい、わかりました。　　　　　hai wa·ka·ri·mash·ta

No, I don't understand.
いいえ、わかりません。　　　　ī·e wa·ka·ri·ma·sen

I understand.
わかりました。　　　　　　　　wa·ka·ri·mash·ta

I don't understand.
わかりません。　　　　　　　　wa·ka·ri·ma·sen

I speak (English).
（英語）が話せます。　　　　　（ē·go) ga ha·na·se·mas

I don't speak (Japanese).
（日本語）が　　　　　　　　　(ni·hon·go) ga
話せません。　　　　　　　　　ha·na·se·ma·sen

I speak a little.
少し話せます。　　　　　　　　su·ko·shi ha·na·se·mas

How do you pronounce this?
これはどう発音しますか。　　　ko·re wa dō ha·tsu·on shi·mas ka

How do you write 'shiatsu'?
「指圧」はどう書きますか？　　shi·a·tsu wa dō ka·ki·mas ka

What does 'deguchi' mean?
「出口」はどういう意味　　　　de·gu·chi wa dō yū i·mi
ですか？　　　　　　　　　　　des ka

Could you please …?	…くれませんか？	… ku·re·ma·sen ka
repeat that	繰り返して	ku·ri·ka·e·shi·te
speak more slowly	もっとゆっくり	mot·to yuk·ku·ri
	話して	ha·na·shi·te
write it down	書いて	kai·te

haiku

Haiku hai·ku（俳句）is a unique form of Japanese poetry. Each haiku consists of 17 syllables grouped in three verses of which two contain five syllables and one seven syllables. There are many rules that govern the form and content of haiku which aspiring haiku-poets, once they master the basic techniques, can use to create their own unique style.

Basho Matsuo (1644–94) – or ma·tsu·o ba·shō（松雄芭蕉）as his name is written in his own language – is commonly considered one of the greatest haiku-poets ever and crucial in the development of this art form. His work explores the beauties of nature and is heavily influenced by Zen Buddhism. His *Narrow Road to the Deep North* o·ku no ho·so·mi·chi（奥の細道）, which was inspired by a five-month journey to the north of the country, is still compulsory reading for most high school students in Japan.

Here's just one of the many haiku written by Basho – the interpretations, as well as the way of translating them into English, abound:

さみだれに	in the seasonal rain
sa·mi·da·re ni	
つるのあし	a crane's legs
tsu·ru no a·shi	
みじかくなれり	have become short
mi·ji·ka·ku na·re·ri	

cardinal numbers

基本数字

The numbers 4, 7 and 9 – and all other numbers containing these numbers – have alternative pronunciations which are completely interchangeable.

1	一	i·chi
2	二	ni
3	三	san
4	四	shi/yon
5	五	go
6	六	ro·ku
7	七	shi·chi/na·na
8	八	ha·chi
9	九	ku/kyū
10	十	jū
11	十一	jū·i·chi
12	十二	jū·ni
13	十三	jū·san
14	十四	jū·shi/jū·yon
15	十五	jū·go
16	十六	jū·ro·ku
17	十七	jū·shi·chi/jū·na·na
18	十八	jū·ha·chi
19	十九	jū·ku/jū·kyū
20	二十	ni·jū
21	二十一	ni·jū·i·chi
22	二十二	ni·jū·ni
30	三十	san·jū
40	四十	yon·jū
50	五十	go·jū
60	六十	ro·ku·jū

70	七十	na·na·jū
80	八十	ha·chi·jū
90	九十	kyū·jū
100	百	hya·ku
200	二百	ni·hya·ku
300	三百	sam·bya·ku
1,000	千	sen
10,000	一万	i·chi·man
1,000,000	百万	hya·ku·man
100,000,000	一億	i·chi·o·ku

Note that Japanese has no unit for 'a million'. Millions are expressed in units of 10 thousand, so one million is 100 ten-thousand units.

ordinal numbers

順番

To use an ordinal number in Japanese, just add ·ban (番) to the end of the corresponding cardinal number.

1st	一番	i·chi·ban
2nd	二番	ni·ban
3rd	三番	sam·ban
4th	四番	yom·ban
5th	五番	go·ban

fractions

分数

a quarter	4分の1	yom·bun no i·chi
a third	3分の1	sam·bun no i·chi
a half	半分	ham·bun
three-quarters	4分の3	yom·bun no san
all	全部	zem·bu
none	なし	na·shi

counters

In Japanese, when expressing a certain number of objects, people or animals, the cardinal number is followed by a counter. Counters, also commonly known as 'classifiers', indicate the size, shape and function of things and distinguish between objects, people and animals.

The following generic counters can be used to count most objects, but not to count people or animals:

1	一つ	hi·to·tsu
2	二つ	fu·ta·tsu
3	三つ	mit·tsu
4	四つ	yot·tsu
5	五つ	i·tsu·tsu
6	六つ	mut·tsu
7	七つ	na·na·tsu
8	八つ	yat·tsu
9	九つ	ko·ko·no·tsu
10	十	tō
numbers higher than 10	…個	…·ko

Note that apart from the last generic counter mentioned in the list above, there's no need to add the cardinal number before the counter as this already makes part of the counter. Eg, the phrase 'Give me an apple, please.' is rin·go o hi·to·tsu ku·da·sai (りんごを一つください), literally 'apple-o one please', not rin·go o i·chi hi·to·tsu ku·da·sai (りんごを一一つください), literally 'apple-o one one please'.

Here are also some basic specific counters frequently used in everyday speech, including the ones for people and animals:

age	···歳	…·sai
animals*	···匹	…·hi·ki/pi·ki/bi·ki
books	···冊	…·sa·tsu
bottles, pens (long objects)*	···本	…·hon/pon/bon
floors (of buildings)	···階	…·kai
objects (small)	···個	…·ko
people	···人	…·nin
scoops, glasses, cups*	···杯	…·hai/pai/bai
sheets (paper, sliced objects)	···枚	…·mai
time	···時	…·ji
vehicles	···台	…·dai

* Note that the pronunciation of these three counters changes according to the preceding number. For these, generally use the first option (·hiki, ·hon, ·hai) but change to ·piki, ·pon, ·pai after the numbers 1, 6 and 10, and to ·biki, ·bon and ·bai after the number 3. Don't forget to add the cardinal number before each of the specific counters listed above!

useful amounts

よく使う分量

How much?	どのくらい?	do·no ku·rai
How many?	いくつ?	i·ku·tsu
Please give me ...	···ください。	… ku·da·sai
(100) grams	(100)グラム	(hya·ku)·gu·ra·mu
half a kilo	500グラム	o·hya·ku·gu·ra·mu
a kilo	1キロ	i·chi·ki·ro
a bottle	ビン1本	bin ip·pon
a jar	ジャー1個	jā ik·ko
a packet	1パック	hi·to·pak·ku
a slice	1枚	i·chi·mai
a tin	1缶	hi·to·kan
less	もっと少ない量	mot·to su·ku·nai ryō
(just) a little	(ほんの)ちょっと	(hon·no) chot·to
a lot	たくさん	ta·ku·san
more	もっと	mot·to
some	いくらか	i·ku·ra ka

telling the time

To specify the hour, add the number of the hour before the word ·ji (時) 'o'clock'. Note that four o'clock is an exception: yo·ji (4時), not shi·ji. The minutes come after the hour and are expressed by adding ·fun/·pun (分) after the number – see **numbers & amounts** for how to form numbers in Japanese. To say 'half past' use ·ji han (時半). For times leading up to the hour (in English 'to') use ma·e des (前です), meaning literally 'before it is' instead of des (です), 'it is'.

What time is it?	何時ですか？	nan·ji des ka
It's (ten) o'clock.	(10)時です。	(jū)·ji des
Five past (ten).	(10)時5分です。	(jū)·ji go·fun des
Quarter past (ten).	(10)時15分です。	(jū)·ji go·fun des
Half past (ten).	(10)時半です。	(jū)·ji han des
Quarter to (ten).	(10)時15分 前です。	(jū)·ji jū·go·fun ma·e des
Twenty to (ten).	(10)時20分 前です。	(jū)·ji ni·jup·pun ma·e des
At what time …?	何時に…	nan·ji ni …
At (ten).	(10時)に。	(jū·ji) ni
At (7.57pm).	(午後7時57分)に。	(go·go shi·chi·ji go·jū·na·na·fun) ni
am	午前	go·zen
pm	午後	go·go

Combining numbers with minutes produces some special forms:

minute(s)					
1	1分	ip·pun	**7**	7分	na·na·fun
2	2分	ni·fun	**8**	8分	hap·pun
3	3分	sam·pun	**9**	9分	kyū·fun
4	4分	yom·pun	**10**	10分	jup·pun

the calendar

days

Monday	月曜日	ge·tsu·yō·bi
Tuesday	火曜日	ka·yō·bi
Wednesday	水曜日	su·i·yō·bi
Thursday	木曜日	mo·ku·yō·bi
Friday	金曜日	kin·yō·bi
Saturday	土曜日	do·yō·bi
Sunday	日曜日	ni·chi·yō·bi

months

January	1月	i·chi·ga·tsu
February	2月	ni·ga·tsu
March	3月	san·ga·tsu
April	4月	shi·ga·tsu
May	5月	go·ga·tsu
June	6月	ro·ku·ga·tsu
July	7月	shi·chi·ga·tsu
August	8月	ha·chi·ga·tsu
September	9月	ku·ga·tsu
October	10月	jū·ga·tsu
November	11月	jū·i·chi·ga·tsu
December	12月	jū·ni·ga·tsu

dates

To express the date, use the cardinal number plus ·ni·chi（日）:

What date is it today?

今日は何月何日ですか?	kyō wa nan·ga·tsu nan·ni·chi des ka

It's (18 October).

（10月18日）です。	(jū·ga·tsu jū·ha·chi·ni·chi) des

There are irregular forms, however, for the 1st to the 10th, the 14th, 20th and 24th when referring to dates:

1st	1日	tsu·i·ta·chi	8th	8日	yō·ka
2nd	2日	fu·tsu·ka	9th	9日	ko·ko·no·ka
3rd	3日	mik·ka	10th	10日	tō·ka
4th	4日	yok·ka	14th	14日	jū·yok·ka
5th	5日	i·tsu·ka	20th	20日	ha·tsu·ka
6th	6日	mu·i·ka	24th	24日	ni·jū·yok·ka
7th	7日	na·no·ka			

seasons

summer	夏	na·tsu
autumn	秋	a·ki
winter	冬	fu·yu
spring	春	ha·ru

present

現在

now	今	i·ma

this ...		
afternoon	今日の午後	kyō no go·go
morning	今朝	ke·sa
month	今月	kon·ge·tsu
week	今週	kon·shū
year	今年	ko·to·shi

today	今日	kyō
tonight	今夜	kon·ya

past

過去

(three days) ago	(3日)前	(mik·ka) ma·e
day before yesterday	おととい	o·to·toy

last ...		
month	先月	sen·ge·tsu
night	ゆうべ	yū·be
week	先週	sen·shū
year	去年	kyo·nen

since (May)	(5月)から	(go·ga·tsu) ka·ra
yesterday ...	きのうの…	ki·nō no ...
afternoon	午後	go·go
evening	夜	yo·ru
morning	朝	a·sa

future

未来

day after tomorrow	あさって	a·sat·te
in (six days)	(6日)後	(mu·i·ka) go
next ...	来…	rai...
month	月	·ge·tsu
week	週	·shū
year	年	·nen
tomorrow ...	明日の…	a·shi·ta no ...
afternoon	午後	go·go
evening	夜	yo·ru
morning	朝	a·sa
until (June)	(6月)まで	(ro·ku·ga·tsu) ma·de

during the day

1日

afternoon	午後	go·go
dawn	夜明け	yo·a·ke
day	日中	nit·chū
evening	夕方	yū·ga·ta
midday	正午	shō·go
midnight	真夜中	ma·yo·na·ka
morning	朝	a·sa
night	夜	yo·ru
sunrise	日の出	hi·no·de
sunset	日の入り	hi·no·i·ri

money

Japan is still a cash-based country, although credit cards are becoming more common – carry some yen with you and don't assume you can use credit cards and checks at restaurants, hotels and shops. For more info on the availibility of various methods of payment, see Lonely Planet's guidebook to Japan.

How much is it?
いくらですか？ i·ku·ra des ka

Can you write down the price?
値段を書いてくれませんか？ ne·dan o kai·te ku·re·ma·sen ka

Do you accept …?	…で払えますか？	… de ha·ra·e·mas ka
credit cards	クレジットカード	ku·re·jit·to·kā·do
debit cards	デビットカード	de·bit·to·kā·do
travellers cheques	トラベラーズ チェック	to·ra·be·rāz· chek·ku

I'd like …, please.	…をお願いします。	… o o·ne·gai shi·mas
a receipt	レシート	re·shī·to
a refund	払い戻し	ha·rai·mo·do·shi
my change	お釣り	o·tsu·ri
to return this	返品	hem·pin

I'd like to …	…をお願い します。	… o o·ne·gai shi·mas
cash a cheque	小切手の 現金化	ko·git·te no gen·kin·ka
change a travellers cheque	トラベラーズ チェックの 現金化	to·ra·be·rāz· chek·ku no gen·kin·ka
change money	両替	ryō·ga·e
get a cash advance	キャッシュ アドバンス	kyas·shu· a·do·ban·su
withdraw money	現金の 引き出し	gen·kin no hi·ki·da·shi

43

Where's ...?	...はどこですか?	... wa do·ko des ka
an automatic teller machine	ATM	ē·tī·e·mu
a foreign exchange office	外国為替 セクション	gai·ko·ku·ka·wa·se· sek·shon

What's the ...?	...はいくらですか?	... wa i·ku·ra des ka
charge	料金	ryō·kin
exchange rate	為替レート	ka·wa·se·rē·to

It's ...	...です。	... des
free	ただ	ta·da
(12) euros	(12)ユーロ	(jū·ni)·yū·ro
(4000) yen	(4000)円	(yon·sen)·en

Do you change money here?
ここで換金できますか?
ko·ko de kan·kin de·ki·mas ka

Do I need to pay upfront?
前払いですか?
ma·e·ba·rai des ka

Do I have to pay?
料金を払わなければ
なりませんか?
ryō·kin o ha·ra·wa·na·ke·re·ba
na·ri·ma·sen ka

Is it coin-operated?
コインを使いますか?
ko·in o tsu·kai·mas ka

There's a mistake in the bill.
請求書に間違いが
あります。
sē·kyū·sho ni ma·chi·gai ga
a·ri·mas

I'd like ..., please.	...をお願いします。	... o o·ne·gai shi·mas
my change	お釣り	o·tsu·ri
a refund	払い戻し	ha·rai·mo·do·shi

getting around

移動する

Which … goes to (Nagasaki)?	(長崎)行きの…はどれですか?	(na·ga·sa·ki)·yu·ki no … wa do·re des ka
boat	船	fu·ne
bus	バス	bas
plane	飛行機	hi·kō·ki
train	電車	den·sha

Is this the … to (Kobe)?	(神戸)行きの…はこれですか?	(kō·be)·yu·ki no … wa ko·re des ka
boat	船	fu·ne
bus	バス	bas
train	電車	den·sha

When's the … (bus)?	…(バス)は何時ですか?	… (bas) wa nan·ji des ka
first	始発の	shi·ha·tsu no
last	最終の	sai·shū no
next	次の	tsu·gi no

What time does it leave?
これは何時に出ますか?   ko·re wa nan·ji ni de·mas ka

What time does it get to (Nagoya)?
これは(名古屋)に
何時に着きますか?   ko·re wa (na·go·ya) ni
nan·ji ni tsu·ki·mas ka

How long will it be delayed?
どのくらい遅れますか?   do·no ku·rai o·ku·re·mas ka

Is this seat free?
この席は空いていますか?   ko·no se·ki wa ai·te i·mas ka

That's my seat.
それは私の
席です。

so·re wa wa·ta·shi no
se·ki des

Please tell me when we get to (Osaka).
(大阪)に着いたら教えて
ください。

(ō·sa·ka) ni tsu·i·ta·ra o·shi·e·te
ku·da·sai

Please stop here.
ここで停めてください。

ko·ko de to·me·te ku·da·sai

tickets

切符

Where do I buy a ticket?
切符はどこで
買えますか？

kip·pu wa do·ko de
ka·e·mas ka

Do I need to book?
予約が必要ですか？

yo·ya·ku ga hi·tsu·yō des ka

A ... ticket (to Tokyo).	（東京行きの） …切符。	(tō·kyō·yu·ki no) ... kip·pu
1st-class (boat)	一等席	it·tō·se·ki
2nd-class (boat)	二等席	ni·tō·se·ki
child's	子ども 料金の	ko·do·mo ryō·kin no
green-class (train)	グリーン席	gu·rīn·se·ki
one-way	片道	ka·ta·mi·chi
return	往復	ō·fu·ku
ordinary-class (train)	普通席	fu·tsū·se·ki
student's	学生料金の	gak·sē ryō·kin no

booklet of tickets	回数券	kai·sū·ken
one-day ticket (line or group of lines)	1日券	i·chi·ni·chi·ken
one-day free ride ticket (area)	フリー切符	frī·kip·pu

PRACTICAL

46

I'd like a/an ... seat.	…席をお願いします。	...·se·ki o o·ne·gai shi·mas
aisle	通路側	tsū·ro·ga·wa
nonsmoking	禁煙	kin·en
smoking	喫煙	kits·en
window	窓側	ma·do·ga·wa

Is there (a toilet)?
(トイレ)はありますか?　(toy·re) wa a·ri·mas ka

How much is it?
いくらですか?　i·ku·ra des ka

How long does the trip take?
時間はどのくらい
かかりますか?　ji·kan wa do·no·ku·rai
ka·ka·ri·mas ka

Is it a direct route?
直行便ですか?　chok·kō·bin des ka

Can I get a stand-by ticket?
スタンドバイチケットは
ありますか?　stan·do·bai·chi·ket·to wa
a·ri·mas ka

Can I get a sleeping berth?
寝台席はありますか?　shin·dai·se·ki wa a·ri·mas ka

What time should I check in?
チェックインは何時ですか?　chek·ku·in wa nan·ji des ka

listen for ...		
a·re	あれ	**that one**
ji·ko·ku·hyō	時刻表	**timetable**
ko·re	これ	**this one**
kyan·se·ru	キャンセル	**cancelled**
ma·do·gu·chi	窓口	**ticket window**
man·se·ki	満席	**full**
o·ku·re	遅れ	**delayed**
pu·rat·to·fō·mu	プラットフォーム	**platform**
ryo·kō·dai·ri·ten	旅行代理店	**travel agent**
sto·rai·ki	ストライキ	**strike**

I'd like to ... my ticket, please.	切符の…を お願いします。	kip·pu no ... o o·ne·gai shi·mas
cancel	キャンセル	kyan·se·ru
change	変更	hen·kō
confirm	コンファーム	kon·fā·mu

luggage

手荷物

Where can I find ...?	…はどこですか?	... wa do·ko des ka
the baggage claim	バッゲージ クレーム	bag·gē·ji· ku·rē·mu
the left-luggage office	手荷物 預かり所	te·ni·mo·tsu· a·zu·ka·ri·sho
a luggage locker	ロッカー	rok·kā
a trolley	トロリー	to·ro·rī

My luggage has been ...	私の 手荷物が…	wa·ta·shi no te·ni·mo·tsu ga ...
damaged	壊れました	ko·wa·re·mash·ta
lost	なくなり ました	na·ku·na·ri· mash·ta
stolen	ぬすまれ ました	nu·su·ma·re· mash·ta

That's mine.
あれは私のです。 a·re wa wa·ta·shi no des

That's not mine.
あれは私の じゃありません。 a·re wa wa·ta·shi no ja a·ri·ma·sen

Can I have some (coins/tokens)?
(コイン/トークン)を ください。 (ko·in/tō·kun) o ku·da·sai

listen for ...		
jū·ryō·ō·bā no te·ni·mo·tsu	重量オーバーの 手荷物	**excess baggage**
ki·nai·mo·chi·ko·mi no te·ni·mo·tsu	機内持込の 手荷物	**carry-on baggage**

plane

飛行機

Where does flight (QF22) …?	(QF22) 便 の…場所は どこですか?	(kyū·e·fu ni·jū·ni)·bin no …·ba·sho wa do·ko des ka
arrive	出発	shup·pa·tsu
depart	到着	tō·cha·ku
Where's …?	…はどこですか?	… wa do·ko des ka
the airport shuttle	シャトルバス	sha·to·ru·bas
arrivals	到着便	tō·cha·ku·bin
departures	出発便	shup·pa·tsu·bin
duty-free	免税店	men·zē·ten
gate number (5)	(5)番ゲート	(go)·ban gē·to

listen for …		
no·ri·ka·e	乗り換え	**transfer**
pas·pō·to	パスポート	**passport**
tō·jō·ken	搭乗券	**boarding pass**
to·ran·jit·to	トランジット	**transit**

bus & coach

バス

How often do buses come?
バスはどのくらい
ひんぱんに来ますか?

bas wa do·no·ku·rai
him·pan ni ki·mas ka

Does it stop at (Yokohama)?
(横浜) に
停まりますか?

(yo·ko·ha·ma) ni
to·ma·ri·mas ka

What's the next stop?
次の停車は
どこですか?

tsu·gi no tē·sha wa
do·ko des ka

I'd like to get off at (Kurashiki).
(倉敷)
で下車します。

(ku·ra·shi·ki)
de ge·sha shi·mas

train

bullet train	新幹線	shin·kan·sen
monorail	モノレール	mo·no·rē·ru
subway	地下鉄	chi·ka·te·tsu
train	電車	den·sha
tram	市電	shi·den

What station is this?
ここは何駅ですか？   ko·ko wa na·ni·e·ki des ka

What's the next station?
次は何駅ですか？   tsu·gi wa na·ni·e·ki des ka

Does it stop at (Nagasaki)?
これは(長崎)に   ko·re wa (na·ga·sa·ki) ni
停まりますか？   to·ma·ri·mas ka

Do I need to change?
乗り換えなければ   no·ri·ka·e·na·ke·re·ba
いけませんか？   i·ke·ma·sen ka

Which line goes to (Roppongi) station?
(六本木)駅は   (rop·pon·gi)·e·ki wa
どの線ですか？   do·no sen des ka

Can I use this ticket on the (Toei) line?
この切符で(都営)線に   ko·no kip·pu de (to·ē)·sen ni
乗れますか？   no·re·mas ka

I need to pay the excess fare.
清算したいのですが。   sē·san shi·tai no des ga

I'd like to go on a bullet train.
新幹線で行きたい   shin·kan·sen de i·ki·tai
のですが。   no des ga

Where's the (east) exit?
(東)口はどこ   (hi·ga·shi)·gu·chi wa do·ko
ですか？   des ka

Where's exit number (2)?
(2)番出口はどこ   (ni)·ban de·gu·chi wa do·ko
ですか？   des ka

Don't push!
押さないで！   o·sa·nai·de

Is it (a/an) …?*	これは…ですか？	ko·re wa … des ka
direct (non-stop)	直行便	chok·kō·bin
limited express train (few stops)	特急	tok·kyū
express	急行	kyū·kō
special rapid train	特別快速	to·ku·be·tsu·kai·so·ku
new rapid train	新快速	shin·kai·so·ku
rapid train	快速	kai·so·ku
local	各駅停車	ka·ku·e·ki·tē·sha

* The trains are listed according to how often they stop, starting with the one that stops the least.

Which carriage is (for) …?	…は 何号車ですか？	… wa nan·gō·sha des ka
dining	食堂車	sho·ku·dō·sha
green class (1st class)	グリーン車	gu·rīn·sha
(Hiroshima)	（広島）行き	(hi·ro·shi·ma)·yu·ki
nonsmoking	禁煙車	kin·en·sha
smoking	喫煙車	ki·tsu·en·sha

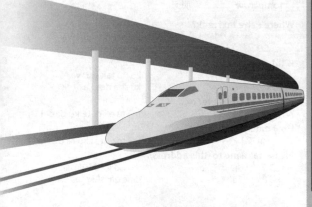

transport

51

boat

船

What's the sea like today?
今日の海の様子は
どうですか？

kyō no u·mi no yō·su wa
dō des ka

Are there life jackets?
救命胴衣はありますか？

kyū·mē·dō·i wa a·ri·mas ka

What (island/beach) is this?
この(島/ビーチ)の
名前は何ですか？

ko·no (shi·ma/bī·chi) no
na·ma·e wa nan des ka

I feel seasick.
船酔いしました。

fu·na·yoy shi·mash·ta

taxi

タクシー

I'd like a taxi …	…タクシーを お願いします。	… tak·shī o o·ne·gai shi·mas
at (9) o'clock	(9)時に	(ku)·ji ni
now	今	i·ma
tomorrow	明日	a·shi·ta

Where's the taxi rank?
タクシー乗り場は
どこですか？

tak·shī·no·ri·ba wa
do·ko des ka

Is this taxi free?
このタクシーは
空車ですか？

ko·no tak·shī wa
kū·sha des ka

Please put the meter on.
メーターを入れてください。

mē·tā o i·re·te ku·da·sai

How much is it (to …)?
(…まで)いくらですか？

(… ma·de) i·ku·ra des ka

Please take me to (this address).
(この住所)まで
お願いします。

(ko·no jū·sho) ma·de
o·ne·gai shi·mas

Please ...	…ください。	... ku·da·sai
slow down	スピードを 落として	spī·do o o·to·shi·te
stop here	ここで 停まって	ko·ko de to·mat·te
wait here	ここで待って	ko·ko de mat·te

car & motorbike hire

レンタカーとオートバイのレンタル

I'd like to hire a/an ...	…を借りたいの ですが。	... o ka·ri·tai no des ga
4WD	四駆	yon·ku
automatic	オートマチック	ō·to·ma·chik·ku
car	自動車	ji·dō·sha
manual	マニュアル	ma·nyu·a·ru
motorbike	オートバイ	ō·to·bai
scooter	スクーター	skū·tā

With ...	…付き	...tsu·ki
air-conditioning	エアコン	air·kon
a driver	運転手	un·ten·shu

How much for ... hire?	…借りると いくらですか?	... ka·ri·ru to i·ku·ra des ka
daily	1日	i·chi·ni·chi
weekly	1週間	is·shū·kan

Does that include (insurance/mileage)?
(保険料/マイレージ)が
含まれていますか?
(ho·ken·ryō/mai·rē·ji) ga fu·ku·ma·re·te i·mas ka

Do you have a guide to the road rules in English?
道路交通法の英語の
ガイドブックがありますか?
dō·ro·kō·tsū·hō no ē·go no gai·do·buk·ku ga a·ri·mas ka

Do you have a road map?
ロードマップがありますか?　rō·do·map·pu ga a·ri·mas ka

What's the speed limit?
制限速度は何キロ
ですか？

sē·gen·so·ku·do wa nan·ki·ro
des ka

How much is the toll for this road?
この道の通行料は
いくらですか？

ko·no mi·chi no tsū·kō·ryō wa
i·ku·ra des ka

Is this the road to (Sapporo)?
この道は（札幌）
まで行きますか？

ko·no mi·chi wa (sap·po·ro)
ma·de i·ki·mas ka

Where's a petrol station?
ガソリンスタンドは
どこですか？

ga·so·rin·stan·do wa
do·ko des ka

Please fill it up.
満タンにしてください。

man·tan ni shi·te ku·da·sai

I'd like ... litres.
…リットルお願いします。

... rit·to·ru o·ne·gai shi·mas

petrol
ガソリン
ga·so·rin

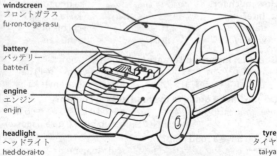

windscreen
フロントガラス
fu·ron·to·ga·ra·su

battery
バッテリー
bat·te·rī

engine
エンジン
en·jin

headlight
ヘッドライト
hed·do·rai·to

tyre
タイヤ
tai·ya

ki·ro	キロ	**kilometres**
mu·ryō	無料	**free (of charge)**
pā·kin·gu·mē·tā	パーキングメーター	**parking meter**
un·ten·men·kyo·shō	運転免許証	**drivers licence**

diesel	ディーゼル	dī·ze·ru
LPG	LPG	e·ru·pī·jī
premium unleaded	ハイオク	hai·o·ku
regular	レギュラー	re·gyu·rā
unleaded	無鉛	mu·en

Can you check	…のチェックを	... no chek·ku o
the ...?	お願いします。	o·ne·gai shi·mas
oil	オイル	oy·ru
tyre pressure	空気圧	kū·ki·a·tsu
water	水	mi·zu

(How long) Can I park here?
（どのくらい）ここに   (do·no·ku·rai) ko·ko ni
駐車できますか？   chū·sha de·ki·mas ka

Do I have to pay?
料金を払わなければ   ryō·kin o ha·ra·wa·na·ke·re·ba
なりませんか？   na·ri·ma·sen ka

car & motorbike problems

自動車とオートバイの故障

I need a mechanic.
整備士が必要です。   sē·bi·shi ga hi·tsu·yō des

I've had an accident.
事故に遭いました。   ji·ko ni ai·mash·ta

The car has broken down (at Minato-ku).
車が（港区で）   ku·ru·ma ga (mi·na·to·ku de)
壊れました。   ko·wa·re·mash·ta

The (car/motorbike) won't start.
（車/オートバイ）の
エンジンがかかりません。

(ku·ru·ma/ō·to·bai) no
en·jin ga ka·ka·ri·ma·sen

I have a flat tyre.
パンクしました。

pan·ku shi·mash·ta

I've lost my car keys.
車の鍵を
無くしました。

ku·ru·ma no ka·gi o
na·ku·shi·mash·ta

I've locked the keys inside.
鍵を中に置いたまま
ロックしてしまいました。

ka·gi o na·ka ni oy·ta ma·ma
rok·ku shi·te shi·mai·mash·ta

I've run out of petrol.
ガス欠です。

gas·ke·tsu des

Can you fix it (today)?
（今日）直せますか？

(kyō) now·se·mas ka

How long will it take?
どのくらい時間が
かかりますか？

do·no·ku·rai ji·kan ga
ka·ka·ri·mas ka

signs		
一時停止	i·chi·ji·tē·shi	Stop Here
一方通行	ip·pō·tsū·kō	One-way
入口	i·ri·gu·chi	Entrance
工事中	kō·ji·chū	Under Construction
立入り禁止	ta·chi·i·ri·kin·shi	No Entry
駐車	chū·sha	Parking
駐車禁止	chū·sha·kin·shi	No Parking
出口	de·gu·chi	Exit (freeway etc)
止まれ	to·ma·re	Stop
料金所	ryō·kin·jo	Toll

bicycle

自転車

I'd like ...	…たいのですが。	…tai no des ga
my bicycle repaired	私の 自転車を 直してもらい	wa·ta·shi no ji·ten·sha o now·shi·te mo·rai
to buy a bicycle	自転車を買い	ji·ten·sha o kai
to hire a bicycle	自転車を借り	ji·ten·sha o ka·ri

I'd like a ...	…が欲しいの ですが。	… ga ho·shī no des ga
mountain bike	マウンテンバイク	ma·un·ten·bai·ku
racing bike	レース用自転車	rē·su·yō·ji·ten·sha
second-hand bike	中古の自転車	chū·ko no ji·ten·sha

How much is it per ...?	…いくらですか?	… i·ku·ra des ka
day	1日	i·chi·ni·chi
hour	1時間	i·chi·ji·kan

Do I need a helmet?
ヘルメットは必要
ですか?

he·ru·met·to wa hi·tsu·yō
des ka

Is there a bicycle-path map?
自転車道の地図が
ありますか?

ji·ten·sha·dō no chi·zu ga
a·ri·mas ka

I have a puncture.
パンクしました。

pan·ku shi·mash·ta

---

on your bike

An originally Japanese cycling discipline, keirin kē·rin (競輪) has made it onto the international stage over the last 20 years. In this 2000 meter track cycling event, each rider cycles behind a motorised derny (a type of motorcycle specifically designed and built for motor-paced track cycling events) that sets the pace for 1400 metres, then pulls off the track and leaves the riders to sprint to the finish – fast, furious and spectacular!

typical addresses

avenue	大通り	ō·dō·ri
lane	路地	ro·ji
street (big, surfaced)	道路	dō·ro
street (smaller than dō·ro)	道	mi·chi
city area (a few blocks)	丁目	chō·me
city area (between chō·me and ku)	町	ma·chi
ward (administrative unit)	区	ku
town	町	ma·chi
city	市	shi
Prefecture	県	ken

Note that Tokyo Prefecture is indicated by adding to（都）to Tokyo – it's often referred to as 'Tokyo Metropolis' – and Osaka and Kyoto Prefectures by adding fu（府）instead of ken（県）to the name of the city. Cities like these with a large population are administratively subdivided in wards ku（区）.

border crossing

出入国

I'm ...	…です。	... des
in transit	トランジット	to·ran·jit·to
on business	ビジネス	bi·ji·nes
on holiday	休暇	kyū·ka

I'm here for ...	私は…	wa·ta·shi wa ...
	滞在します。	tai·zai shi·mas
... days	…日	...·ni·chi
... months	…ヶ月	...·ka·ge·tsu
... weeks	…年	...·nen

I'm going to (Fukuoka).
(福岡)へ行きます。 (fu·ku·o·ka) e i·ki·mas

I'm staying at (Hotel Nikko).
(日航ホテル)に (nik·kō·ho·te·ru) ni
泊まります。 to·ma·ri·mas

The children are on this passport.
子どもはこの ko·do·mo wa ko·no
パスポートに記載 pas·pō·to ni ki·sai
されています。 sa·re·te i·mas

listen for ...		
bi·za	ビザ	visa
gu·rū·pu	グループ	group
hi·to·ri	ひとり	alone
ka·zo·ku	家族	family
pas·pō·to	パスポート	passport

at customs

I have nothing to declare.
何も申請する
ものがありません。

na·ni mo shin·sē su·ru
mo·no ga a·ri·ma·sen

I have something to declare.
申請するものが
あります。

shin·sē su·ru mo·no ga
a·ri·mas

Do I have to declare this?
これを申請
しなければ
なりませんか?

ko·re o shin·sē
shi·na·ke·re·ba
na·ri·ma·sen ka

That's mine.
それは私のです

so·re wa wa·ta·shi no des

That's not mine.
それは私の
じゃありません。

so·re wa wa·ta·shi no
ja a·ri·ma·sen

I didn't know I had to declare it.
これを申請
しなければならないの
を知りませんでした。

ko·re o shin·sē
shi·na·ke·re·ba na·ra·nai no
o shi·ri·ma·sen desh·ta

For duty-free shopping, see **shopping**, pages 73–80, for some
handy phrases.

signs		
移民	i·min	**Immigration**
検疫	ken·e·ki	**Quarantine**
出入国管理	shu·tsu·nyū·ko·ku·kan·ri	**Passport Control**
税関	zē·kan	**Customs**
免税	men·zē	**Duty-free**

Where's (the tourist office)?
(観光案内所)は
どこですか?
(kan·kō·an·nai·jo) wa
do·ko des ka

How do I get there?
そこへはどう行けば
いいですか?
so·ko e wa dō I·ke·ba
ī des ka

How far is it?
どのくらいの距離ですか?
do·no ku·rai no kyo·ri des ka

Can you show me (on the map)?
(地図で)教えて
くれませんか?
(chi·zu de) o·shi·e·te
ku·re·ma·sen ka

What (street) is this?
この(道路)の
名前は何ですか?
ko·no (dō·ro) no
na·ma·e wa nan des ka

What's the address?
住所は何ですか?
jū·sho wa nan des ka

For words that might be used in addresses, see **transport**, page 58.

It's ...	...です。	... des
behind ...	...の後ろ	... no u·shi·ro
close	近く	chi·ka·ku
here	ここ	ko·ko
in front of ...	...の前	... no ma·e
near ...	...の近く	... no chi·ka·ku
next to ...	...のとなり	... no to·na·ri
on the corner	角	ka·do
opposite ...	...の向かい側	... no mu·kai·ga·wa
straight ahead	この先	ko·no sa·ki
there	あそこ	a·so·ko

Turn ...	…まがって ください。	... ma·gat·te ku·da·sai
at the corner	その角を	so·no ka·do o
at the traffic lights	その信号を	so·no shin·gō o
left	左へ	hi·da·ri e
right	右へ	mi·gi e
By ...	…で。	... de
bus	バス	bas
foot	歩き	a·ru·ki
taxi	タクシー	tak·shī
train	電車	den·sha
north	北	ki·ta
south	南	mi·na·mi
east	東	hi·ga·shi
west	西	ni·shi
kilometres	キロ	ki·ro
metres	メートル	mē·to·ru
minutes	分	fun/pun

traffic lights
信号
shin·gō

shop
店
mi·se

pedestrian
crossing
横断歩道
ō·dan·ho·dō

bus
バス
bas

intersection
交差点
kō·sa·ten

corner
角
ka·do

taxi
タクシー
tak·shī

finding accommodation

宿泊場所を見つける

Where's a ...?	…がありますか?	... ga a·ri·mas ka
camping ground	キャンプ場	kyam·pu·jō
capsule hotel	カプセルホテル	ka·pu·se·ru·ho·te·ru
guesthouse	民宿	min·shu·ku
hotel	ホテル	ho·te·ru
Japanese-style inn	旅館	ryo·kan
love hotel	ラブホテル	ra·bu·ho·te·ru
pension	ペンション	pen·shon
youth hostel	ユースホステル	yū·su·ho·su·te·ru

Can you recommend somewhere ...?	おすすめの…ところはありますか?	o·su·su·me no ... to·ko·ro wa a·ri·mas ka
cheap	安い	ya·su·i
good	良い	ī
luxurious	豪華な	gō·ka na
nearby	近くの	chi·ka·ku no
romantic	ロマンチックな	ro·man·chik·ku na

What's the address?
住所は何ですか? jū·sho wa nan des ka

For responses, see **directions**, page 61.

local talk		
dive	いかがわしい	i·ka·ga·wa·shī
rat-infested	ねずみだらけの	ne·zu·mi·da·ra·ke no
top spot	最高の場所	sai·kō no ba·sho

booking ahead & checking in

予約とチェックイン

I'd like to book a room, please.
部屋の予約をお願い
します。

he·ya no yo·ya·ku o o·ne·gai
shi·mas

I have a reservation.
予約があります。

yo·ya·ku ga a·ri·mas

My name's ...
私の名前は
…です。

wa·ta·shi no na·ma·e wa
… des

For (three) nights/weeks.
(3)泊/週間。

(san)·pa·ku/·shū·kan

From (July 2) to (July 6).
(7月2日)から
(7月6日)まで。

(shi·chi·ga·tsu fu·tsu·ka) ka·ra
(shi·chi·ga·tsu mu·i·ka) ma·de

Do I need to pay upfront?
前払いですか?

ma·e·ba·rai des ka

listen for ...		
man·shi·tsu	満室	full
nam·pa·ku des ka	何泊ですか?	How many nights?
pas·pō·to	パスポート	passport

How much is it per ...?	…いくらですか?	… i·ku·ra des ka
night	1泊	ip·pa·ku
person	1人	hi·to·ri
week	1週間	is·shū·kan

Can I pay by ...?	…で払えますか?	… de ha·ra·e·mas ka
credit card	クレジット カード	ku·re·jit·to· kā·do
travellers cheque	トラベラーズ チェック	to·ra·be·rāz· chek·ku

For other methods of payment, see **shopping**, page 74.

PRACTICAL

64

Do you have a … room?	…ルームは ありますか?	…rū·mu wa a·ri·mas ka
double	ダブル	da·bu·ru
single	シングル	shin·gu·ru
twin	ツイン	tsu·in

Can I see it?
見てもいいですか? — mi·te mo ī des ka

I'll take it.
それをお願いします。 — so·re o o·ne·gai shi·mas

signs		
空室	kū·shi·tsu	**vacancy**
バスルーム	bas·rū·mu	**bathroom**
満室	man·shi·tsu	**no vacancy**

requests & queries

依頼と質問

Do you have a/an …?	…がありますか?	… ga a·ri·mas ka
elevator	エレベーター	e·re·bē·tā
laundry service	洗濯サービス	sen·ta·ku·sā·bis
message board	掲示板	kē·ji·ban
safe	金庫	kin·ko
swimming pool	プール	pū·ru

Can I use the …?	…を使ってもいい ですか	… o tsu·kat·te mo ī des ka
kitchen (Japanese)	台所	dai·do·ko·ro
kitchen (Western)	キッチン	kit·chin
laundry	洗濯室	sen·ta·ku·shi·tsu
telephone	電話	den·wa

Could I have ..., please?	…をお願いします。	... o o·ne·gai shi·mas
a receipt	レシート	re·shī·to
an extra blanket	スペアの毛布	spair no mō·fu
my key	鍵	ka·gi

listen for ...

fu·ron·to	フロント	reception
ka·gi	鍵	key
gen·kan	玄関	foyer to leave shoes

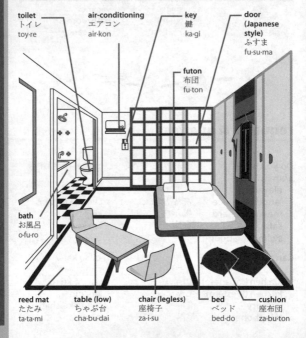

toilet
トイレ
toy·re

air-conditioning
エアコン
air·kon

key
鍵
ka·gi

door (Japanese style)
ふすま
fu·su·ma

futon
布団
fu·ton

bath
お風呂
o·fu·ro

reed mat
たたみ
ta·ta·mi

table (low)
ちゃぶ台
cha·bu·dai

chair (legless)
座椅子
za·i·su

bed
ベッド
bed·do

cushion
座布団
za·bu·ton

When's breakfast served?
朝食はいつですか？　　chō·sho·ku wa i·tsu des ka

Where's breakfast served?
朝食はどこですか？　　chō·sho·ku wa do·ko des ka

Please wake me at (seven) o'clock.
(7)時に起こして　　(shi·chi)·ji ni o·ko·shi·te
ください。　　ku·da·sai

Is there a message for me?
伝言はありますか？　　den·gon wa a·ri·mas ka

Can I leave a message for someone?
伝言を残したいの　　den·gon o no·ko·shi·tai no
ですが。　　des ga

Do you arrange tours here?
ここでツアーに　　ko·ko de tsu·ā ni
申し込めますか？　　mō·shi·ko·me·mas ka

Do you change money here?
ここで換金できますか？　　ko·ko de kan·kin de·ki·mas ka

I'm locked out of my room.
部屋に鍵を残した　　he·ya ni ka·gi o no·ko·shi·ta
まま鍵をかけて　　ma·ma ka·gi o ka·ke te
しまいました。　　shi·mai·mash·ta

Who is it?	どなたですか？	do·na·ta des ka
Just a moment.	ちょっと待って ください。	chot·to mat·te ku·da·sai
Come in.	お入りください。	o·hai·ri ku·da·sai
Come back later, please.	また後できて ください	ma·ta a·to de ki·te ku·da·sai

accommodation

67

complaints

苦情

It's too ...	...すぎます。	... su·gi·mas
bright	明る	a·ka·ru
cold	寒	sa·mu
dark	暗	ku·ra
noisy	うるさ	u·ru·sa
small	小さ	chī·sa

The (fan) doesn't work.
(扇風機)が壊れて
います。
(sem·pū·ki) ga ko·wa·re·te
i·mas

Can I get another (blanket)?
(毛布を)もう一つ
お願いできますか?
(mō·fu o) mō hi·to·tsu
o·ne·gai de·ki·mas ka

This (pillow) isn't clean.
この(枕)はきれい
じゃありません。
ko·no (ma·ku·ra) wa ki·rē
ja a·ri·ma·sen

checking out

チェックアウト

What time is checkout?
チェックアウトは何時
ですか?
chek·ku·ow·to wa nan·ji
des ka

Can I have a late checkout?
チェックアウトを
遅らせたいのですが。
chek·ku·ow·to o
o·ku·ra·se·tai no des ga

Can you call a taxi for me?
タクシーを呼んで
もらえますか?
tak·shī o yon·de
mo·ra·e·mas ka

I'd like a taxi at (11) o'clock.
(11)時にタクシーを呼んで
ください
(jū·i·chi)·ji ni tak·shī o yon·de
ku·da·sai

I'm leaving now.
今、出発します。
i·ma shup·pa·tsu shi·mas

Can I leave my bags here?
ここで荷物を
預かってもらえますか?
ko·ko de ni·mo·tsu o
a·zu·kat·te mo·ra·e·mas ka

There's a mistake in the bill.
請求書に間違いが
あります。
sē·kyū·sho ni ma·chi·gai ga
a·ri·mas

Could I have my ...., please?	…を返して いただきたいの ですが。	... o ka·e·shi·te i·ta·da·ki·tai no des ga
deposit	預かり金	a·zu·ka·ri·kin
passport	パスポート	pas·pō·to
valuables	貴重品	ki·chō·hin

I'll be back ...	…もどります	... mo·do·ri·mas
in (three) days	(3)日後に	(mik)·ka·go ni
on (Tuesday)	(火曜日)に	(ka·yō·bi) ni

I had a great stay, thank you.
たいへんくつろげました。
tai·hen ku·tsu·ro·ge·mash·ta

I'll recommend it to my friends.
友達に薦めます。
to·mo·da·chi ni su·su·me·mas

camping

キャンピング

Do you have ...?	…がありますか?	... ga a·ri·mas ka
electricity	電気	den·ki
a laundry	コインランドリー	ko·in·ran·do·rī
shower facilities	シャワー	sha·wā
a site	キャンプサイト	kyam·pu·sai·to
tents for hire	貸しテント	ka·shi·ten·to

How much is it per ...?	…いくらですか?	... i·ku·ra des ka
caravan	キャラバン1台	kya·ra·ban i·chi·dai
person	1人	hi·to·ri
tent	テント1つ	ten·to hi·to·tsu
vehicle	車1台	ku·ru·ma i·chi·dai

Can I ...?	…してもいい ですか?	... shi·te mo ī des ka
camp here	ここでキャンプ	ko·ko de kyam·pu
park next to my tent	テントのとなりに 駐車	ten·to no to·na·ri ni chū·sha

Is the water drinkable?
水は飲めますか?   mi·zu wa no·me·mas ka

Is it coin-operated?
コインを使いますか?   ko·in o tsu·kai·mas ka

Where's the caretaker's office?
管理事務所はどこですか? kan·ri·ji·mu·sho wa do·ko des ka

Could I borrow ...?
…を貸して
もらえませんか?   ... o ka·shi·te
mo·ra·e·ma·sen ka

renting

賃貸

Do you have a/an ... for rent?	賃貸の ための… がありますか?	chin·tai no ta·me no ... ga a·ri·mas ka
apartment	マンション	man·shon
house	家	i·e
room	部屋	he·ya
monthly	マンスリー	man·su·rī·
apartment	マンション	man·shon
villa	別荘	bes·sō
weekly	ウィークリー	wī·ku·rī·
apartment	マンション	man·shon
(partly) furnished	一部家具付き	(i·chi·bu) ka·gu·tsu·ki
unfurnished	家具なし	ka·gu·na·shi

staying with locals

ホームステイ

Can I stay at your place?
お宅に泊めて
いただけませんか?

o·ta·ku ni to·me·te
i·ta·da·ke·ma·sen ka

Is there anything I can do to help?
何か手伝うことは
ありませんか?

na·ni ka te·tsu·dow ko·to wa
a·ri·ma·sen ka

I have my own ...	私は…を 持っています。	wa·ta·shi wa … o mot·te i·mas
mattress	マットレス	mat·to·res
sleeping bag	寝袋	ne·bu·ku·ro

Can I ...?	…ましょうか?	…ma·shō ka
bring anything for the meal	食事を運び	sho·ku·ji o ha·ko·bi
clear the table	テーブルの 片付けをし	tē·bu·ru no ka·ta·zu·ke o shi
do the dishes	食器を洗い	shok·ki o a·rai
set the table	テーブルの 準備をし	tē·bu·ru no jum·bi o shi
take out the rubbish	外にごみを 持っていき	so·to ni go·mi o mot·te i·ki

Thanks for your hospitality.
たいへんお世話に
なりました。

tai·hen o·se·wa ni
na·ri·mash·ta

For dining-related expressions, see **food**, page 162.

shoes off!

It's customary in Japan to bring a small gift when visiting someone's home. Cakes, chocolates, fruit and flowers are common and relatively safe gifts. Something for the kids or from your country will go down a treat – and it doesn't need to be big.

When entering a Japanese home, take your shoes off in the entrance hall or gen·kan (玄関), the foyer that specifically serves this purpose – make sure your socks don't have holes! Slippers are usually provided to guests but remember that it's strictly socks only on the ta·ta·mi (たたみ), the straw matting you'll see in Japanese houses.

Wait until your host indicates where to sit before sitting down. For women it's best to sit with the legs to one side rather than cross-legged. The sē·za (正座) position in which you tuck your knees directly underneath you is required in very formal situations only. If unsure, simply follow your hosts' example.

If you stay over, remember that body-washing takes place before entering the bath – a shower, tap or tub will be provided for this.

For some dining-related etiquette, see **eating out**, page 162.

looking for ...

…を探す

Where's a (supermarket)?
（スーパー）はどこですか？　(sū·pā) wa do·ko des ka

Where can I buy (a padlock)?
（鍵）はどこで　(ka·gi) wa do·ko de
買えますか？　ka·e·mas ka

signs		
営業中	ē·gyō·chū	**Open**
閉店	hē·ten	**Closed**
押す	o·su	**Push**
引く	hi·ku	**Pull**

To find your way to the shops, see **directions**, page 61.

making a purchase

買う

I'm just looking.
見ているだけです。　mi·te i·ru da·ke des

I'd like to buy (an adaptor plug).
（電源プラグ）をください。　(den·gen·pu·ra·gu) o ku·da·sai

How much is it?
いくらですか？　i·ku·ra des ka

Can you write down the price?
値段を書いて　ne·dan o kai·te
もらえますか？　mo·ra·e·mas ka

Does this price include …?
この値段に…が
含まれますか？
ko·no ne·dan ni … ga
fu·ku·ma·re·mas ka

Do you have any others?
ほかに何かありますか？
ho·ka ni na·ni ka a·ri·mas ka

Can I look at it?
それを見てもいいですか？
so·re o mi·te mo ī des ka

Could I have it wrapped?
包んでもらえますか？
tsu·tsun·de mo·ra·e·mas ka

Does it have a guarantee?
保証はありますか？
ho·shō wa a·ri·mas ka

Can I have it sent overseas/abroad?
海外に郵送して
もらえますか？
kai·gai ni yū·sō shi·te
mo·ra·e·mas ka

Can you order it for me?
注文してもらえますか？
chū·mon shi·te mo·ra·e·mas ka

Can I pick it up later?
受け取りは後で
できますか？
u·ke·to·ri wa a·to de
de·ki·mas ka

It's faulty.
不良品です。
fu·ryō·hin des

Do you accept …?	…で支払えます か？	… deshi·ha·ra·e·mas ka
credit cards	クレジット カード	ku·re·jit·to· kā·do
debit cards	デビット カード	de·bit·to· kā·do
travellers cheques	トラベラーズ チェック	to·ra·be·rāz· chek·ku

Could I have a …, please?	…をください。	… o ku·da·sai
bag	袋	fu·ku·ro
receipt	レシート	re·shī·to

I'd like …, please.	…をお願い します。	… o o·ne·gai shi·mas
my change	お釣り	o·tsu·ri
a refund	払い戻し	ha·rai·mo·do·shi
to return this	返品	hem·pin

bargaining

値切る

That's too expensive.
高すぎます。 ta·ka·su·gi·mas

Can you lower the price?
安くして ya·su·ku shi·te
もらえませんか? mo·ra·e·ma·sen ka

Do you have something cheaper?
もっと安いものが mot·to ya·su·i mo·no ga
ありますか? a·ri·mas ka

Can you give me a discount?
ディスカウントできますか? dis·kown·to de·ki·mas ka

I'll give you (5000 yen).
(5千円)払います。 (go·sen·en) ha·rai·mas

local talk		
bargain	バーゲン	bā·gen
rip-off	ばか高い	ba·ka·da·kai
sale	セール	sē·ru
specials	特売品	to·ku·bai·hin

clothes

服

My size is ...	私のサイズは	wa·ta·shi no sai·zu wa
	…です。	… des
(40)	(40)号	(yon·jū)·gō
large	L	e·ru
medium	M	e·mu
small	S	e·su

Can I try it on?
試着できますか? shi·cha·ku de·ki·mas ka

It doesn't fit.
体にフィットしません。 ka·ra·da ni fit·to shi·ma·sen

For clothing items, see the **dictionary**.

shopping

repairs

Can I have my ...	…を直して	... o na·o·shi·te
repaired here?	もらえますか?	mo·ra·e·mas ka
When will my ...	…はいつ	... wa i·tsu
be ready?	できますか?	de·ki·mas ka
backpack	バックパック	bak·ku·pak·ku
camera	カメラ	ka·me·ra
glasses	眼鏡	me·ga·ne
shoes	靴	ku·tsu
sunglasses	サングラス	san·gu·ra·su

hairdressing

I'd like (a) ...	…をお願いします。	... o o·ne·gai shi·mas
blow wave	ブロー	bu·rō
colour	カラーリング	ka·rā·rin·gu
haircut	ヘアカット	hair·kat·to
shave	シェービング	shē·bin·gu
trim	トリミング	to·ri·min·gu

Don't cut it too short.
短く切りすぎないで
ください。

mi·ji·ka·ku ki·ri·su·gi·nai de
ku·da·sai

Please use a new blade.
新しい刃を使って
ください。

a·ta·ra·shī ha o tsu·kat·te
ku·da·sai

Shave it all off!
全部剃り落として
ください。

zem·bu so·ri·o·to·shi·te
ku·da·sai

I should never have let you near me!
あなたに頼まなければ
よかった!

a·na·ta ni ta·no·ma·na·ke·re·ba
yo·kat·ta

For colours, see the **dictionary**.

books & reading

Do you have …?	…はありますか?	… wa a·ri·mas ka
a book by (Yukio Mishima)	(三島由紀夫)の本	(mi·shi·ma yu·ki·o) no hon
an entertainment guide	エンターテイメントガイド	en·tā·tē·men·to·gai·do
Is there an English-language …?	英語の…はありますか?	ē·go no … wa a·ri·mas ka
bookshop	本屋	hon·ya
section	セクション	sek·shon
I'd like a …	…をください。	… o ku·da·sai
dictionary	辞書	ji·sho
newspaper (in English)	(英字)新聞	(ē·ji) shim·bun
notepad	ノート	nō·to

music

音楽

I'd like a ...   ...をください。   ... o ku·da·sai
  blank tape   ブランクテープ   bu·ran·ku tē·pu
  CD   CD   shī·dī

I'm looking for something by (Southern Allstars).
(サザンオールスターズ)   (sa·zan·ō·ru·stāz)
の曲を探しています。   no kyo·ku o sa·ga·shi·te i·mas

What's their best recording?
どの曲がいちばん   do·no kyo·ku ga i·chi·ban
ですか?   des ka

Can I listen to this?
これを聴いてもいいですか? ko·re o kī·te mo ī des ka

DVD & video

DVDとビデオ

Does this have an English-language preference?
これには英語設定が   ko·re ni wa ē·go·set·tē ga
ありますか?   a·ri·mas ka

Will this work on any DVD player?
これはどんな   ko·re wa don·na
DVDプレーヤー   dī·vī·dī·pu·rē·yā
でも大丈夫ですか?   de·mo dai·jō·bu des ka

Is this a (PAL/NTSC) system?
これは (PAL/NTSC)   ko·re wa (pa·ru/e·nu·tī·e·su·shī)
システムですか?   shis·te·mu des ka

Is this the latest model?
これは新製品ですか?   ko·re wa shin·sē·hin des ka

Is this (240) volts?
(240) ボルト   (ni·hya·ku yon·jū) bo·ru·to
ですか?   des ka

Where can I buy duty-free electronic goods?
電気製品の免税品   den·ki·sē·hin no men·zē·hin
はどこで買えますか?   wa do·ko de ka·e·mas ka

photography

I need … film for this camera.	このカメラに合う…フィルムをください。	ko·no ka·me·ra ni a·u … fi·ru·mu o ku·da·sai
APS	APS	ē·pī·es
B&W	白黒	shi·ro·ku·ro
colour	カラー	ka·rā
slide	スライド	su·rai·do
… speed	ISO/ASA…の	ai·es·ō/ā·sā … no

Can you …?	…できますか?	… de·ki·mas ka
develop this film	このフィルムを現像	ko·no fi·ru·mu o gen·zō
load my film	フィルムを挿入	fi·ru·mu o sō·nyū
develop digital photos	デジタル写真を現像	de·ji·ta·ru·sha·shin o gen·zō
recharge the battery for my digital camera	デジカメの電池を充電	de·ji·ka·me no den·chi o jū·den
transfer photos from my camera to CD	デジカメからCDに写真をコピー	de·ji·ka·me ka·ra shī·dī ni sha·shin o ko·pī

I would like my photos …	写真は…でお願いします。	sha·shin wa … de o·ne·gai shi·mas
glossy	光沢	kō·ta·ku
matt	無光沢	mu·kō·ta·ku

When will it be ready?
いつ出来上がりますか?　i·tsu de·ki·a·ga·ri·mas ka

I need a passport photo taken.
パスポート用の写真が必要です。　pas·pō·to·yō no sha·shin ga hi·tsu·yō des

I'm not happy with these photos.
この写真の現像に満足していません。　ko·no sha·shin no gen·zō ni man·zo·ku shi·te i·ma·sen

souvenirs

antiques (Japanese)	骨董品	kot·tō·hin
art books	美術の本	bi·ju·tsu no hon
carp banners	こいのぼり	koy·no·bo·ri
ceramics	陶芸	tō·gē
cotton bathrobe	浴衣	yu·ka·ta
electrical goods	電化製品	den·ka·sē·hin
fan (hand-held, nonfolding)	うちわ	u·chi·wa
fan (folding)	扇子	sen·su
folding screen	屏風	byō·bu
foodstuffs	食品	sho·ku·hin
furniture	家具	ka·gu
gifts	おみやげ	o·mi·ya·ge
handmade paper	和紙	wa·shi
high-heel boots	ハイヒールのブーツ	hai·hī·ru no bū·tsu
Japanese dolls	日本人形	ni·hon nin·gyō
Japanese swords	刀	ka·ta·na
Japanese tea	日本茶	ni·hon·cha
Japanese umbrella:		
generic term	傘	ka·sa
for sun	日傘	hi·ga·sa
for rain	番傘	ban·ga·sa
kimono	きもの	ki·mo·no
kitchenware	台所用品	dai·do·ko·ro·yō·hin
lacquerware	漆器	shik·ki
pearl jewellery	真珠	shin·ju
pottery	陶芸	tō·gē
scrolls	掛け軸	ka·ke·ji·ku
sword guards	鍔	tsu·ba
tea set	茶器	cha·ki
textiles	生地	ki·ji
woodblock prints	浮世絵	u·ki·yo·e
wooden toys	木のおもちゃ	ki no o·mo·cha

post office

郵便局

I want to send a/an ...	…を送りたいのですが。	... o o·ku·ri·tai no des ga
fax	ファックス	fak·kus
letter	手紙	te·ga·mi
parcel	小包	ko·zu·tsu·mi
postcard	はがき	ha·ga·ki
I want to buy a/an ...	…をください。	... o ku·da·sai
aerogram	エアログラム	air·ro·gu·ra·mu
envelope	封筒	fū·tō
stamp	切手	kit·te
customs declaration	関税申告	kan·zē·shin·ko·ku
domestic	国内	ko·ku·nai
fragile	壊れ物	ko·wa·re·mo·no
international	国際	ko·ku·sai
mail	郵便	yū·bin
mailbox	ポスト	pos·to
postcode	郵便番号	yū·bin·ban·gō
post office	郵便局	yū·bin·kyo·ku

snail mail		
air	航空便	kō·kū·bin
express	速達	so·ku·ta·tsu
registered	書留	ka·ki·to·me
sea	船便	fu·na·bin
surface	普通便	fu·tsū·bin

Please send it by airmail to (Australia).
(オーストラリア)まで
航空便でお願いします。
(ō·sto·ra·rya) ma·de
kō·kū·bin de o·ne·gai shi·mas

Please send it by surface mail to (England).
(イギリス)まで
普通便でお願いします。
(i·gi·ri·su) ma·de
fu·tsū·bin de o·ne·gai shi·mas

It contains (souvenirs).
(お土産)が入っています。
(o·mi·ya·ge) ga hait·te i·mas

Where's the poste restante section?
局留め郵便の
セクションはどこですか?
kyo·ku·do·me·yū·bin no
sek·shon wa do·ko des ka

Is there any mail for me?
私宛の
郵便物はありますか?
wa·ta·shi·a·te no
yū·bin·bu·tsu wa a·ri·mas ka

phone

電話

What's your phone number?
あなたの電話番号は
何番ですか?
a·na·ta no den·wa·ban·gō wa
nam·ban des ka

Where's the nearest public phone?
いちばん近くの
公衆電話は
どこですか?
i·chi·ban chi·ka·ku no
kō·shū·den·wa wa
do·ko des ka

Can I look at a phone book?
電話帳を見てもいい
ですか?
den·wa·chō o mi·te mo ī
des ka

Can you help me find the number for …?
…の電話番号を
見つけてくれませんか?
… no den·wa·ban·gō o
mi·tsu·ke·te ku·re·ma·sen ka

I want to …	…たいのですが。	…tai no des ga
buy a phonecard	テレフォンカードを買い	te·re·fon·kā·do o kai
call (Singapore)	(シンガポール)に電話し	(shin·ga·pō·ru) ni den·wa shi
make a (local) call	(市内)に電話し	(shi·nai) ni den·wa shi
reverse the charges	コレクトコールで電話し	ko·re·ku·to·kō·ru de den·wa shi
speak for (three) minutes	(3分間)話し	(sam·pun·kan) ha·na·shi

How much does … cost?	…はいくらですか?	… wa i·ku·ra des ka
each extra minute	1分間の加算料金	ip·pun·kan no ka·san·ryō·kin
a (three)-minute call	(3)分間の通話料金	(sam)·pun·kan no tsū·wa·ryō·kin

The number is …
電話番号は…です。
den·wa·ban·gō wa … des

What's the area code for (Osaka)?
(大阪)の市内局番は何番ですか?
(ō·sa·ka) no shi·nai·kyo·ku·ban wa nam·ban des ka

What's the country code for (New Zealand)?
(ニュージーランド)の国番号は何番ですか?
(nyū·jī·ran·do) no ku·ni·ban·gō wa nam·ban des ka

It's engaged.
お話中です。
o·ha·na·shi·chū des

I've been cut off.
電話が切れました。
den·wa ga ki·re·mash·ta

The connection's bad.
電話のかかりが悪いです。
den·wa no ka·ka·ri ga wa·ru·i des

Hello.
もしもし。
mo·shi·mo·shi

It's ...
…です。 … des

Can I speak to ...?
…をお願いします。 … o o·ne·gai shi·mas

Is ... there?
…はいらっしゃいますか? … wa i·ras·shai·mas ka

Please tell him/her I called.
私が電話したと wa·ta·shi ga den·wa shi·ta to
お伝えください。 o·tsu·ta·e ku·da·sai

Can I leave a message?
伝言をお願い den·gon o o·ne·gai
できますか? de·ki·mas ka

My number is ...
私の wa·ta·shi no
電話番号は…です。 den·wa·ban·gō wa … des

I don't have a contact number.
電話番号はありません。 den·wa·ban·gō wa a·ri·ma·sen

I'll call back later.
また後で電話します。 ma·ta a·to de den·wa shi·mas

---

listen for ...

chot·to mat·te ku·da·sai ちょっと待ってください。	**One moment.**
do·na·ta des ka どなたですか?	**Who's calling?**
do·na·ta ni ka·wa·ri·ma·shō ka どなたに代わりましょうか?	**Who do you want to speak to?**
ka·no·jo wa i·ma·sen 彼女はいません。	**She's not here.**
ka·re wa i·ma·sen 彼はいません。	**He's not here.**
ma·chi·gai·den·wa des 間違い電話です。	**Wrong number.**

mobile/cell phone

I'd like a ...	…をお願いします。	... o o·ne·gai shi·mas
charger for my phone	携帯電話の 充電器	kē·tai·den·wa no jū·den·ki
mobile/cell phone for hire	携帯電話の レンタル	kē·tai·den·wa no ren·ta·ru
prepaid mobile/ cell phone	プリペイドの 携帯電話	pu·ri·pē·do no kē·tai·den·wa
SIM card	SIMカード	shi·mu·kā·do

What are the rates?
通話料金はいくら
ですか?

tsū·wa·ryō·kin wa i·ku·ra des ka

(10) yen per (1) minute.
(1)分間(10)円。

(ip)·pun·kan (jū)·en

the internet

Where's the local Internet cafe?
インターネットカフェは
どこですか？
in·tā·net·to·ka·fe wa
do·ko des ka

I'd like to ... …したいのですが。 ... shi·tai no des ga
check my email Eメールを ī·mē·ru o
チェック chek·ku
get Internet インターネット in·tā·net·to
access にアクセス ni ak·ses
use a printer プリント prin·to
use a scanner スキャン skyan

Do you have ...? …がありますか？ ... ga a·ri·mas ka
Macs マッキントッシュ mak·kin·tos·shu
PCs PC pī·shī
a Zip drive ジップドライブ jip·pu·do·rai·bu

How much per ...? …いくらですか？ ... i·ku·ra des ka
hour 1時間 i·chi·ji·kan
(five)-minutes (5) 分間 (go)·fun·kan
page 1ページ i·chi·pē·ji

How do I log on?
どうすればログオン
できますか？
dō·su·re ba ro·gu·on
de·ki·mas ka

Please change it to the English-language setting.
英語のセッティングに
してください。
ē·go no set·tin·gu ni
shi·te ku·da·sai

It's crashed.
クラッシュしています。 ku·ras·shu shi·te i·mas

I've finished.
終わりました。 o·wa·ri·mash·ta

What time does the bank open?
銀行は何時に
開きますか？
gin·kō wa nan·ji ni
hi·ra·ki·mas ka

Where can I withdraw money?
どこで現金の
引き出しができますか？
do·ko de gen·kin no
hi·ki·da·shi ga de·ki·mas ka?

I'd like to withdraw money.
現金の引き出しを
お願いします。
gen·kin no hi·ki·da·shi o
o·ne·gai shi·mas

Where can I ...?	どこで…できますか？	do·ko de … de·ki·mas ka
I'd like to ...	…をお願いします。	… o o·ne·gai shi·mas
cash a cheque	小切手の現金化	ko·git·te no gen·kin·ka
change a travellers cheque	トラベラーズチェックの現金化	to·ra·be·rāz·chek·ku no gen·kin·ka
change money	両替	ryō·ga·e
get a cash advance	キャッシュアドバンス	kyas·shu· a·do·ban·su
What's the ...?	…はいくらですか？	… wa i·ku·ra des ka
charge for that	手数料	te·sū·ryō
exchange rate	為替レート	ka·wa·se·rē·to
Where's ...?	…はどこですか？	… wa do·ko des ka
an automated teller machine	ATM	ē·tī·e·mu
a foreign exchange office	外国為替の窓口	gai·ko·ku·ka·wa·se no ma·do·gu·chi

The automated teller machine took my card.

ATMにカードを取られて
しまいました。

ē·tī·e·mu ni kā·do o to·ra·re·te
shi·mai·mash·ta

I've forgotten my PIN.

暗証番号を
忘れました。

an·shō·ban·gō o
wa·su·re·mash·ta

Can I use my credit card to withdraw money?

クレジットカードで現金を
引き出せますか？

ku·re·jit·to·kā·do de gen·kin o
hi·ki·da·se·mas ka

Can I have smaller notes?

お金をくずして
もらえませんか？

o·ka·ne o ku·zu·shi·te
mo·ra·e·ma·sen ka

Has my money arrived yet?

お金は届いていますか？

o·ka·ne wa to·doy·te i·mas ka

How long will it take to arrive?

お金が届くのに時間
はどのくらいかかりますか？

o·ka·ne ga to·do·ku no ni ji·kan
wa do·no ku·rai ka·ka·ri·mas ka

listen for ...		
mi·bun·shō·mē·sho	身分証明書	**identification**
pas·pō·to	パスポート	**passport**
chot·to mon·dai ga a·ri·mas 　ちょっと問題があります。		**There's a problem.**
de·ki·ma·sen 　できません。		**We can't do that.**
ko·ko ni sain o o·ne·gai shi·mas 　ここにサインをお願いします。		**Sign here.**
zan·da·ka ga a·ri·ma·sen 　残高がありません。		**You have no funds left.**

PRACTICAL

88

I'd like a/an ...	…をお願いします	... o o·ne·gai shi·mas
audio set	オーディオセット	ō·di·o·set·to
catalogue	パンフレット	pan·fu·ret·to
guide	ガイド	gai·do
guidebook	英語の	ē·go no
in English	ガイドブック	gai·do·buk·ku
(local) map	(市街)地図	(shi·gai) chi·zu

Do you have information on ... sights?	…についての案内 はありますか?	... ni tsu·i·te no an·nai wa a·ri·mas ka
cultural	文化的 見どころ	bun·ka·te·ki mi·do·ko·ro
historical	史跡	shi·se·ki
religious	宗教的 見どころ	shū·kyō·te·ki mi·do·ko·ro

I'd like to see ...
…を見ようと思います。   ... o mi·yō to o·moy·mas

What's that?
あれは何ですか?   a·re wa nan des ka

Who made it?
誰が作りましたか?   da·re ga tsu·ku·ri·mash·ta ka

How old is it?
どのくらい古いですか?   do·no ku·rai fu·ru·i des ka

Could you take a photo of me?
私の写真を   wa·ta·shi no sha·shin o
撮ってもらえませんか?   tot·te mo·ra·e·ma·sen ka

Can I take a photo (of you)?
（あなたの）写真を
撮ってもいいですか？

(a·na·ta no) sha·shin o
tot·te mo ī des ka

I'll send you the photo.
写真を送ります。

sha·shin o o·ku·ri·mas

getting in

入場

What time does it open?
何時に開きますか？

nan·ji ni a·ki·mas ka

What time does it close?
何時に閉まりますか？

nan·ji ni shi·ma·ri·mas ka

What's the admission charge?
入場料はいくらですか？

nyū·jō·ryō wa i·ku·ra des ka

Is there a dress code?
服装規定はありますか？

fu·ku·sō·ki·tē wa a·ri·mas ka

Can I take photos?
写真を撮ってもいいですか？

sha·shin o tot·temo ī des ka

Is there a discount for ...?	…割引が ありますか？	…wa·ri·bi·ki ga a·ri·mas ka
children	子供	ko·do·mo
families	家族	ka·zo·ku
groups	グループ	gu·rū·pu
older people	高齢者	kō·rē·sha
pensioners	年金者	nen·kin·sha
students	学生	gak·sē

tours

Can you recommend a ...?	おすすめの…は ありますか?	o·su·su·me no ... wa a·ri·mas ka
When's the next ...?	次の…はいつ ですか?	tsu·gi no ... wa i·tsu des ka
boat-trip	ボートツアー	bō·to·tsu·ā
day trip	1日観光	i·chi·ni·chi kan·kō
tour	ツアー	tsu·ā
Is ... included?	…は含まれて いますか?	... wa fu·ku·ma·re·te i·mas ka
accommodation	宿泊料	shu·ku·ha·ku·ryō
food	食事代	sho·ku·ji·dai
transport	交通費	kō·tsū·hi

The guide will pay.
ガイドが払います。
gai·do ga ha·rai·mas

The guide has paid.
ガイドが払いました。
gai·do ga ha·rai·mash·ta

How long is the tour?
ツアーにかかる時間は
どのくらいですか?
tsu·ā ni ka·ka·ru ji·kan wa
do·no ku·rai des ka

What time should we be back?
何時に戻ればいいですか?
nan·ji ni mo·do·re·ba ī des ka

I'm with them.
彼らと一緒です。
ka·re·ra to is·sho des

I've lost my group.
グループから。
はぐれました
gu·rū·pu ka·ra
ha·gu·re·mash·ta

signs

入口	i·ri·gu·chi	Entrance
インフォメーション	in·fo·mē·shon	Information
営業中	ē·gyō·chū	Open (shops, restaurants etc)
エレベータ	e·re·bē·ta	Lift/Elevator
男	o·to·ko	Men
女	on·na	Women
開館	kai·kan	Open (theatres, museums etc)
危険	ki·ken	Danger
喫煙	ki·tsu·en	Smoking
禁煙	kin·en	Nonsmoking
さわるな	sa·wa·ru·na	Do Not Touch
準備中	jum·bi·chū	In Preparation (restaurants)
立入り禁止	ta·chī·ri·kin·shi	No Entry
出口	de·gu·chi	Exit
トイレ	toy·re	Toilets
止まれ	to·ma·re	Stop
入場無料	nyū·jō·mu·ryō	Free Admission
非常口	hi·jō·gu·chi	Emergency Exit
閉館	hē·kan	Closed (theatres, museums etc)
閉店	hē·ten	Closed (shops, restaurants etc)

doing business

仕事をする

I'm attending a …	…に出席 します。	… ni shus·se·ki shi·mas
conference	会議	kai·gi
course	コース	kōs
meeting	ミーティング	mī·tin·gu
trade fair	展示会	ten·ji·kai
I'm with …	…といっしょです。	… to is·sho des
(Mr Suzuki)	(鈴木さん)	(su·zu·ki·san)
my colleague(s)	同僚	dō·ryō
(two) others	ほかの（２人）	ho·ka no (fu·ta·ri)
(UNICEF)	(ユニセフさん)	(yu·ni·se·fu)
Here's my …	これが私の …です。	ko·re ga wa·ta·shi no … des
What's your …?	あなたの …は何ですか?	a·na·ta no … wa nan des ka
address	住所	jū·sho
business card	名刺	mē·shi
email address	Eメールアドレス	ī·mē·ru·a·do·res
fax number	ファックス番号	fak·kus·ban·gō
mobile number	携帯番号	kē·tai·ban·gō
pager number	ポケベル番号	po·ke·be·ru·ban·gō
work number	仕事の 電話番号	shi·go·to no den·wa·ban·gō
Where's the …?	…はどこですか?	… wa do·ko des ka
business centre	ビジネスセンター	bi·ji·nes·sen·tā
conference	会議	kai·gi
meeting	ミーティング	mī·tin·gu

I need …	…が必要です。	… ga hi·tsu·yō des
a computer	コンピュータ	kom·pyū·ta
an Internet	インターネットの	in·tā·net·to no
connection	接続	se·tsu·zo·ku
an interpreter	通訳	tsū·ya·ku
more business	もっと名刺	mot·to mē·shi
cards		
some space	セットアップ	set·to·ap·pu
to set up	するスペース	su·ru spēs
to send a fax	ファックス送信	fak·kus·sō·shin

I have an appointment with …
…とアポがあります。 … to a·po ga a·ri·mas

Thank you for your time.
お時間をどうもありがとう o·ji·kan o dō·mo a·ri·ga·tō
ございました。 go·zai·mash·ta

Shall we go for a drink?
食事に行きましょうか? no·mi ni i·ki·ma·shō ka

Shall we go for a meal?
飲みに行きましょうか? sho·ku·ji ni i·ki·ma·shō ka

It's on me.
私のおごりです。 wa·ta·shi no o·go·ri des

---

cards on the table

If you're in Japan on business, make sure you master the art of exchanging business cards or mē·shi (名刺).

Cards are exchanged at the start of the meeting. Make sure you carry enough for everyone attending and try to start with the most important or senior person present. Hand over your card with the writing facing the receiver so he or she can read it, and preferably give and receive cards with both hands.

Always read the card you're given on the spot, and treat it with care. Never write on the card, fold it or leave it behind as this is interpreted as a sign of disrespect.

During a meeting, it's best to keep the card in front of you on the table so you have all details handy – file it appropriately at the end of the meeting keeping it in a place where it won't get creased or dirty.

looking for a job

Where are jobs advertised?
求人広告はどこ
ですか？
kyū·jin·kō·ko·ku wa do·ko
des ka

I'm enquiring about the position advertised.
求人広告で
見つけた仕事に
ついてお電話しました。
kyū·jin·kō·ko·ku de
mi·tsu·ke·ta shi·go·to ni
tsu·i·te o·den·wa shi·mash·ta

I'm looking for ... work.	…の仕事を 探しています。	... no shi·go·to o sa·ga·shi·te i·mas
bar	バー	bā
casual	臨時	rin·ji
English-teaching	英語教師	ē·go·kyō·shi
full-time	正社員	sē·shain
hostess	ホステス	hos·tes
labouring/ construction	建築現場	ken·chi·ku·gem·ba
modelling	モデル	mo·de·ru
office	事務	ji·mu
part-time	アルバイト	a·ru·bai·to
waitering	ウェイター	wē·tā

Here's my ...	これが私の …です。	ko·re ga wa·ta·shi no ... des
CV	履歴書	ri·re·ki·sho
visa	ビザ	bi·za
work permit	就業許可	shū·gyō·kyo·ka

Do I need ...?	…は必要ですか？	... wa hi·tsu·yō des ka
a contract	連絡先	ren·ra·ku·sa·ki
experience	経験	kē·ken
insurance	保険	ho·ken
paperwork	書類	sho·ru·i
a uniform	制服	sē·fu·ku
a work permit	就業許可	shū·gyō·kyo·ka

business

95

I've had experience.
経験があります。   kē·ken ga a·ri·mas

What's the wage?
給料はいくらですか？   kyū·ryō wa i·ku·ra des ka

Do you cover my transport cost?
交通費は支給   kō·tsū·hi wa shi·kyū
されますか？   sa·re·mas ka

I can start ...	…始められます。	… ha·ji·me·ra·re·mas
at (eight) o'clock	(8)時に	(ha·chi)·ji ni
next week	次の週から	tsu·gi no shū ka·ra
today	今日から	kyō ka·ra
tomorrow	明日から	a·shi·ta ka·ra

advertisement	広告	kō·ko·ku
contract	契約	kē·ya·ku
employee	従業員	jū·gyō·in
employer	雇い主	ya·toy·nu·shi
job	仕事	shi·go·to
work experience	職業経験	sho·ku·gyō·kē·ken

business etiquette

Always give ample notice of your visit and start the meeting by exchanging business cards. A small present representing your country or company always goes down well.

The seating is linked to status, so wait to be directed to your seat and don't sit (or stand) before the person highest in the pecking order does. Never initiate the use of first names – let your Japanese contacts decide. It's more likely that titles will be used instead.

Japanese business people are interested in establishing long-term relationships, so don't try to rush or push decisions. Entertainment makes part of this process – try not to skip these occasions. Be aware though that talking business during a meal is a no-no and that controversial topics are better avoided.

senior & disabled travellers
高齢の旅行者と障害をもつ旅行者

I have a disability.
私は障害者です。   wa·ta·shi wa shō·gai·sha des

I need assistance.
手を貸してください。   te o ka·shi·te ku·da·sai

What services do you have for people with a disability?
障害者のために   shō·gai·sha no ta·me ni
どんな設備が   don·na se·tsu·bi ga
ありますか?   a·ri·mas ka

Are there disabled toilets?
障害者用トイレは   shō·gai·sha·yō·toy·re wa
ありますか?   a·ri·mas ka

Are there disabled parking spaces?
障害者優先の   shō·gai·sha yū·sen no
駐車場はありますか?   chū·sha·jō wa a·ri·mas ka

Is there wheelchair access?
車椅子で入れますか?   ku·ru·ma·i·su de hai·re·mas ka

How wide is the entrance?
入口はどのくらいの   i·ri·gu·chi wa do·no ku·rai no
広さですか?   hi·ro·sa des ka

I'm deaf.
私は聴覚障害   wa·ta·shi wa chō·ka·ku·shō·gai
があります。   ga a·ri·mas

I have a hearing aid.
補聴器をしています。   ho·chō·ki o shi·te i·mas

Are guide dogs permitted?
盲導犬は入れますか?   mō·dō·ken wa hai·re·mas ka

How many steps are there?
段差は何段ありますか?   dan·sa wa nan·dan a·ri·mas ka

Is there a lift?
エレベータはありますか?   e·re·bē·ta wa a·ri·mas ka

senior & disabled

Are there rails in the bathroom?

バスルームに手すりは
ありますか？

bas·rū·mu ni te·su·ri wa
a·ri·mas ka

Could you call me a disabled taxi?

障害者用タクシーを
呼んでもらえますか？

shō·gai·sha·yō·tak·shī o
yon·de mo·ra·e·mas ka

Are there train carriages for people with a disability?

障害者のための
車両はありますか？

shō·gai·sha no ta·me no
sha·ryō wa a·ri·mas ka

Could you help me cross the street safely?

道を渡るのを
手伝ってもらえますか？

mi·chi o wa·ta·ru no o
te·tsu·dat·te mo·ra·e·mas ka

Is there somewhere I can sit down?

座れるところは
ありますか？

su·wa·re·ru to·ko·ro wa
a·ri·mas ka

guide dog	盲導犬	mō·dō·ken
older person	高齢者	kō·rē·sha
person with a disability	障害者	shō·gai·sha
ramp	傾斜路	kē·sha·ro
seat reserved for an older or disabled person	優先席	yū·sen·se·ki
walking frame	歩行車	ho·kō·sha
walking stick	杖	tsu·e
wheelchair	車椅子	ku·ru·ma·i·su

Is there a …?	…はありますか?	… wa a·ri·mas ka
baby change room	授乳室	ju·nyū·shi·tsu
child discount	子供割引	ko·do·mo·wa·ri·bi·ki
child-minding service	託児サービス	ta·ku·ji·sā·bis
child's portion	子供の 分量	ko·do·mo no bun·ryō
children's menu	子供の メニュー	ko·do·mo no me·nyū
crèche	託児所	ta·ku·ji·sho
family ticket	家族チケット	ka·zo·ku·chi·ket·to
I need a/an …	…が必要です。	… ga hi·tsu·yō des
baby seat	ベビーシート	be·bī·shī·to
(English-speaking) babysitter	(英語のできる) ベビーシッター	(ē·go no de·ki·ru) be·bī·shit·tā
booster seat	ジュニアシート	ju·nya·shī·to
cot	ベビーベッド	be·bī·bed·do
highchair	ベビーチェア	be·bī·chair
potty	おまる	o·ma·ru
pram	乳母車	u·ba·gu·ru·ma
sick bag	乗り物酔いの の袋	no·ri·mo·no·yoy no fu·ku·ro
stroller	ベビーカー	be·bī·kā
Where's the nearest …?	この近くの …はどこですか?	ko·no chi·ka·ku no … wa do·ko des ka
drinking fountain	水のみ場	mi·zu·no·mi·ba
park	公園	kō·en
playground	遊び場	a·so·bi·ba
swimming pool	プール	pū·ru
tap	水道	su·i·dō
theme park	テーマパーク	tē·ma·pā·ku
toyshop	おもちゃ屋	o·mo·cha·ya

Do you sell ...?	...はありますか？	... wa a·ri·mas ka
baby wipes	おしり拭き	o·shi·ri·fu·ki
baby painkillers	子供用の 鎮痛剤	ko·do·mo·yō no chin·tsū·zai
disposable nappies	紙おむつ	ka·mi·o·mu·tsu
tissues	ティッシュ	tis·shu

Do you hire out ...?	...のレンタルは ありますか？	... no ren·ta·ru wa a·ri·mas ka
prams	乳母車	u·ba·gu·ru·ma
strollers	ベビーカー	be·bī·kā

Are there any good places to take children around here?

この近くに子供
が喜ぶような
所がありますか？

ko·no chi·ka·ku ni ko·do·mo
ga yo·ro·ko·bu yō·na
to·ko·ro ga a·ri·mas ka

Are children allowed?

子供は入れますか？　ko·do·mo wa hai·re·mas ka

Where can I change a nappy?

おむつはどこで
換えられますか？

o·mu·tsu wa do·ko de
ka·e·ra·re·mas ka

Do you mind if I breast-feed here?

ここで母乳をあげて
もいいですか？

ko·ko de bo·nyū o a·ge·te
mo ī des ka

Could I have some paper and pencils please?

紙とエンピツを
お願いできますか？

ka·mi to em·pi·tsu o
o·ne·gai de·ki·mas ka

Is this suitable for ... year old children?

これは...歳の
子供向きですか？

ko·re wa ...·sai no
ko·do·mo·mu·ki des ka

Do you know a (dentist/doctor) who is good with children?

子供の扱いが上手
な(歯医者/お医者)さんを
知っていますか？

ko·do·mo no a·tsu·kai ga jō·zu
na (ha·i·sha/oy·sha)·san o
shit·te i·mas ka

For health issues, see **health**, page 199.

basics

基本

Yes.	はい。	hai
No.	いいえ。	ī·e
Please. (asking)	ください	ku·da·sai
Please. (offering)	どうぞ。	dō·zo
Thank you (very much).	(どうも)ありがとう (ございます)。	(dō·mo) a·ri·ga·tō (go·zai·mas)
You're welcome.	どういたしまして。	dō i·ta·shi·mash·te
Excuse me. (to get attention)	すみません。	su·mi·ma·sen
Sorry.	ごめんなさい。	go·men·na·sai

a degree in politeness

Reflecting the hierarchy in all Japanese relationships where someone's position is determined by factors like age, job, and experience as well as the social context of a conversation, Japanese shows different degrees of formality by using particular words and verb froms. This phrasebook uses the standard polite ·mas (ます) forms which are suitable for most situations you're likely to encounter.

greetings & goodbyes

あいさつ

Hello/Hi.	こんにちは。	kon·ni·chi·wa
Good ...		
afternoon	こんにちは。	kon·ni·chi·wa
day	こんにちは。	kon·ni·chi·wa
evening	こんばんは。	kom·ban·wa
morning	おはよう (ございます)。	o·ha·yō (go·zai·mas)

How are you?		
お元気ですか?		o·gen·ki des ka

Fine. And you?		
はい、元気です。		hai, gen·ki des
あなたは?		a·na·ta wa

(Excuse me,) What's your name?		
(失礼ですが、)		(shi·tsu·rē des ga)
お名前は何ですか?		o·na·ma·e wa nan des ka

My name is …		
私の名前は…		wa·ta·shi no na·ma·e wa …
です。		des

I'd like to introduce you to …		
…を紹介します。		… o shō·kai shi·mas

This is my …	こちらは	ko·chi·ra wa
	私の…です。	wa·ta·shi no … des
child	子供	ko·do·mo
colleague	同僚	dō·ryo
friend	友達	to·mo·da·chi
husband	主人	shu·jin
partner (intimate)	パートナー	pā·to·nā
wife	妻	tsu·ma

For family members, see **family**, page 108.

like a rice stalk in the wind

The most common gesture used when greeting is the bow – introducing yourself, greeting, thanking and saying goodbye are all done bowing. Timing, posture and movement of the bow are meant to be a reflection of sincerity, respect and maturity. In Japan a beautiful bow is often compared to a ripe rice stalk swaying in the wind – the more mature the person, the deeper the head is lowered. An improper bow on the other hand, hints a lack of education and maturity.

As a visitor to Japan you're not expected to emulate this ritual faithfully; a gentle nod will do. Kissing and hugging in Japan are still rare, except with close friends or family. For handshakes, it's best to let the locals take the lead so wait and let them instigate this process if they feel comfortable doing so.

I'm pleased to meet you.	お会いできて うれしいです。	o·ai de·ki·te u·re·shī des
See you later.	また会いましょう。	ma·ta ai·ma·shō
Goodbye.	さようなら。	sa·yō·na·ra
Bye.	じゃ、また。	ja ma·ta
Good night.	おやすみ（なさい）。	o·ya·su·mi (na·sai)
Bon voyage!	よい旅を！	yoy·ta·bi o

addressing people

話しかける

| Mr/Ms/Mrs/Miss | …さん | …san |
| Sir/Madam | …さま | …sama |

everyone's a san

In Japan people normally call each other by their surname and add the suffix ·san（さん）, eg su·zu·ki·san（鈴木さん）– avoid using first names unless invited to do so. It's also common to call people by their title instead of their name, like sha·chō（社長）for a company president and sen·sē（先生）for a doctor or teacher (literally meaning 'master'). You may also notice older people addressing children or young women with the suffix ·chan（ちゃん）as a term of endearment.

Avoid using all forms of the second person pronoun 'you' altogether in Japanese speech as it can sound too direct – it will be understood from context who you're referring to when speaking (for more information regarding pronouns, see the **phrasebuilder**, page 27).

meeting people

making conversation

The Japanese love a chat – just avoid criticising aspects of the Japanese culture too vigorously as your comments might be taken quite personally. Never get visibly angry or shout as this leaves a bad impression. For more info on conversation topics, see **politics & social issues**, page 116.

Isn't it (hot) today?
今日は(暑い)ですね。   kyō wa (a·tsu·i) des ne

What a beautiful day.
素晴らしい日ですね。   su·ba·ra·shī hi des ne

(Nice/Awful/Strange) weather, isn't it?
(いい/ひどい/変な)   (ī/hi·doy/hen·na)
天気ですね。   ten·ki des ne

Do you live here?
ここに住んでいますか?   ko·ko ni sun·de i·mas ka

Where are you going?
どこに行きますか?   do·ko ni i·ki·mas ka

What are you doing?
何をしていますか?   na·ni o shi·te i·mas ka

Do you like it here?
ここが好きですか?   ko·ko ga su·ki des ka

I love it here.
ここが大好きです。   ko·ko ga dai·su·ki des

What's this called?
これは何といいますか?   ko·re wa nan to ī·mas ka

Can I take a photo (of you)?
(あなたの)写真を   (a·na·ta no) sha·shin o
撮ってもいいですか?   tot·te mo ī des ka

That's (beautiful), isn't it?
(きれい)ですね。   (ki·rē) des ne

Are you here on holidays?
休暇でここに   kyū·ka de ko·ko ni
来ましたか?   ki·mash·ta ka

Hey! (In an argument)	おい！	oy
Hey! (for attention)	ちょっと、	chot·to
	ちょっと！	chot·to
Great!	すごい！	su·goy
Sure.	もちろん。	mo·chi·ron
Maybe.	たぶん。	ta·bun
So-so.	まあまあ。	mā·mā
No way!	だめ！	da·me
Just a minute.	ちょっと	chot·to
	待って。	mat·te
It's OK.	いいよ。	ī·yo
No problem.	だいじょうぶ。	dai·jō·bu
Good luck.	がんばって。	gam·bat·te
Totally/For sure!	絶対！	zet·tai
No kidding?	マジ？	ma·ji
Just joking.	冗談です。	jō·dan des
Really?	ほんと？	hon·to
What?	なに？	na·ni

I'm here …	…ここに	… ko·ko ni
	来ました。	ki·mash·ta
for a holiday	休暇で	kyū·ka de
on business	仕事で	shi·go·to de
to study	勉強のために	ben·kyō no ta·me ni

How long are you here for?
いつまでここにいますか？　i·tsu ma·de ko·ko ni i·mas ka

I'm here for (two) weeks.
ここに (2) 週間います。　ko·ko ni (ni)·shū·kan i·mas

I'm here for (four) days.
ここに (4) 日間います。　ko·ko ni (yok)·ka·kan i·mas

nationalities

Where are you from?
どちらから来ましたか？　　　do·chi·ra ka·ra ki·mash·ta ka

I'm from ...　　　　　　…から来ました。　　　… ka·ra ki·mash·ta
　Australia　　　　　　オーストラリア　　　ō·sto·ra·rya
　Canada　　　　　　　カナダ　　　　　　　ka·na·da
　Singapore　　　　　　シンガポール　　　　shin·ga·pō·ru

age

Talking about age did not use to be a big issue, but more recently, the topic is best avoided when speaking to women.

How old are you?
おいくつですか？　　　　　oy·ku·tsu des ka

How old is your (son/daughter)?
(息子/娘)さんは　　　　　　(mu·su·ko/mu·su·me)·san wa
おいくつですか？　　　　　oy·ku·tsu des ka

I'm ... years old.
私は…歳です。　　　　　　wa·ta·shi wa …·sai des

He's ... years old.
彼は…歳です。　　　　　　ka·re wa …·sai des

She's ... years old.
彼女は…歳です。　　　　　ka·no·jo wa …·sai des

Too old!
もう歳です。　　　　　　　mō to·shi des

I'm younger than I look.
私は見た目より　　　　　　wa·ta·shi wa mi·ta·me yo·ri
若いです。　　　　　　　　wa·kai des

For your age, see **numbers & amounts**, page 35.

occupations & studies

What's your occupation?
お仕事は何ですか?　　　　o·shi·go·to wa nan des ka

I work in (sales & marketing).
私は(営業)の　　　　　　wa·ta·shi wa (ē·gyō) no
仕事をしています。　　　　shi·go·to o shi·te i·mas

I'm a ...	私は…です。	wa·ta·shi wa ... des
businessperson	ビジネスマン	bi·ji·nes·man
chef	シェフ	she·fu
employee (private company)	会社員	kai·sha·in
farmer	農民	nō·min
fisherman	漁師	ryō·shi
homemaker	主夫/主婦 m/f	shu·fu/shu·fu
journalist	ジャーナリスト	jā·na·ris·to
public servant	公務員	kō·mu·in
teacher	教師	kyō·shi

I'm ...	私は…です。	wa·ta·shi wa ... des
retired	退職者	tai·sho·ku·sha
self-employed	自営業者	ji·ē·gyō·sha
unemployed	失業者	shi·tsu·gyō·sha

I've been made redundant.
リストラされました。　　　ri·su·to·ra sa·re·mash·ta

What are you studying?
何を勉強していますか?　　na·ni o ben·kyō shi·te i·mas ka

I'm studying (science).
私は　　　　　　　　　　wa·ta·shi wa
(自然科学)を　　　　　　(shi·zen·ka·ga·ku) o
勉強しています。　　　　ben·kyō shi·te i·mas

family

Japanese uses different forms for certain words and verbs depending on social context and the specific relationship between the speaker and the listener. One category of such words are the kinship terms which take different forms depending on whether you're talking about your own family or the listener's family. Use the words in the 'my' column to refer to your own family, those in the 'your' column to refer to someone else's relatives.

	my		your	
brother	兄弟	kyō·dai	ご兄弟	go·kyō·dai
daughter	娘	mu·su·me	娘さん	mu·su·me·san
family	家族	ka·zo·ku	ご家族	go·ka·zo·ku
father	父	chi·chi	お父さん	o·tō·san
granddaughter	孫娘	ma·go· mu·su·me	孫娘さん	ma·go· mu·su·me·san
grandfather	祖父	so·fu	おじいさん	o·jī·san
grandmother	祖母	so·bo	おばあさん	o·bā·san
grandson	孫	ma·go	お孫さん	o·ma·go·san
husband	夫	ot·to	ご主人	go·shu·jin
mother	母	ha·ha	お母さん	o·kā·san
partner	パートナー	pā·to·nā	パートナー	pā·to·nā
sister	姉妹	shi·mai	ご姉妹	go·shi·mai
son	息子	mu·su·ko	息子さん	mu·su·ko·san
wife	妻	tsu·ma	奥さん	o·ku·san

Do you have a (brother)?
(ご兄弟) がいますか?　　　(go·kyō·dai) ga i·mas ka

I have a (daughter).
(娘) がいます。　　　(mu·su·me) ga i·mas

I don't have a (partner).
(パートナー) がいません。　　　(pā·to·nā) ga i·ma·sen

Are you married?
結婚していますか?　　　　kek·kon shi·te i·mas ka

I live with someone.
同棲しています。　　　　　dō·sē shi·te i·mas

I'm ...　　　　　　　私は…　　　　　　　wa·ta·shi wa ...
   married　　　　　結婚しています　　　kek·kon shi·te i·mas
   separated　　　　離婚しました　　　　ri·kon shi·mash·ta
   single　　　　　　独身です　　　　　　do·ku·shin des

---

kids' talk

When's your birthday?
お誕生日はいつ?　　　　　o·tan·jō·bi wa i·tsu

Do you go to (school/kindergarten)?
(学校/幼稚園)に行って　　(gak·kō/yō·chi·en) ni it·te
いるの?　　　　　　　　　i·ru no

What grade are you in?
何年生?　　　　　　　　　nan·nen·sē

Do you like ...?　　　…は好き?　　　　　…wa su·ki
   school　　　　　学校　　　　　　　gak·kō
   sport　　　　　　スポーツ　　　　　spōts
   your teacher　　先生　　　　　　　sen·sē

What do you do after school?
放課後は何をするの?　　　hō·ka·go wa na·ni o su·ru no

Do you learn English?
英語を勉強してる?　　　　ē·go o ben·kyō shi·te·ru

I come from very far away.
私はとても遠く　　　　　wa·ta·shi wa to·te·mo tō·ku
からきたの。　　　　　　ka·ra ki·ta no

Are you lost?
迷子になっちゃったの?　　mai·go ni nat·chat·ta no

farewells

Tomorrow is my last day here.
明日がここにいる　　　　a·shi·ta ga ko·ko ni i·ru
最後の日です。　　　　　sai·go no hi des

Here's my ...　　　　これが私　　　　ko·re ga wa·ta·shi
　　　　　　　　　　　　の…です。　　　no ... des
What's your ...?　　　あなたの…は　　a·na·ta no ... wa
　　　　　　　　　　　　何ですか?　　　nan des ka

　address　　　　　　住所　　　　　　jū·sho
　email address　　　Eメールアドレス　ī·mē·ru·a·do·res
　phone number　　　電話番号　　　　den·wa·ban·gō

Keep in touch.
連絡をとりましょう。　　ren·ra·ku o to·ri·ma·shō

It's been great meeting you.
あなたに会えてとても　　a·na·ta ni a·e·te to·te·mo
よかったです。　　　　　yo·kat·ta des

well wishing		
Bon voyage!	よい旅を!	yoy ta·bi o
Congratulations!	おめでとう	o·me·de·tō
	(ございます)。	(go·zai·mas)
Good luck!	がんばって!	gam·bat·te
Happy birthday!	誕生日	tan·jō·bi
	おめでとう	o·me·de·tō
	(ございます)。	(go·zai·mas)
Happy New Year!	明けまして	a·ke·mash·te
	おめでとう	o·me·de·tō
	(ございます)。	(go·zai·mas)
Hooray!	万歳!	ban·zai
Merry Christmas!	メリー	me·rī·
	クリスマス!	ku·ri·su·mas
Look after yourself.	お大事に。	o·dai·ji ni
(to a sick person)		

Note that when you're in a more formal situation, you can add go·zai·mas (ございます), 'very much', after some of these wishes.

common interests

共通の趣味

What do you do in your spare time?
ひまなとき何を　　　　　hi·ma na to·ki na·ni o
しますか?　　　　　　　shi·mas ka

Do you like ...?	…が好きですか?	... ga su·ki des ka
I like ...	…が好きです。	... ga su·ki des
I don't like ...	…が好きじゃ ありません。	... ga su·ki ja a·ri·ma·sen

billiards	ビリヤード	bi·ri·yā·do
calligraphy	書道	sho·dō
computer games	コンピュータゲーム	kom·pyū·ta·gē·mu
cooking	料理	ryō·ri
dancing	ダンス	dan·su
drawing	スケッチ	sket·chi
films	映画	ē·ga
gardening	庭仕事	ni·wa·shi·go·to
hiking	ハイキング	hai·kin·gu
music	音楽	on·ga·ku
painting	絵画	kai·ga
photography	写真	sha·shin
reading	読書	do·ku·sho
shopping	買い物	kai·mo·no
socialising	おしゃべり	o·sha·be·ri
sport	スポーツ	spō·tsu
surfing the Internet	インターネットサーフィン	in·tā·net·to· sā·fin
travelling	旅行	ryo·kō
watching TV	テレビ	te·re·bi

For sporting activities, see **sport**, page 139.

While you're in Japan why not try your hand at these pastimes:

bonsai (miniature trees)	盆栽	bon·sai
go (board game)	碁	go
ikebana (flower arranging)	生け花	i·ke·ba·na
manga (cartoons)	漫画	man·ga
origami (paper folding)	折り紙	o·ri·ga·mi
pachinko (vertical pinball game)	パチンコ	pa·chin·ko
shogi (Japanese chess)	将棋	shō·gi

music

音楽

Do you ...?	…ますか?	…mas ka
dance	ダンスをし	dan·su o shi
go to concerts	コンサートに行き	kon·sā·to ni i·ki
listen to music	音楽を聴き	on·ga·ku o ki·ki
play an instrument	楽器を演奏し	gak·ki o en·sō shi
sing	歌い	u·tai
What ... do you like?	どんな…が 好きですか?	don·na … ga su·ki des ka
bands	バンド	ban·do
music	音楽	on·ga·ku
singers	歌手	ka·shu

blues	ブルース	bu·rū·su
classical music	クラシック	ku·ra·shik·ku
electronic music	エレクトロニック	e·re·ku·to·ro·nik·ku·
	ミュージック	myū·jik·ku
enka (genre of popular songs)	演歌	en·ka
ethnic music	民族音楽	min·zo·ku·on·ga·ku
folk music	フォーク	fō·ku
hip hop	ヒップホップ	hip·pu·hop·pu
Japanese folk music	民謡	min·yō
Japanese pop (until late 80s)	歌謡曲	ka·yō·kyo·ku
Japanese pop (90s onwards)	J-ポップ	jē·pop·pu
Japanese traditional music	邦楽	hō·ga·ku
jazz	ジャズ	ja·zu
'noise' music	ノイズ	noyz
pop	ポップ	pop·pu
rock	ロック	rok·ku
world music	ワールド	wā·ru·do·
	ミュージック	myū·jik·ku

Planning to go to a concert? See **tickets**, page 46 and **going out**, page 123.

cinema & theatre

映画と演劇

I feel like going to a ...	…に行こうと 思います。	… ni i·kō to o·moy·mas
Did you like the ...?	…はよかった ですか?	… wa yo·kat·ta des ka
ballet	バレエ	ba·rē
film	映画	ē·ga
play	劇	ge·ki

What's showing at the ... tonight?	今晩はどんな …がありますか?	kom·ban wa don·na ... ga a·ri·mas ka
cinema	映画	ē·ga
theatre	舞台	bu·tai

Is it in English?
英語ですか?   ē·go des ka

Does it have (English) subtitles?
(英語の)字幕が
ありますか?   (ē·go no) ji·ma·ku ga a·ri·mas ka

Is this seat vacant?
この席は空いていますか?   ko·no se·ki wa ai·te i·mas ka

Have you seen ...?
…をもう観ましたか?   ... o mō mi·mash·ta ka

Who's in it?
だれが演じていますか?   da·re ga en·ji·te i·mas ka

It stars ...
主役は…です。   shu·ya·ku wa ... des

I thought it was ...	…と思います。	... to o·moy·mas
excellent	素晴らしかった	su·ba·ra·shi·kat·ta
long	長すぎた	na·ga·su·gi·ta
OK	まあまあだった	mā·mā dat·ta

I like ...	…は好きです。	... wa su·ki des
I don't like ...	…は好きじゃありません。	... wa su·ki ja a·ri·ma·sen
action movies	アクションムービー	a·ku·shon·mū·bī
animé films	アニメ	a·ni·me
comedies	コメディ	ko·me·di
documentaries	ドキュメンタリー	do·kyu·men·ta·rī
drama	ドラマ	do·ra·ma
horror movies	ホラー映画	ho·rā·ē·ga
Japanese cinema	日本映画	ni·hon·ē·ga
kung fu movies	カンフー映画	kan·fū·ē·ga
samurai dramas	時代劇	ji·dai·ge·ki
sci-fi	SF	e·su·e·fu
short films	短編映画	tam·pen·ē·ga
thrillers	スリラー	su·ri·rā
war movies	戦争映画	sen·sō·ē·ga
yakuza movies	ヤクザ映画	ya·ku·za·ē·ga

feelings

感情

Are you …?	あなたは…か?	a·na·ta wa … ka
I'm …	私は…	wa·ta·shi wa …
cold	寒いです	sa·mu·i des
disappointed	がっかり	gak·ka·ri
	しました	shi·mash·ta
embarrassed	恥ずかしいです	ha·zu·ka·shī des
happy	幸せです	shi·a·wa·se des
hot	暑いです	a·tsu·i des
hungry	お腹が	o·na·ka ga
	すきました	su·ki·mash·ta
in a hurry	急いでいます	i·so·i·de i·mas
sad	悲しいです	ka·na·shī des
thirsty	のどが	no·do ga
	渇きました	ka·wa·ki·mash·ta
tired	疲れました	tsu·ka·re·mash·ta
worried	心配して	shim·pai shi·te
	います	i·mas

If feeling unwell, see **health**, page 199.

mixed emotions		
a little	ちょっと	chot·to
I'm a little sad.	ちょっと悲しい	chot·to ka·na·shī
	です。	des
extremely	本当に	hon·tō ni
I'm extremely sorry.	本当に	hon·tō ni
	すみません。	su·mi·ma·sen
very	とても	to·te·mo
I feel very lucky.	とても運が	to·te·mo un ga
	良かったと	yo·kat·ta to
	思います。	o·moy·mas

opinions

意見

Did you like it?
好きですか?　　　　　　　su·ki des ka

What do you think of it?
どう思いますか?　　　　　dō o·moy·mas ka

I thought it was …	…と思いました。	… to o·moy·mash·ta
It's …	…です。	… des
awful	ひどい	hi·doy
beautiful	美しい	u·tsu·ku·shī
boring	つまらない	tsu·ma·ra·nai
great	素晴らしい	su·ba·ra·shī
interesting	面白い	o·mo·shi·roy
too expensive	高すぎる	ta·ka·su·gi·ru

I thought it was …	…だと 思いました。	… da to o·moy·mash·ta
It's …	…です。	… des
OK	まあまあ	mā·mā
strange	変	hen

politics & social issues

政治と社会情勢

The Japanese generally tend not to discuss politics openly and avoid mentioning which party they support. Be aware that bold statements regarding Japan and Japanese culture might be taken quite personally and are better avoided altogether.

Who do you vote for?
だれに投票しますか?　　　da·re ni tō·hyō shi·mas ka

I support the ... party.	私は…党を支持します。	wa·ta·shi wa ...·tō o shi·ji shi·mas
I'm a member of the ... party.	私は…党員です。	wa·ta·shi wa ...·tō·in des
communist	共産	kyō·san
conservative	保守	ho·shu
democratic	民主	min·shu
green	緑の	mi·do·ri no
liberal (progressive)	由	ji·yū
liberal democratic	自民	ji·min
social democratic	社会民主	sha·kai·min·shu
socialist	社会	sha·kai

political landscape		
DPJ (Democratic Party of Japan)	民主党	min·shu·tō
JCP (Japanese Communist Party)	共産党	kyō·san·tō
LDP (Liberal Democratic Party)	自民党	ji·min·tō
New Komeito	公明党	kō·mē·tō
SDP (Social Democratic Party)	社民党	sha·min·tō

Did you hear about ...?
…について聞きましたか？
... ni tsu·i·te ki·ki·mash·ta ka

Do you agree with it?
それに賛成しますか？
so·re ni san·sē shi·mas ka

I agree with ...
…に賛成します。
... ni san·sē shi·mas

I don't agree with ...
…に賛成しません。
... ni san·sē shi·ma·sen

How do people feel about ...?
みんなは…についてどう思っていますか？
min·na wa ... ni tsu·i·te dō o·mot·te i·mas ka

abortion	避妊	hi·nin
animal rights	動物の権利	dō·bu·tsu no ken·ri
corruption	汚職	o·sho·ku
crime	犯罪	han·zai
discrimination	差別	sa·be·tsu
drugs	麻薬	ma·ya·ku
the economy	経済	kē·zai
education	教育	kyōy·ku
the environment	環境	kan·kyō
equal opportunity	機会均等	ki·kai·kin·tō
euthanasia	安楽死	an·ra·ku·shi
globalisation	グローバル化	gu·rō·ba·ru·ka
human rights	人権	jin·ken
immigration	移民	i·min
indigenous issues	先住民問題	sen·jū·min·mon·dai
inequality	不平等	fu·byō·dō
North Korean issues	北朝鮮問題	ki·ta·chō·sen· mon·dai
party politics	政党政治	sē·tō·sē·ji
privatisation	民営化	min·ē·ka
racism	人種差別	jin·shu·sa·be·tsu
sexism	性差別	sē·sa·be·tsu
social welfare	社会福祉	sha·kai·fu·ku·shi
suicide	自殺問題	ji·sa·tsu·mon·dai
terrorism	テロリズム	te·ro·ri·zu·mu
unemployment	失業問題	shi·tsu·gyō·mon·dai
US bases	アメリカ軍基地	a·me·ri·ka·gun·ki·chi
the war in ...	…戦争	...sen·sō

the environment

環境

Is there a ... problem here?
ここには…の問題
がありますか?

ko·ko ni wa ... no mon·dai
ga a·ri·mas ka

What should be done about ...?
…について何を
しなければなりませんか?

... ni tsu·i·te na·ni o
shi·na·ke·re·ba na·ri·ma·sen ka

conservation	自然保護	shi·zen·ho·go
deforestation	森林伐採	shin·rin·bas·sai
dioxin	ダイオキシン	dai·o·ki·shin
drought	干害	kan·gai
ecosystem	エコシステム	e·ko·shi·su·te·mu
endangered species	絶滅に 瀕している 生物	ze·tsu·me·tsu ni hin·shi·te i·ru sē·bu·tsu
genetically modified food	遺伝子組み換え 食品	i·den·shi ku·mi·ka·e sho·ku·hin
hunting	狩猟	shu·ryō
hydroelectricity	水力発電	su·i·ryo·ku· ha·tsu·den
irrigation	灌漑	kan·gai
nuclear energy	原子力	gen·shi·ryo·ku
nuclear testing	核実験	ka·ku·jik·ken
ozone layer	オゾン層	o·zon·sō
pesticides	殺虫剤	sat·chū·zai
pollution	公害	kō·gai
poverty	貧困	hin·kon
recycling programme	リサイクル	ri·sai·ku·ru
toxic waste	有害廃棄物	yū·gai·hai·ki·bu·tsu
water supply	水資源	mi·zu·shi·gen
whaling	捕鯨	ho·gē

Is this a protected …?	これは保護されて いる…ですか?	ko·re wa ho·go sa·re·te i·ru … des ka
forest	森	mo·ri
park	公園	kō·en
species	生物	sē·bu·tsu

a pat on the back

The Japanese will warm easily to anyone who has some knowledge of their country or language. A few words in Japanese will get you a long way – you'll be complimented on your language skills when making even the slightest effort to speak Japanese. If you're able to respond to these pats on the back in a typically modest Japanese fashion, you'll be even more sure to impress. When they say:

Your Japanese is so good.
日本語がお上手ですね。　　ni·hon·go ga o·jō·zu des ne

you could answer with:

It's nothing really.
それほどでも。　　　　　　so·re·ho·do de·mo

Similarly, it's good manners to exchange some niceties when giving or receiving presents. The lucky recipient of the present could add the following phrase to a simple 'Thank you very much.', dō·mo a·ri·ga·tō go·zai·mas (どうも ありがとうございます):

You shouldn't have bothered.
そんなに気を　　　　　　　son·na ni ki o
使わなくて　　　　　　　　tsu·ka·wa·na·ku·te
もよかったのに。　　　　　mo o·kat·ta no ni

to which the person giving the present could reply:

It's my pleasure.
どういたしまして。　　　　dō i·ta·shi mash·te

It's nothing really.
つまらないものですが。　　tsu·ma·ra·nai mo·no des ga

where to go

どこに行く

Eating, drinking, karaoke, going to the theatre and nightclubbing are popular forms of social activity in Japan. Baseball games and sumo tournaments, which draw huge crowds, are also important opportunities for social outings. Whatever the form of entertainment, city-dwellers tend to time their outings around the availability of trains which stop running around 12.30am.

What's there to do in the evenings?
夜は何ができますか?　　　yo·ru wa na·ni ga de·ki·mas ka

What's on ...?	…は何が	… wa na·ni ga
	ありますか?	a·ri·mas ka
locally	近所に	kin·jo ni
this weekend	今週の	kon·shū no
	週末	shū·ma·tsu
today	今日	kyō
tonight	今夜	kon·ya
Where can I	どこに行けば	do·ko ni i·ke·ba
find ...?	…がありますか?	… ga a·ri·mas ka
clubs	クラブ	ku·ra·bu
gay venues	ゲイの場所	gē no ba·sho
Japanese-style	居酒屋	i·za·ka·ya
pubs		
places to eat	食事が	sho·ku·ji ga
	できる所	de·ki·ru to·ko·ro
pubs	パブ	pa·bu

Is there a local ... guide?	地元の…ガイド はありますか?	ji·mo·to no ...gai·do wa a·ri·mas ka
entertainment	エンターテ イメント	en·tā·tē· men·to
film	映画	ē·ga
gay	ゲイ	gē
music	音楽	on·ga·ku

I did it my way

Hugely popular around the world, karaoke is a uniquely Japanese invention. Taken from the words ka·ra (空), 'empty' and ō·kes·to·ra (オーケストラ), 'orchestra', it literally means 'empty orchestra'.

If you're in the mood for a croon you'll first have to decide on a venue for your performance. The most expensive is the 'hostess bar', simply called bā (バー), where the staff serve you drinks, assist in the selection of music and, at times, will even sing with you. Karaoke boxes, ka·ra·o·ke·bok·kus (カラオケボックス) – rooms that can be booked on an hourly basis – are hugely popular. Drinks and music are self-serve. The karaoke bar, ka·ra·o·ke (カラオケ), which is a drinking place with a stage and a karaoke machine, is another option.

Wherever you'd like to take centre stage, the following phrases might come in handy:

Let's sing together.
いっしょに歌いましょう。 is·sho ni u·tai·ma·shō

Are there English songs?
英語の曲がありますか? ē·go no kyo·ku ga a·ri·mas ka

I don't know this song.
この曲は知りません。 ko·no kyo·ku wa shi·ri·ma·sen

I'm not good at singing.
歌は上手じゃありません。 u·ta wa jō·zu ja a·ri·ma·sen

Only if you sing with me.
いっしょに歌って くれれば歌います。 is·sho ni u·tat·te ku·re·re·ba u·tai·mas

I'm a shy person.
恥ずかしいです。 ha·zu·ka·shī des

I feel like going to a ...	…に行きたい 気分です。	... ni i·ki·tai ki·bun des
ballet	バレエ	ba·rē
bar	バー	bā
café	カフェ	ka·fe
concert	コンサート	kon·sā·to
film	映画	ē·ga
karaoke bar	カラオケ	ka·ra·o·ke
nightclub	ナイトクラブ	nai·to·ku·ra·bu
party	パーティー	pā·tī
performance	パフォーマンス	pa·fō·man·su
play	劇	ge·ki
pub	パブ	pa·bu
restaurant	レストラン	res·to·ran

For more on bars and drinks, see **eating out**, page 164.

invitations

招待

What are you doing ...?	…何をする予定 ですか?	... na·ni o su·ru yo·tē des ka
now	これから	ko·re·ka·ra
this weekend	今週の 週末	kon·shū no shū·ma·tsu
tonight	今夜	kon·ya

Would you like to go (for a) ...?	…に 行きませんか?	... ni i·ki·ma·sen ka
I feel like going (for a) ...	…に行きたい 気分です。	... ni i·ki·tai ki·bun des
coffee	コーヒー	kō·hī
dancing	ダンス	dan·su
drink	飲み	no·mi
meal	食事	sho·ku·ji
out somewhere	どこか外	do·ko ka so·to
walk	散歩	sam·po

My round.
私の番です。
wa·ta·shi no ban des

Do you know a good restaurant?
いいレストランを知って
いますか?
ī res·to·ran o shit·te
i·mas ka

Do you want to come to the concert with me?
いっしょにコンサートに
行きませんか?
is·sho ni kon·sā·to ni
i·ki·ma·sen ka

We're having a party.
パーティーをします。
pā·tī o shi·mas

You should come.
来てください。
ki·te ku·da·sai

responding to invitations

Sure!
もちろん!
mo·chi·ron

Yes, I'd love to.
はい、ぜひとも。
hai, ze·hi to·mo

That's very kind of you.
親切にありがとう。
shin·se·tsu ni a·ri·ga·tō

Where shall we go?
どこに行きましょうか?
do·ko ni i·ki·ma·shō ka

No, I'm afraid I can't.
すみませんが、ちょっと
都合が悪いんです。
su·mi·ma·sen ga, chot·to
tsu·gō ga wa·ru·in des

What about tomorrow?
明日はどうですか?
a·shi·ta wa dō des ka

Sorry, I can't ... ごめんなさい、 go·men·na·sai,
　　　　　　…ないんです。 …nain des
  dance 踊れ o·do·re
  sing 歌え u·ta·e

arranging to meet

What time will we meet?
何時に会いましょうか？　　　　nan·ji ni ai·ma·shō ka

Where will we meet?
どこで会いましょうか？　　　　do·ko de ai·ma·shō ka

Let's meet ...　　　　…会いましょう。　… ai·ma·shō
　at (eight) o'clock　　(8)時に　　　　　(ha·chi)·ji ni
　at (the entrance)　　（入口）で　　　　(i·ri·gu·chi) de

I'll pick you up.
迎えに行きます。　　　　　　　mu·ka·e ni i·ki·mas

Are you ready?
準備はいいですか？　　　　　　jum·bi wa ī des ka

I'm ready.
準備はいいです。　　　　　　　jum·bi wa ī des

I'll be coming later.
遅れて行きます。　　　　　　　o·ku·re·te i·ki·mas

Where will you be?
どこにいますか？　　　　　　　do·ko ni i·mas ka

If I'm not there by (nine), don't wait for me.
(9)時までに私が　　　　　　　(ku)·ji ma·de ni wa·ta·shi ga
行かなかったら　　　　　　　　i·ka·na·kat·ta·ra
待たないでください。　　　　　ma·ta·nai de ku·da·sai

OK!
OK！　　　　　　　　　　　　ō·kē

I'll see you then.
じゃ、そこで会いましょう。　　ja, so·ko de ai·ma·shō

See you later.
あとで会いましょう。　　　　　a·to de ai·ma·shō

See you tomorrow.
　明日会いましょう。　　　　　　a·shi·ta ai·ma·shō

I'm looking forward to it.
　楽しみにしています。　　　　　ta·no·shi·mi ni shi·te i·mas

Sorry I'm late.
　遅れてすみません。　　　　　　o·ku·re·te su·mi·ma·sen

Never mind.
　だいじょうぶです。　　　　　　dai·jō·bu des

drugs

麻薬

I don't take drugs.
　麻薬はやりません。　　　　　　ma·ya·ku wa ya·ri·ma·sen

I take … occasionally.
　ときどき … をやります。　　　to·ki·do·ki … o ya·ri·mas

Do you want to have a smoke?
　吸いたいですか?　　　　　　　su·i·tai des ka

Do you have a light?
　火はありますか?　　　　　　　hi wa a·ri·mas ka

I'm high.
　ぶっとんでます。　　　　　　　but·ton·de·mas

asking someone out

デートに誘う

Would you like to do something (tomorrow)?
(明日)何か
しませんか?
(a·shi·ta) na·ni ka
shi·ma·sen ka

Where would you like to go (tonight)?
(今晩)どこに行きたい
ですか?
(kom·ban) do·ko ni i·ki·tai
des ka

Yes, I'd love to.
はい、ぜひとも。
hai, ze·hi to·mo

Sorry, I can't.
すみません、
行けません。
su·mi·ma·sen,
i·ke·ma·sen

local talk		
He's (a) ...	彼は…です。	ka·re wa ... des
bastard	ひどいやつ	hi·doy ya·tsu
cute	かわいい	ka·wa·ī
good looking	かっこいい	kak·ko·ī
handsome	ハンサム	han·sa·mu
hot	セクシー	sek·shī
She's (a) ...	彼女は…です。	ka·no·jo wa ... des
bad woman	悪い	wa·ru·i
beautiful	きれい	ki·rē
cute	かわいい	ka·wa·ī
good looking	美人	bi·jin
hot	セクシー	sek·shī

pick-up lines

Would you like a drink?
何か飲みませんか？
na·ni ka no·mi·ma·sen ka

You look like someone I know.
私の知っている人に
よく似ています。
wa·ta·shi no shit·te i·ru hi·to ni
yo·ku ni·te i·mas

You're a fantastic dancer.
踊りがすごく
うまいですね。
o·do·ri ga su·go·ku
u·mai des ne

How about some tea?
お茶しませんか？
o·cha shi·ma·sen ka

Do you want to come to my place?
うちに来ない？
u·chi ni ko·nai

Can I ...?　…もいいですか？　… mo ī des ka
　dance with you　いっしょに踊って　is·sho ni o·dot·te
　sit here　ここに座って　ko·ko ni su·wat·te
　take you home　お宅まで　o·ta·ku ma·de
　　送って　o·kut·te

rejections

断る

I'm here with my boyfriend.
彼氏と一緒なんです。
ka·re·shi to is·sho nan des

I'm here with my girlfriend.
彼女と一緒なんです。
ka·no·jo to is·sho nan des

Excuse me, I have to go now.
すみませんが、もう
行かなくてはなりません。
su·mi·ma·sen ga, mō
i·ka·na·ku·te wa na·ri·ma·sen

No, thank you.
いいえ、けっこうです。
ī·e, kek·kō des

No way!
やだ！
ya da

Leave me alone, please.
独りにしておいて
ください。
hi·to·ri ni shi·te oy·te
ku·da·sai

I'm with someone.
連れがいますので。
tsu·re ga i·mas no·de

Go away! あっちへ行け! at·chi e i·ke
**You're a pain
  in the neck!** うざい! u·zai
You're annoying! しつこい! shi·tsu·koy
Piss off! ほっといて! hot·toy·te
Fat chance! まさか! ma·sa·ka
Stop it! やめて! ya·me·te

getting closer

親密になる

I like you very much.
あなたがとても好き。
a·na·ta ga to·te·mo su·ki

You're great.
すごい。
su·goy

Can I kiss you?
キスしてもいい?
ki·su shi·te mo ī

Do you want to come inside for a while?
ちょっと、うちに寄って
いきませんか?
chot·to u·chi ni yot·te
i·ki·ma·sen ka

Do you want a massage?
マッサージしましょうか?
mas·sā·ji shi·ma·shō ka

Can I stay over?
泊まってもいいですか?
to·mat·te mo ī des ka

セックス

Kiss me.
キスして。   ki·su shi·te

I want you.
あなたが欲しい。   a·na·ta ga ho·shī

Let's go to bed.
ベッドに行きましょう。   bed·do ni i·ki·ma·shō

Touch me here.
ここを触って。   ko·ko o sa·wat·te

Do you like this?
これは好き?   ko·re wa su·ki

I like that.
それは好きです。   ko·re wa su·ki des

I don't like that.
それは好きじゃありません。   ko·re wa su·ki ja a·ri·ma·sen

I think we should stop now.
これ以上はやめましょう。   ko·re i·jō wa ya·me·ma·shō

Do you have a (condom)?
（コンドーム）はありますか?   (kon·dō·mu) wa a·ri·mas ka

Let's use a (condom).
（コンドーム）を使いましょう。   (kon·dō·mu) o tsu·kai·ma·shō

I won't do it without protection.
避妊具なしでは   hi·nin·gu na·shi de wa
しません。   shi·ma·sen

Don't worry, I'll do it myself.
だいじょうぶ、   dai·jō·bu,
自分でやるから。   ji·bun de ya·ru ka·ra

It's my first time.
初めてです。   ha·ji·me·te des

It helps to have a sense of humour.
肩の力を抜いて   ka·ta no chi·ka·ra o nu·i·te
やろうよ。   ya·rō yo

Oh my god!	すごい！	su·goy
That's great!	素晴らしい！	su·ba·ra·shī
Easy tiger!	ちょっと待って！	chot·to mat·te
That was ...		
amazing	すばらしかった です。	su·ba·ra·shi·kat·ta des
romantic	ロマンチック でした。	ro·man·chik·ku desh·ta
wild	ワイルドでした。	wai·ru·do desh·ta

love

ラブ

I love you.
愛しています。　　　　　　　ai shi·te i·mas

I think we're good together.
いいカップルだと思います。　ī kap·pu·ru da to o·moy·mas

Will you ...?	…ませんか？	…ma·sen ka
go out with me	付き合い	tsu·ki·ai
marry me	結婚し	kek·kon shi
meet my	私の親	wa·ta·shi no o·ya
parents	に会い	ni ai

terms of endearment

The Japanese are generally more reserved about expressing emotions than many other cultures, so pet names are a lot less used than elsewhere.

However, some couples use nicknames derived from their first name. They might affectionately abbreviate each other's first name and add the suffix ·chan（ちゃん）expressing endearment: eg ta·ke·chan（たけちゃん）for ta·ke·shi（たけし）or ha·na·chan（はなちゃん）for ha·na·ko（はなこ）.

problems

Are you seeing someone else?
他の人と付き合って
いますか?
ho·ka no hi·to to tsu·ki·at·te
i·mas ka

He's just a friend.
彼はただの
友達です。
ka·re wa ta·da no
to·mo·da·chi des

She's just a friend.
彼女はただの
友達です。
ka·no·jo wa ta·da no
to·mo·da·chi des

You're just using me for sex.
私をセックスのため
だけに使っています。
wa·ta·shi o sek·kus no ta·me
da·ke ni tsu·kat·te i·mas

I don't think it's working out.
もう、うまくいかないと
思います。
mō u·ma·ku i·ka·nai to
o·moy·mas

We'll work it out.
どうにかしましょう。
dō ni ka shi·ma·shō

I never want to see you again.
もう2度と会いたくないです。 mō ni·do to ai·ta·ku nai des

leaving

I have to leave (tomorrow).
(明日)別れなければ
なりません。
(a·shi·ta) wa·ka·re·na·ke·re·ba
na·ri·ma·sen

I'll come and visit you.
あなたに会いに来ます。
a·na·ta ni ai ni ki·mas

I'll keep in touch.
連絡します。
ren·ra·ku shi·mas

I'll miss you.
さびしくなります。
sa·bi·shi·ku na·ri·mas

religion

宗教

What's your religion?
あなたの宗教は
何ですか？
a·na·ta no shū·kyō wa
nan des ka

I'm not religious.
私はあまり
宗教的ではありません。
wa·ta·shi wa a·ma·ri
shū·kyō·te·ki de wa a·ri·ma·sen

I'm ...	私は…です。	wa·ta·shi wa ... des
agnostic	不可知論者	fu·ka·chi·ron·ja
atheist	無神論者	mu·shin·ron·ja
Buddhist	仏教徒	buk·kyō·to
Catholic	カトリック教徒	ka·to·rik·ku·kyō·to
Christian	キリスト教徒	ki·ri·su·to·kyō·to
Hindu	ヒンドゥー教徒	hin·dū·kyō·to
Jewish	ユダヤ教徒	yu·da·ya·kyō·to
Muslim	イスラム教徒	i·su·ra·mu·kyō·to
Shinto	神道の信者	shin·tō no shin·ja

I believe in ... …を信じています。 ... o shin·ji·te i·mas
I don't believe …を信じて ... o shin·ji·te
in ... いません。 i·ma·sen

astrology	星占い	ho·shi·u·ra·nai
fate	運命	um·mē
God	神	ka·mi

Where can I ...? どこで… do·ko de ...
できますか？ de·ki·mas ka

attend a service	礼拝に参加	rē·hai ni san·ka
attend mass	ミサに参加	mi·sa ni san·ka
meditate	瞑想	mē·sō
pray	お祈り	oy·no·ri
worship	礼拝	rē·hai

cultural differences

文化の違い

Is this a local or national custom?
これは地元の習慣
ですか、それとも
全国的な習慣
ですか?

ko·re wa ji·mo·to no shū·kan
des ka, so·re·to·mo
zen·ko·ku·te·ki na shū·kan
des ka

I don't want to offend you.
不愉快な思いを
させたくありません。

fu·yu·kai na o·moy o
sa·se·ta·ku a·ri·ma·sen

I didn't mean to do anything wrong.
悪意でやったわけでは
ありません。

a·ku·i de yat·ta wa·ke de wa
a·ri·ma·sen

I'm not used to this.
これに慣れていません。

ko·re ni na·re·te i·ma·sen

I'd rather not join in.
参加を辞退したいと
思います。

san·ka o ji·tai shi·tai to
o·moy·mas

I'll try it.
やってみます。

yat·te mi·mas

I'm sorry, it's against my ...	すみませんが、それは私の…に反します。	su·mi·ma·sen ga so·re wa wa·ta·shi no ... ni han·shi·mas
beliefs	信仰	shin·kō
religion	宗教	shū·kyō
This is ...	これは…	ko·re wa ...
different	変わっています	ka·wat·te i·mas
fun	楽しいです	ta·no·shī des
interesting	おもしろいです	o·mo·shi·roy des

When's the ...	...はいつ	wa i·tsu
open?	開きますか?	... hi·ra·ki·mas ka
gallery	ギャラリー	gya·ra·rī
museum	美術館	bi·ju·tsu·kan

What kind of art are you interested in?

| どんな芸術に興味が | don·na gē·ju·tsu ni kyō·mi ga |
| ありますか? | a·ri·mas ka |

What's in the collection?

| 所蔵品には何が | sho·zō·hin ni wa na·ni ga |
| ありますか? | a·ri·mas ka |

What do you think of (Takashi Murakami)?

| (村上隆)をどう | (mu·ra·ka·mi ta·ka·shi) o dō |
| 思いますか? | o·moy·mas ka |

It's a/an ... exhibition.

| ...の展覧会です。 | ... no ten·ran·kai des |

I'm interested in ...

| ...に興味があります。 | ... ni kyō·mi ga a·ri·mas |

I like the works of ...

| ...の作品が好きです。 | ... no sa·ku·hin ga su·ki des |

... art	...アート	...ā·to
Edo	江戸	e·do
graphic	グラフィック	gu·ra·fik·ku
impressionist	印象派	in·shō·ha
modern	モダン	mo·dan
Momoyama	桃山	mo·mo·ya·ma
performance	パフォーマンス	pa·fō·man·su
Renaissance	ルネッサンス	ru·nes·san·su

antique (European)	アンティーク	an·tī·ku
antique (Japanese)	骨董品	kot·tō·hin
architecture	建築	ken·chi·ku
artwork	芸術作品	gē·ju·tsu·sa·ku·hin
calligraphy	書道	sho·dō
ceramics	陶芸	tō·gē
curator	キュレーター	kyu·rē·tā
design	デザイン	de·zain
etching	エッチング	et·chin·gu
exhibit	展覧	ten·ran
exhibition hall	展覧会場	ten·ran·kai·jō
film	映画	ē·ga
flower arranging	生け花	i·ke·ba·na
folk art	民芸	min·gē
garden design	造園	zō·en
haiku (17-syllable poem)	俳句	hai·ku
installation	インスタレーション	in·sta·rē·shon
ink painting	水墨画	su·i·bo·ku·ga
Japanese dolls	日本人形	ni·hon nin·gyō
Japanese handmade paper	和紙	wa·shi
lacquerware	漆器	shik·ki
literature	文学	bun·ga·ku
manga (cartoons)	漫画	man·ga
narrative epics	物語	mo·no·ga·ta·ri
opening	オープニング	ō·pu·nin·gu
painter	画家	ga·ka
painting (artwork)	絵	e
painting (technique)	絵画	kai·ga
period	時代	ji·dai
permanent collection	平常陳列	hē·jō·chin·re·tsu
print	印刷	in·sa·tsu
sculptor	彫刻家	chō·ko·ku·ka

sculpture	彫刻	chō·ko·ku
statue	像	zō
studio	スタジオ	sta·ji·o
style	スタイル	stai·ru
tattoo art	刺青	i·re·zu·mi
tea ceremony	茶道	sa·dō
technique	技術	gi·ju·tsu
textiles	生地	ki·ji
theatre	演劇	en·ge·ki
ukiyo-e prints (a type of wood-block prints)	浮世絵	u·ki·yo·e
waka (31-syllable poem)	和歌	wa·ka
woodblock prints	版画	han·ga
yamato-e (Japanese painting)	大和絵	ya·ma·to·e

For a night at the theatre, choose from the many forms of contemporary or classical theatre, like for example:

bunraku 文楽 bun·ra·ku
Japan's traditional puppet theatre involving large puppets manipulated by up to three silent puppeteers – a seated narrator tells the story while also providing the voices of the characters

buto 舞踏 bu·tō
modern dance form often dealing with taboo topics such as sexuality and death; dancers use their bodies (sometimes naked or semi-naked) to express elemental and intense human emotions – performances tend to be more underground than the more established forms of theatre

kabuki 歌舞伎 ka·bu·ki
traditional art form performed exclusively by men – on·na·ga·ta（女形）or o·ya·ma（女形）are *kabuki* players who even specialise in female roles – and in which the acting is a combination of dancing and speaking in conventional intonation patterns

kyogen 狂言 kyō·gen
comic vignettes performed in everyday language in which the characters are ordinary people; they're performed in between nō（能）performances

no 能 nō
Zen-influenced classical dance-drama including a chorus, drummers and a flautist

manzai 漫才 man·zai
a comic dialogue in which clever witticisms on up-to-the-minute themes from everyday life are exchanged

rakugo 落語 ra·ku·go
literally meaning 'dropped word' *rakugo* is a traditional style of comic monologue ending in a punch line – this form dates back to the early 17th century

sporting interests

スポーツへの関心

Spurred on by the success of Japanese players in the USA league, baseball is undoubtedly the most popular sport played and watched in Japan. Soccer has also gained in popularity in recent years, especially since Japan hosted the World Cup in 2002. Golf (particularly popular among businessmen), hiking and of course sumo wrestling further complete the list of Japan's most popular sports.

What sport do you play?
どんなスポーツをしますか?　don·na spō·tsu o shi·mas ka

What sport do you follow?
どのスポーツのファン　　　　do·no spō·tsu no fan
ですか?　　　　　　　　　　des ka

I play/do ...	…をします。	... o shi·mas
I follow ...	…のファンです。	... no fan des
aikido	合気道	ai·ki·dō
athletics	陸上	ri·ku·jō
baseball	野球	ya·kyū
basketball	バスケット	bas·ket·to
football (soccer)	サッカー	sak·kā
Japanese archery	弓道	kyū·dō
judo	柔道	jū·dō
karate	空手	ka·ra·te
kendo	剣道	ken·dō
martial arts	武道	bu·dō
ninjutsu	忍術	nin·ju·tsu
sumo	相撲	su·mō
table tennis	卓球	tak·kyū
tennis	テニス	te·nis
volleyball	バレー	ba·rē

I ...	...をします。	... o shi·mas
cycle	サイクリング	sai·ku·rin·gu
run	ジョギング	jo·gin·gu
walk	散歩	sam·po

Do you like (sumo)?
(相撲)が好きですか?　　　　　　(su·mō) ga su·ki des ka

Yes, very much.
はい、とても好きです。　　　　　hai, to·te·mo su·ki des

Not really.
あまり好きじゃありません。　　　a·ma·ri su·ki ja a·ri·ma·sen

I like watching it.
観るのが好きです。　　　　　　　mi·ru no ga su·ki des

Who's your favourite ...?	どの…がいちばん好きですか?	do·no ... ga i·chi·ban su·ki des ka
sportsperson	選手	sen·shu
team	チーム	chī·mu

listen for this sumo jargon ...

ba·sho	場所	tournament
do·hyō	土俵	ring/arena
do·hyō·i·ri	土俵入り	opening ceremony
gum·bai	軍配	fan held by the referee
gyō·ji	行司	referee
he·ya	部屋	stable/school of wrestlers
hi·ga·shi	東	east end (arena)
hi·ki·o·to·shi	引き落とし	pull down the opponent
mat·ta	まった!	'Wait!'
ma·wa·shi	まわし	loincloth
ni·shi	西	west end (arena)
no·kot·ta	のこった!	'Continue!'
o·shi·da·shi	押し出し	push the opponent out of the arena
o·shi·tow·shi	押し倒し	knock or throw down the opponent
ri·ki·shi	力士	wrestler
shi·ko	四股	stomping
tsu·ri·da·shi	つり出し	carry the opponent out of the arena
yo·ri·ki·ri	寄り切り	drive the opponent out of the arena

going to a game

試合に行く

Would you like to go to a game?
試合に行きたいですか?　　　shi·ai ni i·ki·tai des ka

Who are you supporting?
だれを応援していますか?　　da·re o ō·en shi·te i·mas ka

What's the score?
スコアはどうですか?　　　　sko·a wa dō des ka

Who's ...?	だれが…か?	da·re ga … ka
playing	プレーしています	pu·rē shi·te i·mas
winning	勝っています	kat·te i·mas

That was a ... game!	…試合でしたね!	… shi·ai desh·ta ne
bad	悪い	wa·ru·i
boring	つまらない	tsu·ma·ra·nai
great	素晴らしい	su·ba·ra·shī

playing sport

スポーツをする

Do you want to play?
プレーしたいですか?　　　　pu·rē shi·tai des ka

Can I join in?
いっしょにやってもいい　　　is·sho ni yat·te mo ī
ですか?　　　　　　　　　　des ka

That would be great.
それはいいですね。　　　　　so·re wa ī des ne

I can't.
できません。 de·ki·ma·sen

Your point.
あなたの点。 a·na·ta no ten

My point.
私の点。 wa·ta·shi no ten

Kick it to me!
こっちにキック！ kot·chi ni kik·ku

Pass it to me!
こっちにパス！ kot·chi ni pas

You're a good player.
うまいですね。 u·mai des ne

Thanks for the game.
試合、ありがとう。 shi·ai, a·ri·ga·tō

Where's the nearest ...?	いちばん近い…はどこですか？	i·chi·ban chi·kai … wa do·ko des ka
golf course	ゴルフ場	go·ru·fu·jō
gym	ジム	ji·mu
swimming pool	プール	pū·ru
tennis court	テニスコート	te·nis kō·to

What's the charge per ...?	…の料金はいくらですか？	… no ryō·kin wa i·ku·ra des ka
day	1日	i·chi·ni·chi
game	1ゲーム	i·chi·gē·mu
hour	1時間	i·chi·ji·kan
visit	1回	ik·kai

sports talk

What a ...!	すごい…！	su·goy …
goal	ゴール	gō·ru
hit	ヒット	hit·to
kick	キック	kik·ku
pass	パス	pas
performance	パフォーマンス	pa·fō·man·su

Can I hire a ...?	…を貸して もらえませんか?	... o ka·shi·te mo·ra·e·ma·sen ka
ball	ボール	bō·ru
bat	バット	bat·to
bicycle	自転車	ji·ten·sha
court	コート	kō·to
racquet	ラケット	ra·ket·to
table-tennis table	卓球台	tak·kyū·dai
Where are the ...?	…はどこですか?	... wa do·ko des ka
changing rooms	更衣室	kō·i·shi·tsu
showers	シャワー	sha·wā

Can I take lessons?
レッスンを受けられますか?   res·sun o u·ke·ra·re·mas ka

Can I book a lesson?
レッスンの予約が   res·sun no yo·ya·ku ga
できますか?   de·ki·mas ka

Do I have to be a member to attend?
メンバーじゃないと参加   mem·bā ja nai to san·ka
できませんか?   de·ki·ma·sen ka

Do we have to pay?
お金を   o·ka·ne o
払わなければ   ha·ra·wa·na·ke·re·ba
なりませんか?   na·ri·ma·sen ka

Is there a women-only session?
女性だけのセッションは   jo·sē da·ke no ses·shon wa
ありますか?   a·ri·mas ka

Is the equipment secure?
道具は安全ですか?   dō·gu wa an·zen des ka

baseball

base	塁	ru·i
baseball	野球	ya·kyū
batter	バッター	bat·tā
Central League	セリーグ	se·rī·gu
curve ball	カーブ	kā·bu
dugout	ベンチ	ben·chi
fastball	速球	sok·kyū
grand slam	満塁ホームラン	man·ru·i·hō·mu·ran
home plate	ホームベース	hō·mu·bē·su
home run	ホームラン	hō·mu·ran
infielder	内野手	nai·ya·shu
inning	イニング	i·nin·gu
out a/n	アウト	ow·to
outfielder	外野手	gai·ya·shu
Pacific League	パリーグ	pa·rī·gu
pitcher	ピッチャー	pit·chā
run n	ラン	ran
safe	セーフ	sē·fu
strike n	ストライク	sto·rai·ku

diving

Where's a good diving site?
いいダイビングスポットは
どこですか？
ī dai·bin·gu·spot·to wa
do·ko des ka

Is the visibility good?
視界はいいですか？
shi·kai wa ī des ka

How deep is the dive?
深さはどの
くらいですか？
fu·ka·sa wa do·no
ku·rai des ka

Are there currents?
海流がありますか？
kai·ryū ga a·ri·mas ka

Are there …?	…がいますか?	… ga i·mas ka
dolphins	イルカ	i·ru·ka
sharks	サメ	sa·me
whales	クジラ	ku·ji·ra
Is it a … dive?	…ダイビング ですか?	…dai·bin·gu des ka
boat	ボート	bō·to
shore	岸	ki·shi
I'd like to …	…したいのですが。	… shi·tai no des ga
explore caves	ケーブを探検	kē·bu o tan·ken
explore wrecks	沈没船を 探検	chim·bo·tsu·sen o tan·ken
go night diving	ナイト ダイビングを	nai·to· dai·bin·gu o
go scuba diving	スキューバ ダイビングを	skyū·ba· dai·bin·gu o
go snorkelling	シュノーケ リングを	shu·nō·ke· rin·gu o
join a diving tour	ダイビングの ツアーに参加	dai·bin·gu no tsu·ā ni san·ka
learn to dive	ダイビングを 修得	dai·bin·gu o shū·to·ku
I want to hire (a) …	…をレンタル したいのですが。	… o ren·ta·ru shi·tai no des ga
buoyancy vest	BCD	bī·shī·dī
diving equipment	ダイビング用具	dai·bin·gu·yō·gu
flippers	フィン	fin
mask	マスク	mas·ku
regulator	レギュレーター	re·gu·rē·tā
snorkel	シュノーケル	shu·nō·ke·ru
tank	タンク	tan·ku
weight belt	ウェイトベルト	wē·to·be·ru·to
wetsuit	ウェットスーツ	wet·to·sū·tsu

I need an air fill.

タンク充填が必要です。　　tan·ku·jū·ten ga hi·tsu·yō des

golf

How much …?	…はいくらですか?	… wa i·ku·ra des ka
for a round	1ラウンド	i·chi·rown·do
to play 9 holes	9ホール	nain·hō·ru
to play 18 holes	18ホール	jū·ha·chi·hō·ru

Do I need to hire a …?	…をつけないと いけませんか?	… o tsu·ke·nai to i·ke·ma·sen ka
golf cart	乗用カート	jō·yō kā·to
caddie (person)	キャディー	kya·dī
caddie cart	キャディーカート	kya·dī·kā·to

Can I hire golf clubs?
クラブはレンタル
できますか?
ku·ra·bu wa ren·ta·ru
de·ki·mas ka

What's the dress code?
ドレスコードはなんですか? do·re·su·kō·do wa nan des ka

Do I need golf shoes?
ゴルフシューズは必要
ですか?
go·ru·fu·shū·zu wa hi·tsu·yō
des ka

Soft or hard spikes?
スパイクはソフトですか、
ハードですか?
spai·ku wa so·fu·to des ka,
hā·do des ka

bunker	バンカー	ban·kā
flag	フラッグ	fu·rag·gu
golf ball	ゴルフボール	go·ru·fu·bō·ru
golf course	ゴルフコース	go·ru·fu·kō·su
green	グリーン	gu·rīn
hole	ホール	hō·ru
iron	アイアン	ai·an
putter	パター	pa·tā
tee	ティー	tī
teeing ground	ティーグラウンド	tī·gu·rown·do
wood	ウッド	ud·do

Fore!	フォア!	fo·a

146

hiking

ハイキング

For phrases about hiking, see **outdoors**, page 151.

skiing

スキー

I'd like to hire ...	…を借りたいの ですが。	... o ka·ri·tai no des ga
boots	ブーツ	bū·tsu
gloves	手袋	te·bu·ku·ro
goggles	ゴーグル	gō·gu·ru
poles	ストック	stok·ku
skis	スキー	skī
a ski suit	スキースーツ	skī·sū·tsu
Is it possible to go ...?	…に行けますか?	... ni i·ke·mas ka
Alpine skiing	アルペンスキー	a·ru·pen·skī
cross-country skiing	クロスカントリー	ku·ros·kan·to·rī
snowboarding	スノーボード	su·nō·bō·do
tobogganing	そり	so·ri

How much is a pass?
券はいくらですか?   ken wa i·ku·ra des ka

What are the conditions like (at Niseko)?
(ニセコの)コンディション   (ni·se·ko no) kon·di·shon
はどうですか?   wa dō des ka

What level is that slope?
このゲレンデはどの   ko·no ge·ren·de wa do·no
レベルですか?   re·be·ru des ka

Which are the ... slopes?	...レベルの ゲレンデはどこ ですか?	... re·be·ru no ge·ren·de wa do·ko des ka
advanced	上級	jō·kyū
beginner	初級	sho·kyū
intermediate	中級	chū·kyū

cable car	ケーブルカー	kē·bu·ru·kā
chairlift	リフト	ri·fu·to
instructor	インストラクター	in·sto·rak·tā
resort	リゾート	ri·zō·to
ski-lift	リフト	ri·fu·to
sled	そり	so·ri

soccer

サッカー

Who plays for (Urawa Reds)?
だれが(浦和レッズ)で
プレーしていますか?
da·re ga (u·ra·wa rez·zu) de
pu·rē shi·te i·mas ka

Which team is at the top of the league?
どのチームがリーグの
トップですか?
do·no chī·mu ga rī·gu no
top·pu des ka

corner	コーナー	kō·nā
foul	ファウル	fow·ru
free kick	フリーキック	fu·rī·kik·ku
goal	ゴール	gō·ru
goalkeeper	ゴールキーパー	gō·ru·kī·pā
J-league	Jリーグ	jē·rī·gu
offside	オフサイド	of·sai·do
penalty	ペナルティ	pe·na·ru·tī
player	プレーヤー	pu·rē·yā
red card	レッドカード	red·do·kā·do
referee	審判	shim·pan
throw in	スローイン	srō·in
yellow card	イエローカード	ye·rō·kā·do

What a ... team!	...チームだ！	... chī·mu da
great	素晴らしい	su·ba·ra·shī
terrible	だめな	da·me na

tennis & table tennis

テニスと卓球

I'd like to play tennis.
テニスをしたいのですが。 te·nis o shi·tai no des ga

Can we play at night?
夜、プレーできますか？ yo·ru pu·rē de·ki·mas ka

Do you have a table-tennis table?
卓球台はありますか？ tak·kyū·dai wa a·ri·mas ka

Can I book a table ?
卓球台を予約 tak·kyū·dai o yo·ya·ku
したいのですが。 shi·tai no des ga

ace	エース	ē·su
bat (table tennis)	バット	bat·to
clay	クレイ	ku·rē
fault	フォルト	fo·ru·to
grass	グラス	gu·ra·su
hard court	ハードコート	hā·do·kō·to
net	ネット	net·to
ping-pong ball	ピンポン球	pim·pon·da·ma
play doubles	ダブルスを	da·bu·ru·su o
	します	shi·mas
racquet	ラケット	ra·ket·to
serve	サーブ	sā·bu
table-tennis table	卓球台	tak·kyū·dai
tennis ball	テニスボール	te·nis·bō·ru

water sports

ウォータースポーツ

Can I hire (a) ...?	…をレンタルしたいのですが。	… o ren·ta·ru shi·tai no des ga
boat	ボート	bō·to
canoe	カヌー	ka·nū
kayak	カヤック	ka·yak·ku
life jacket	救命胴衣	kyū·mē·dō·i
snorkelling gear	シュノーケル用具	shu·nō·ke·ru·yō·gu
water-skis	水上スキー	su·i·jō·skī
wetsuit	ウェットスーツ	wet·to·sū·tsu
Are there any ...?	…がありますか？	… ga a·ri·mas ka
reefs	リーフ	rī·fu
rips	リップ	rip·pu
water hazards	危険水域	ki·ken·su·i·ki

guide	ガイド	gai·do
motorboat	モーターボート	mō·tā·bō·to
oars	オール	ō·ru
sailing boat	帆船	han·sen
surfboard	サーフボード	sā·fu·bō·do
surfing	サーフィン	sā·fin
wave	波	na·mi
windsurfing	ウィンドサーフィン	win·do·sā·fin

hiking

ハイキング

Where can I …?	どこで…ますか?	do·ko·de ….mas ka
buy supplies	食料が買え	sho·ku·ryō ga ka·e
find someone	この地域を良く	ko·no chī·ki o yo·ku
who knows	知っている人が	shīt·te I·ru hi·to ga
this area	見つかり	mi·tsu·ka·ri
get a map	地図が手に入り	chī·zu ga te ni hai·ri
hire hiking gear	登山用品が	to·zan·yō·hin ga
	買え	ka·e

How …?	どのくらい…が	do·no·ku·rai … ga
	ありますか?	a·ri·mas ka
high is the climb	高度差	kō·do·sa
long is the trail	距離	kyo·ri

Do we need to	…を持っていく	… o mot·te i·ku
take …?	必要が	hi·tsu·yō ga
	ありますか?	a·ri·mas ka
bedding	シーツ	shī·tsu
food	食料	sho·ku·ryō
water	水	mi·zu

Do we need a guide?
ガイドが必要ですか?　　　gai·do ga hi·tsu·yō des ka

Are there guided treks?
ガイドが同行してくれる　　gai·do ga dō·kō shi·te ku·re·ru
ルートがありますか?　　　rū·to ga a·ri·mas ka

Is it safe?
安全ですか?　　　　　　　　an·zen des ka

Is there a hut?
山小屋がありますか?　　　ya·ma·go·ya ga a·ri·mas ka

Is the track ...?	山道は…か?	ya·ma·mi·chi wa ... ka
(well-)marked	標識が	hyō·shi·ki ga
	(きちんと)	(ki·chin·to)
	あります	a·ri·mas
open	開通しています	kai·tsū shi·te i·mas
scenic	眺めがいいです	na·ga·me ga ī des
Which is the	どのルートが…	do·no rū·to ga ...
... route?	ですか?	des ka
easiest	いちばん簡単	i·chi·ban kan·tan
shortest	いちばん短い	i·chi·ban mi·ji·kai
Where can I find	…はどこに	... wa do·ko ni
the ...?	ありますか?	a·ri·mas ka
camping ground	キャンプ場	kyam·pu·jō
showers	シャワー	sha·wā
toilets	トイレ	toy·re

Does this path go to ...?
この道は…に
行きますか?
ko·no mi·chi wa ... ni
i·ki·mas ka

Can I go through here?
ここを通り抜け
できますか?
ko·ko o tō·ri·nu·ke
de·ki·mas ka

Is the water OK to drink?
水を飲んでも
だいじょうぶですか?
mi·zu o non·de mo
dai·jō·bu des ka

I'm lost.
道に迷いました。
mi·chi ni ma·yoy·mash·ta

beach

ビーチ

Where's the	…ビーチはどこ	... bī·chi wa do·ko
... beach?	ですか?	des ka
best	いちばんいい	i·chi·ban ī
nearest	いちばん近い	i·chi·ban chi·kai
public	公共の	kō·kyo no

Is it safe to ... here?	ここは安全に …ますか?	ko·ko wa an·zen ni …mas ka
dive	飛び込め	to·bi·ko·me
swim	泳げ	o·yo·ge

What time is ... tide?	…は何時ですか?	... wa nan·ji des ka
high	満潮	man·chō
low	干潮	kan·chō

How much for a/an ...?	…はいくらですか?	... wa i·ku·ra des ka
chair	いす	i·su
hut	小屋	ko·ya
umbrella	パラソル	pa·ra·so·ru

weather

天気

What's the weather like?
天気はどうですか?　　　　　ten·ki wa dō des ka

What will the weather be like tomorrow?
明日の天気はどうですか?　　a·shi·ta no ten·ki wa dō des ka

It's ...	…です。	... des
cloudy	曇り	ku·mo·ri
cold	寒い	sa·mu·i
hot	暑い	a·tsu·i
humid	蒸し暑い	mu·shi·a·tsu·i
raining	雨	a·me
snowing	雪	yu·ki
sunny	晴れ	ha·re
warm	暖かい	a·ta·ta·kai
windy	風が強い	ka·ze ga tsu·yoy

outdoors

earthquake	地震	ji·shin
rainy season	雨季	u·ki
tsunami (giant wave)	津波	tsu·na·mi
typhoon	台風	tai·fū
volcanic eruption	噴火	fun·ka
volcano	火山	ka·zan

flora & fauna

動物と植物

What ... is that?	あれはなんと言う…ですか?	a·re wa nan to yū ... des ka
animal	動物	dō·bu·tsu
plant	植物	sho·ku·bu·tsu
tree	木	ki

Is it ...?		
common	普通に見られますか?	fu·tsū ni mi·ra·re·mas ka
dangerous	危険ですか?	ki·ken des ka
endangered	絶滅しそうですか?	ze·tsu·me·tsu shi·sō des ka
protected	保護されていますか?	ho·go sa·re·te i·mas ka

wild thing

alps (alpine region)	アルプス	a·ru·pus
bamboo	竹	ta·ke
bear	クマ	ku·ma
brown bear	ヒグマ	hi·gu·ma
cat	ネコ	ne·ko
cherry blossom	桜	sa·ku·ra
chrysanthemum	菊	ki·ku
conifer	杉	su·gi
crane	鶴	tsu·ru
Japanese river otter	カワウソ	ka·wa·u·so
macaque	ニホンザル	ni·hon·za·ru
pine tree	松	ma·tsu
plum tree	梅	u·me

key language

基本の言葉

breakfast*	朝食/朝ごはん	chō·sho·ku/a·sa·go·han
lunch*	昼食/昼ごはん	chū·sho·ku/hi·ru·go·han
dinner*	夕食/晩ごはん	yū·sho·ku/ban·go·han
snack*	間食/スナック	kan·sho·ku/su·nak·ku
to eat	食べます	ta·be·mas
to drink	飲みます	no·mi·mas
I'd like …	…をください。	… o·ku·da·sai
I'm starving!	お腹がすいた。	o·na·ka ga su·i·ta

* alternative terms are commonly used, the first ones being slightly more formal

mix 'n' match

Traditional Japanese breakfasts usually consist of rice go·han (ご飯), miso-soup mi·so·shi·ru (味噌汁), raw egg na·ma·ta·ma·go (生卵), dried fish hi·mo·no (干物), fermented soy bean nat·tō (納豆), dried seaweed no·ri (海苔) and pickles tsu·ke·mo·no (漬物). Western breakfasts are also common.

Set-menu lunches, mostly served in lunch boxes ben·tō (弁当) are popular and often include rice, soup sū·pu (スープ), pickles, a main dish and fruit ku·da·mo·no (くだもの). Noodles – so·ba (そば), sō·men (そうめん), rā·men (ラーメン) or u·don (うどん) – are also common fare for lunch.

Dinner is the main meal of the day and whether taken at home or at a restaurant, will include rice, soup and a side dish o·ka·zu (おかず).

For more Japanese dishes and ingredients, see the **culinary reader**, page 175.

eating out

finding a place to eat

Can you recommend a ...?	どこかいい…を 知っていますか?	do·ko ka ī ... o shit·te i·mas ka
bar	バー	bā
café	カフェ	ka·fe
restaurant	レストラン	res·to·ran

Where would you go for ...?	…ならどこに 行きいますか?	... na·ra do·ko ni i·ki·mas ka
a celebration	お祝いをする	oy·wai o su·ru
a cheap meal	安い食事 をする	ya·su·i sho·ku·ji o su·ru
local specialities	名物を 食べる	mē·bu·tsu o ta·be·ru

I'd like to reserve a table for ...	…の予約を お願いします。	... no yo·ya·ku o o·ne·gai shi·mas
one person/ two people	1人/2人	hi·to·ri/fu·ta·ri
(eight) o'clock	(8)時	(ha·chi)·ji

listen for ...

hē·ten des 閉店です。	We're closed.
man·se·ki des 満席です。	We're full.
nan·mē·sa·ma 何名様?	How many people?
shō·shō o·ma·chi ku·da·sai 少々お待ちください。	One moment.
do·chi·ra no se·ki ga yo·ro·sī de·shō ka どちらのお席がよろしい でしょうか?	Where would you like to sit?
o·ki·ma·ri de·shō ka お決まりでしょうか?	What can I get for you?
dō·zo どうぞ。	Here you go!

I'd like ..., please.	…をお願いします。	… o o·ne·gai shi·mas
a children's menu	子供の メニュー	ko·do·mo no me·nyū
the drink list	飲み物の メニュー	no·mi·mo·no no me·nyū
a half portion	半人前	han·nim·ma·e
the menu	メニュー	me·nyū
a menu in English	英語のメニュー	ē·go no me·nyū
nonsmoking	禁煙席	kin·en·se·ki
smoking	喫煙席	ki·tsu·en·se·ki
a table for (five)	(5)人分の テーブル	(go)·nim·bun no tē·bu·ru

tea for two

If you reserve a table for more than three, you'll always be seated at a table. When you make a booking for two or less, make sure you insist on getting a table, or you might end up sitting at the counter.

A table for one person, please.

1人、テーブルで
お願いします。

hi·to·ri, tē·bu·ru de
o·ne·gai shi·mas

A table for two people, please.

2人、テーブルで
お願いします。

fu·ta·ri, tē·bu·ru de
o·ne·gai shi·mas

Are you still serving food?

まだ食事ができますか?　　ma·da sho·ku·ji ga de·ki·mas ka

How long is the wait?

どのくらい待ちますか?　　do·no ku·rai ma·chi·mas ka

tuck in

Many eating places specialise in serving up one particular
type of dish. Look for the ·ya (屋) after the name of a dish
and that's where you'll find it!

For example, ton·ka·tsu·ya (とんかつ屋) specialise in
ton·ka·tsu (pork cutlet), sha·bu·sha·bu·ya (しゃぶしゃぶ屋) in
sha·bu·sha·bu hot pot, so·ba·ya (そば屋) in so·ba (buckwheat
noodles) and su·shi·ya (すし屋) in su·shi, to name a few. Other
popular alternatives are ro·ba·ta·ya·ki (ろばた焼き), where
food is grilled, ya·ki·to·ri (焼き鳥) restaurants specialising in
variations of skewered chicken, and o·den (おでん) shops,
whipping up stewed hot pot.

For a quick bite and booze, try the i·za·ka·ya (居酒屋) which
are relatively cheap places where colleagues often retire at the
end of the day to eat and drink, or kis·sa·ten (喫茶店) coffee
shops or café-style establishments. Other options are the
sho·ku·dō (食堂), cheap restaurants or dining halls dishing
up filling and inexpensive food, or kai·ten·zu·shi (回転ずし)
where su·shi comes on a rotating conveyer belt. For a more
upmarket experience you can try a kap·pō (割烹), usually a
small but expensive upmarket version of the i·za·ka·ya. If you
feel you have yen to spare, try the ryō·tē (料亭) for a traditional, top-notch luxury dining experience.

at the restaurant

レストランで

What would you recommend?
なにがおすすめですか?　　　　　na·ni ga o·su·su·me des ka

What's in that dish?
あの料理に何が入って　　　　　a·no ryō·ri ni na·ni ga hait·te
いますか?　　　　　　　　　　i·mas ka

I'll have that.
あれをください。　　　　　　　a·re o ku·da·sai

Please decide for me.
おまかせします。　　　　　　　o·ma·ka·se shi·mas

Does it take long to prepare?
料理に時間が
かかりますか?
ryō·ri ni ji·ka
ka·ka·ri·mas

Is it self-serve?
セルフサービスですか?
se·ru·fu·sā·bis

Is service included in the bill?
サービス料込みですか?
sā·bis·ryō ko·mi des ka

Are these complimentary?
これはただですか?
ko·re wa ta·da des ka

I'd like ...
…をお願いします。
... o o·ne·gai shi·mas

　the chicken
鶏肉
to ri·ni·ku

　a local speciality
地元の
名物
ji·mo·to no
mē·bu·tsu

　a meal fit for
　a king
大ごちそう
ō·go·chi·sō

Do you have ...?
…がありますか?
... ga a·ri·mas ka

I'd like it with ...
…を付けてお願いします。
... o tsu·ke·te o·ne·gai shi·mas

I'd like it without ...
…を抜きでお願いします。
... o nu·ki de o·ne·gai shi·mas

---

listen for ...

... wa o·su·ki des ka
　…はお好きですか?
Do you like ...?

... o o·su·su·me shi·mas
　…をおすすめします。
I suggest the ...

do·no yō ni ryō·ri i·ta·shi·ma·shō ka
　どのように料理
　いたしましょうか?
How would you like
that cooked?

eating out

159

	唐辛子	tō·ga·ra·shi
~~nger~~	ニンニク	nin·ni·ku
	ショウガ	shō·ga
sauce	ソース	sō·su
seaweed	のり	no·ri
sesame seeds	ゴマ	go·ma
seven-spice chilli	七味唐辛子	shi·chi·mi·tō·
powder		ga·ra·shi
soy sauce	しょう油	shō·yu
spring onions	ネギ	ne·gi
horseradish (green)	わさび	wa·sa·bi

For other specific meal requests, see **vegetarian & special
meals**, page 173.

For other specific meal requests, see **vegetarian & special
meals**, page 173.

look for ...

前菜	zen·sai	**appetisers**
スープ	sū·pu	**soups**
アントレー	an·to·rē	**entrees**
サラダ	sa·ra·da	**salads**
メインコース	mēn·kō·su	**main courses**
デザート	de·zā·to	**desserts**
一品料理	ip·pin·ryō·ri	**à la carte**
麺	men	**noodles**
鍋	na·be	**hot pot**
食前酒	sho·ku·zen·shu	**apéritifs**
飲み物	no·mi·mo·no	**drinks**
ソフトドリンク	so·fu·to·do·rin·ku	**soft drinks**
スピリット	spi·rit·to	**spirits**
ビール	bī·ru	**beers**
スパークリング	spā·ku·rin·gu·	**sparkling wines**
ワイン	wain	
白ワイン	shi·ro·wain	**white wines**
赤ワイン	a·ka·wain	**red wines**
デザートワイン	de·zā·to·wain	**dessert wines**
食後酒	sho·ku·go·shu	**digestifs**

For more words you might see on a menu, see the **culinary
reader**, page 175.

For more words you might see on a menu, see the **culinary
reader**, page 175.

FOOD

at the table

Please bring ...	…をください。	... o ku·da·sai
an ashtray	灰皿	hai·za·ra
the bill	お勘定	o·kan·jō
a cloth	フキン	fu·kin
a fork	フォーク	fō·ku
a glass	グラス	gu·ra·su
a knife	ナイフ	nai·fu
a serviette	ナプキン	na·pu·kin
a spoon	スプーン	spūn
a wineglass	ワイングラス	wain·gu·ra·su

This is ...	これは…です	ko·re wa ... des
cold	冷たい	tsu·me·tai
spicy	スパイシー	spai·shī
superb	素晴らしい	su·ba·ra·shī

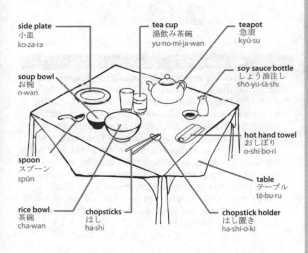

side plate
小皿
ko·za·ra

tea cup
湯飲み茶碗
yu·no·mi·ja·wan

teapot
急須
kyū·su

soup bowl
お椀
o·wan

soy sauce bottle
しょう油注し
shō·yu·sa·shi

spoon
スプーン
spūn

hot hand towel
おしぼり
o·shi·bo·ri

table
テーブル
tē·bu·ru

rice bowl
茶碗
cha·wan

chopsticks
はし
ha·shi

chopstick holder
はし置き
ha·shi·o·ki

talking food

I love this dish.
この料理が大好きです。   ko·no ryō·ri ga dai·su·ki des

I love the local cuisine.
地元料理が大好きです。   ji·mo·to·ryō·ri ga dai·su·ki des

That was delicious!
おいしかった。   oy·shi·kat·ta

My compliments to the chef.
シェフにおいしかったと
伝えてください。   she·fu ni oy·shi·kat·ta to
tsu·ta·e·te ku·da·sai

It was a real feast.
ごちそうさま   go·chi·sō·sa·ma

I'm full.
お腹がいっぱいです。   o·na·ka ga ip·pai des

mind your manners

Traditional restaurants generally have a tatami floor or area –
strictly no shoes is the message. A hand towel o·shi·bo·ri
(おしぼり) will be given to you upon sitting down. With
a little bit of practice you'll soon manage the art of eating
with chopsticks ha·shi (はし), but if you're struggling never-
theless, don't be afraid to ask for cutlery. Don't wave your
chopsticks around, rather put them down if you need to
make hand gestures. Never leave them standing up in your
food either – this position is associated with death because
of the similarity with incense sticks offered to the dead.

Note that people generally do not walk and eat on the
streets in Japan and that blowing your nose in public is seen
as somewhat uncanny.

methods of preparation

準備

I'd like it …	…ください。	… ku·da·sai
boiled (in hot water)	ゆでて	yu·de·te
boiled (in stock)	煮て	ni·te
broiled	あぶって	a·but·te
deep-fried	揚げて	a·ge·te
fried	炒めて	i·ta·me·te
grilled	グリルして	gu·ri·ru shi·te
mashed	つぶして	tsu·bu·shi·te
medium	ミディアムにして	mi·dya·mu ni shi·te
rare	レアにして	rair ni shi·te
re-heated	温めなおして	a·ta·ta·me·now·shi·te
steamed	蒸して	mu·shi·te
well-done	ウェルダンにして	we·ru·dan ni shi·te
with the dressing on the side	ドレッシングを別にして	do·res·shin·gu o be·tsu ni shi·te
without …	…抜きにして	…nu·ki ni shi·te
I don't want it …	…ください。	… ku·da·sai
deep-fried	揚げないで	a·ge·nai·de
fried	炒めないで	i·ta·me·nai·de
re-heated	温めなおさないで	a·ta·ta·me·now·sa·nai·de

listen for …

i·ta·da·ki·mas	いただきます	**Bon appétit!** (lit: I receive)

eating out

163

in the bar

Excuse me.
すみません。 su·mi·ma·sen

I'm next.
次は私です。 tsu·gi wa wa·ta·shi des

I'll have …
…をお願いします。 … o o·ne·gai shi·mas

Same again, please.
同じのをお願いします。 o·na·ji no o o·ne·gai shi·mas

No ice, thanks.
氷なしでお願い kō·ri·na·shi de o·ne·gai
します。 shi·mas

I'll buy you a drink.
1杯おごります。 ip·pai o·go·ri·mas

What would you like?
何を飲みますか? na·ni o no·mi·mas ka

It's my round.
次は私の tsu·gi wa wa·ta·shi no
番です。 ban des

Do you serve meals here?
食事はできますか? sho·ku·ji wa de·ki·mas ka

nan ni shi·mas ka
何にしますか? **What are you having?**

mō jū·bun de shō
もうじゅうぶんでしょう。 **I think you've had enough.**

ras·to·ō·dā des
ラストオーダーです。 **Last orders.**

nonalcoholic drinks

… mineral water	…ミネラルウォーター	…mi·ne·ra·ru·wō·tā
sparkling	炭酸	tan·san
still	炭酸なしの	tan·san·na·shi no
hot water	お湯	o·yu
lemonade	レモネード	re·mo·nē·do
milk	ミルク	mi·ru·ku
orange juice	オレンジジュース	o·ren·ji·jū·su
soft drink	ソフトドリンク	so·fu·to·do·rin·ku
water	水	mi·zu
(cup of) tea …	…紅茶(1杯)	… kō·cha (ip·pai)
(cup of) coffee …	…コーヒー(1杯)	… kō·hī (ip·pai)
with (milk)	(ミルク)入り	(mi·ru·ku)·i·ri
without (sugar)	(砂糖)なし	(sa·tō)·na·shi

coffee

black	ブラック	bu·rak·ku
cappucino	カプチーノ	ka·pu·chī·no
decaffeinated	デカフェ	de·ka·fe
espresso	エスプレッソ	es·pres·so
iced	アイス	ai·su
latte	カフェラテ	ka·fe·ra·te
strong	濃い	koy
weak	薄い	u·su·i
white	ホワイト	ho·wai·to

アルコール飲料

...a's 泡盛		a·wa·mo·ri
	ビール	bī·ru
	ブランデー	bu·ran·dē
champagne	シャンペン	sham·pen
chilled *sake*	冷酒	rē·shu
cocktail	カクテル	ka·ku·te·ru
ginjo-style *sake*	吟醸	gin·jō
local *sake*	地酒	ji·za·ke
plum wine	梅酒	u·me·shu
sake	酒	sa·ke
shochu highball	酎ハイ	chū·hai
shochu spirit	焼酎	shō·chū
warm *sake*	お燗	o·kan
a shot of ...	…をワンショット	... o wan·shot·to
rum	ラム	ra·mu
vodka	ウォッカ	wok·ka
whisky	ウィスキー	wis·kī
a bottle of	…ワインを	…wain o
... wine	ボトルで	bo·to·ru de
a glass of	…ワインを	…wain o
... wine	グラスで	gu·ra·su de
dessert	デザート	de·zā·to
red	赤	a·ka
rosé	ロゼ	ro·ze
sparkling	スパークリング	spā·ku·rin·gu
white	白	shi·ro
a ... of beer	ビールを…で	bī·ru o ... de
glass	グラス	gu·ra·su
jug	ジャグ	ja·gu
large bottle	大ビン	ō·bin
large mug	大ジョッキ	dai·jok·ki
small bottle	中ビン	chū·bin

drinking up

呑む

Cheers!
乾杯！
kam·pai

This is hitting the spot.
お腹に染みます。
o·na·ka ni shi·mi·mas

I feel fantastic!
気分がいいです。
ki·bun ga ī des

I think I've had one too many.
ちょっと飲みすぎました。
chot·to no·mi·su·gi·mash·ta

I'm feeling drunk.
酔いました。
yoy·mash·ta

I'm pissed.
酔っ払った。
yop·pa·rat·ta

I feel ill.
気分が悪いです。
ki·bun ga wa·ru·i des

pot or pint?

Make sure how much to ask for when ordering drinks using these typical local measurements:

for *sake* and *shochu*:

1 cup (180ml)	1合	i·chi·gō
2 cups (360ml)	2合	ni·gō
large bottle (1.8L)	1升	is·shō

for bottled beer:

medium bottle (500ml)	中ビン	chū·bin
large bottle (633ml)	大ビン	ō·bin

for draft beer – although the amounts vary from shop to shop:

small glass (400ml)	小ジョッキ	shō·jok·ki
medium glass (500ml)	中ジョッキ	chū·jok·ki
large glass (700ml)	大ジョッキ	daï·jok·ki

Where's the toilet?
トイレはどこですか？

toy·re wa do·ko des ka

I'm tired, I'd better go home.
疲れました、
うちに帰ります。

tsu·ka·re·mash·ta,
u·chi ni ka·e·ri·mas

Can you call a taxi for me?
タクシーを呼んで
くれますか？

tak·shī o yon·de
ku·re·mas ka

I don't think you should drive.
運転しないほうがいいと
思います。

un·ten shi·nai hō ga ī to
o·moy·mas

---

titbits

If you fancy a bite with your booze, check out which bar
snacks o·tsu·ma·mi （おつまみ） are on offer.

buying food

食料を買う

What's the local speciality?
地元料理は何があ
りますか?
ji·mo·to·ryō·ri wa na·ni ga
a·ri·mas ka

What's that?
それは何ですか?
so·re wa nan des ka

Can I taste it?
味見してもいいですか?
a·ji·mi shi·te mo ī des ka

Can I have a bag, please?
1袋ください。
hi·to·fu·ku·ro ku·da·sai

How much is a kilo of (rice)?
(米)1キロいくら
ですか?
(ko·me) i·chi·ki·ro i·ku·ra
des ka

How much?
いくら?
i·ku·ra

food stuff		
cooked	火が通った	hi ga tōt·ta
cured	保存	ho·zon
dried	乾燥	kan·sō
fresh	新鮮	shin·sen
frozen	冷凍	rē·tō
raw	なま	na·ma
smoked	燻製	kun·sē

I'd like …	…ください。	… ku·da·sai
(200) grams	(200)グラム	(ni·hya·ku)·gu·ra·mu
half a dozen	半ダース	han·dās
a dozen	1ダース	i·chi·dās
half a kilo	500グラム	go·hya·ku·gu·ra·mu
a kilo	1キロ	i·chi·ki·ro
(two) kilos	(2)キロ	(ni)·ki·ro
a bottle	ビン1本	bin ip·pon
a jar	ジャー1つ	jā hi·to·tsu
a packet	1パック	hi·to·pak·ku
a piece	1個	ik·ko
(three) pieces	(3)個	(san)·ko
a slice	1枚	i·chi·mai
(six) slices	(6)枚	(ro·ku)·mai
a tin	1缶	hi·to·kan
(just) a little	(ほんの)少し	(hon·no) su·ko·shi
more	もっと	mot·to
some …	…をいくらか	… o i·ku·ra ka
that one	あれを	a·re o
this one	これを	ko·re o

Less.	少なく。	su·ku·na·ku
A bit more.	もうちょっと多く。	mō chot·to ō·ku
Enough.	充分です。	jū·bun des

---

listen for …

i·ras·shai·ma·se いらっしゃいませ。		**Can I help you?**
na·ni o o·sa·ga·shi des ka なにをお探しですか?		**What would you like?**
ho·ka ni na·ni ka o·sa·ga·shi des ka 他に何かお探しですか?		**Anything else?**
go·zai·ma·sen ございません。		**There isn't any.**
(go·sen·en) des (5千円)です。		**That's (5000 yen).**

Do you have …?	…がありますか？	… ga a·ri·mas ka
anything cheaper	安いもの	ya·su·i mo·no
other kinds	他のもの	ho·ka no mo·no

Where can I find the … section?	…のコーナーは どこですか？	… no kō·nā wa do·ko des ka
dairy	乳製品	nyū·sē·hin
fish	魚	sa·ka·na
frozen goods	冷凍食品	rē·tō·sho·ku·hin
fruit and vegetable	果物と 野菜	ku·da·mo·no to ya·sai
meat	肉	ni·ku
poultry	鳥肉	to·ri·ni·ku

cooking utensils

料理の道具

Could I please borrow a (bottle opener)?
（栓抜き）を貸して
もらえませんか？
(sen·nu·ki) o ka·shi·te
mo·ra·e·ma·sen ka

I need a (can opener).
（缶切り）が必要です。
(kan·ki·ri) ga hi·tsu·yō des

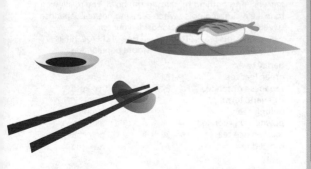

bowl	ボール	bō·ru
chopping knife	包丁	hō·chō
corkscrew	コーク	kō·ku·
	スクリュー	sku·ryū
miso-soup bowl	お椀	o·wan
pair of chopsticks	箸	ha·shi
pair of disposable chopsticks	割り箸	wa·ri·ba·shi
rice cooker	炊飯器	su·i·han·ki
wok	中華鍋	chū·ka·na·be

For more cooking implements, see the **dictionary**.

the art of drinking tea

The sha·no·yu (茶の湯), or sa·do (茶道) as they're more commonly known, which take place in the traditional tea-houses, are quite elaborate tea ceremonies governed by a set of centuries-old rules and conventions. As a foreigner you're not expected to be completely au fait with the ins and outs of a sa·do – if you're lucky enough to experience one, observe, relax and go with the flow and it will be a memorable experience. You'll be served the powdered green tea variety in a tea bowl that's larger and more elaborate than the standard tea cup, often a special piece of art in itself. Drink it by positioning the 'front' of the bowl away from the mouth and taking three or four large sips of tea, ensuring nothing remains in the bowl. You're allowed to make a slurping noise when drinking hot tea. Japanese sweets will also be served alongside your tea.

In restaurants tea is often served free of charge, refills are also generally free. These are the more popular teas:

barley tea	麦茶	mu·gi·cha
green leaf tea	煎茶	sen·cha
Japanese green tea (generic term)	緑茶	ryo·ku·cha
oolong tea	ウーロン茶	ū·ron·cha
powdered green tea	抹茶	mat·cha
roasted rice tea	玄米茶	gem·mai·chai
roasted tea	焙じ茶	hō·ji·cha

vegetarian & special meals
ベジタリアンと特殊な料理

ordering food

食事の注文

Halal and kosher food might be hard to come by, even in the big smoke, but you might want to try your luck with these phrases:

Is there a …	この近くに…	ko·no chi·ka·ku ni …
restaurant	レストランは	res·to·ran wa
near here?	ありますか?	a·ri·mas ka
halal	イスラム教徒の	i·su·ra·mu·kyō·to no
	ためのハラル	ta·me no ha·ra·ru
kosher	ユダヤ教徒の	yu·da·ya·kyō·to no
	ためのコーシャー	ta·me no kō·shā
vegetarian	ベジタリアン	be·ji·ta·ri·an

I don't eat …	…は食べません。	… wa ta·be·ma·sen
Could you prepare a meal without …?	…抜きの料理をお願いできますか?	…·nu·ki no ryō·ri o o·ne·gai shi·mas ka
butter	バター	ba·tā
eggs	卵	ta·ma·go
fish	魚	sa·ka·na
fish stock	魚のだし	sa·ka·na no da·shi
meat stock	肉のだし	ni·ku no da·shi
oil	油	a·bu·ra
pork	豚肉	bu·ta·ni·ku
poultry	鳥肉	to·ri·ni·ku
red meat	赤身の肉	a·ka·mi no ni·ku

Is this (free of animal produce)?
これは(動物性
成分抜きの)
食品ですか?
ko·re wa (dō·bu·tsu·sē
sē·bun·nu·ki no)
sho·ku·hin des ka

decaffeinated	デカフェの	de·ka·fe no
free-range	放し飼いの	ha·na·shi·gai no
genetically	遺伝子	i·den·shi·
modified	組み替えの	ku·mi·ka·e no
gluten-free	グルテン抜きの	gu·ru·ten·nu·ki no
low-fat	脂肪分が低い	shi·bō·bun ga hi·ku·i
low in sugar	糖分が低い	tō·bun ga hi·ku·i
organic	オーガニックの	ō·ga·nik·ku no
salt-free	塩分抜きの	em·bun·nu·ki no

special diets & allergies

特殊な食餌制限とアレルギー

I'm on a special diet.

| 私は特殊な | wa·ta·shi wa to·ku·shu na |
| 食餌制限をしています。 | sho·ku·ji·sē·gen o shi·te i·mas |

I'm (a) ...	私は…です。	wa·ta·shi wa ... des
Buddhist	仏教徒	buk·kyō·to
Hindu	ヒンズー教徒	hin·zū·kyō·to
Jewish	ユダヤ教徒	yu·da·ya·kyō·to
Muslim	イスラム教徒	i·su·ra·mu·kyō·to
vegan	厳格な	gen·ka·ku na
	菜食主義者	sai·sho·ku·shu·gi·sha
vegetarian	ベジタリアン	be·ji·ta·ri·an

I'm allergic to ...	私は…に	wa·ta·shi wa ... ni
	アレルギーが	a·re·ru·gī ga
	あります。	a·ri·mas
dairy produce	乳製品	nyū·sē·hin
eggs	卵	ta·ma·go
gelatine	ゼラチン	ze·ra·chin
gluten	グルテン	gu·ru·ten
honey	蜂蜜	ha·chi·mi·tsu
MSG	グルタミン	gu·ru·ta·min·
	酸ソーダ	san·sō·da
nuts	ナッツ類	nat·tsu·ru·i
peanuts	ピーナッツ	pī·nat·tsu
seafood	海産物	kai·sam·bu·tsu

These Japanese dishes and ingredients are listed alphabetically, by pronunciation, so you can easily understand what's on offer and ask for what takes your fancy. A more detailed food glossary can be found in Lonely Planet's *World Food Japan*.

A

a·ba·ra あばら *ribs*

a·be·ka·wa·mo·chi 安倍川もち *rice cakes covered with* ki·na·ko *& sugar (Shizuoka Prefecture)*

a·bo·ga·do アボガド *avocado*

a·bu·ra 油 *oil*

a·bu·ra·a·ge 油揚げ *deep-fried, thinly sliced* tō·fu

… a·e …和え *dishes dressed with …, eg* go·ma·a·e *(dish dressed with sesame seeds)*

a·e·mo·no 和え物 *food blended with a dressing*

…·a·ge …揚げ *fried …*

a·ge·da·shi·dō·fu 揚げだし豆腐 *deep-fried* tō·fu *in fish stock*

a·ge·mo·no 揚げ物 *deep-fried food*

a·hi·ru アヒル *duck*

ai·ga·mo 合鴨 *Japanese duck*

ai·na·me あいなめ *green ling · ling cod (type of fish)*

ais·ku·rī·mu アイスクリーム *ice cream*

a·ji アジ *horse mackerel · scad (type of fish)*

a·ka·a·ma·dai 赤アマダイ *red* a·ma·dai

a·ka·chi·ko·ri 赤チコリー *radicchio*

a·ka·gai 赤貝 *ark shell · bearded clam · red clam*

a·ka·ga·rê アカガレイ *plaice*

a·ka·in·gen 赤インゲン *red kidney bean*

a·ka·ji·so 赤しそ *red* shi·so

a·ka·kya·be·tsu 赤キャベツ *red cabbage*

a·ka·ren·zu·ma·me 赤レンズマメ *red lentil*

a·ka·ta·ma·ne·gi 赤たまねぎ *red onion*

a·ka·wain 赤ワイン *red wine*

a·ka·za·ke 赤酒 *reddish wine made of rice, barley and/or wheat, to which wood ash is added (Kumamoto Prefecture)*

a·ki·a·ji 秋味 *see* a·ra·ma·ki·za·ke

a·ki·ta·gai アキタ貝 *North Japan term for scallop*

a·ma·dai アマダイ *blanquillo (type of fish) · ocean whitefish · tilefish (also called* gu·ji*)*

a·ma·e·bi 甘エビ *sweet prawn*

a·mai 甘い *sweet (taste)*

a·ma·nat·tō 甘納豆 *sugar-coated beans boiled in syrup*

a·ma·za·ke 甘酒 *sweet, warm* sa·ke

a·ma·zu 甘酢 *vinegar sweetened with sugar*

am·bai 塩梅 *literally 'salt-plum', meaning 'balance' – a term used by the older generation in reference to food*

a·me 飴 *candy · lolly*

a·mi·ga·sa·ta·ke アミガサタケ *morel (type of mushroom)*

a·mi·ya·ki 網焼き *cooked on a griddle*

am·mi·tsu あんみつ *a dessert made from fruit, boiled red peas, diced Japanese gelatine &* an·ko *with syrup on top*

am·pan アンパン *baked bun filled with* an·ko

an あん *sweet bean paste*

a·na·kyū アナキュウ no·ri*-rolled* su·shi *with conger eel & cucumber*

a·na·go アナゴ *conger eel*

an·cho·bi アンチョビ *anchovy*

an·ka·ke あんかけ *dishes topped with a sauce thickened with cornstarch*

an·ko 餡子 a·zu·ki *beans boiled with sugar*

an·kō アンコウ *angler · goosefish · monkfish*

an·ko·ro·mo·chi あんころ餅 *rice cake filled with sweetened* a·zu·ki *beans*

an·zu あんず *apricot*

an·zu·ta·ke アンズタケ chanterelle

a·o·ji·so 青じそ green beefsteak plant

a·o·no·ri あおのり a strong green type of no·ri seaweed, produced in flake form & sprinkled on o·ko·no·mi·ya·ki & ya·ki·so·ba

a·o·to あおと green peppers

a·o·ya·gi あおやぎ sunray surf clam · trough shell

a·o·yu あおゆ green yu·zu

a·ra アラ grouper · type of sea bass · rock cod that reaches up to 1m in length

a·ra あら left-over fish head, bones & offal used in hotpot, clear soups & stock

a·rai あらい a style of sa·shi·mi where raw, white-fleshed fish is thinly sliced & washed in cold water to keep the meat firm

a·ra·ma·ki·za·ke 新巻鮭 salted whole salmon

a·ra·na·be アラ鍋 hotpot made with sea bass (island of Kyūshū)

a·ra·re あられ baked cracker made from mo·chi

a·sa no mi 麻の実 hemp seed

a·sa·ri あさり baby clam

a·sa·tsu·ki あさつき very thin spring onion

a·sa·zu·ke 浅漬け lightly salted pickles

as·sa·ri あっさり general term for light (not greasy)

a·ta·ma·ryō·ri 頭料理 'head cuisine' using fish entrails (Taketa City)

ā·ti·chō·ku アーティチョーク artichoke

a·tsu·a·ge 厚揚げ fried tō·fu

a·wa アワ Italian millet · foxtail millet (rice substitute)

a·wa·bi あわび abalone

a·wa·bi no ka·su·zu·ke あわびの粕漬け abalone pickled in sa·ke·ka·su (Iwate Prefecture)

a·wa·mo·ri 泡盛 alcoholic spirit made from rice (Okinawa Prefecture)

a·yu アユ sweetfish · smelt (salmonoid food fish)

a·yu·ryō·ri アユ料理 sweetfish cuisine

a·zu·ki 小豆 red bean – ingredient for the sweet paste used as a filling in many Japanese cakes & confections

B

bai·gai バイ貝 bloody clam

ba·ka·gai バカ貝 see a·o·ya·gi

ban·cha 番茶 everyday tea made from the second tea harvest

ba·ni·ra バニラ vanilla

ba·ni·ku 馬肉 horse meat

ba·ra no mi·cha バラの実茶 rosehip tea

bas バス bass · sea perch

ba·sa·shi 馬刺し horse meat sa·shi·mi (Nagano Prefecture)

ba·tā バター butter

ba·tā·mi·ru·ku バターミルク buttermilk

bat·te·ra·zu·shi バッテラずし vinegared fish on pressed su·shi

be·bī·kōn ベビーコーン baby corn

bē·kon ベーコン bacon

bē·ku·do·po·te·to ベークドポテト baked potatoes

be·ni·ba·na·in·gen ベニバナインゲン runner bean

be·ni·shō·ga 紅しょうが red pickled ginger

be·ni·ta·de 紅たで water pepper, a dark red peppery garnish

ben·tō 弁当 lunch box normally containing rice with different vegetables, meat, fish & sometimes fruit

be·ra べら wrasse (type of fish)

be·rī ベリー berries

bet·ta·ra·zu·ke べったらづけ pickled dai·kon

bī·fu ビーフ beef

bī·fu·jā·kī ビーフジャーキー beef jerky

bī·fu·ka·tsu ビーフカツ beef cutlet

bi·fu·te·ki ビフテキ beef steak

bin·na·ga ビンナガ longfin tuna

bī·ru ビール beer · ale

bi·to·rū·to ビートルート beetroot

bi·wa びわ loquat (small yellow plum-like fruit)

bo·ra ボラ mullet

bo·ta·mo·chi 牡丹もち rice cake made from half sticky rice & half nonglutinous rice

bu·chi·in·gem·ma·me ブチインゲンマメ pinto bean

bu·dō ブドウ grapes

bu·na·shi·me·ji ぶなしめじ *a small, yellow mushroom variety*

bu·rak·ku·be·rī ブラックベリー *blackberry*

bu·rak·ku·pu·din·gu ブラックプディング *black pudding*

bu·ri ブリ amberjack • yellowtail *(types of fish)*

bu·ri·ko ブリコ ha·ta·ha·ta *eggs (Akita Prefecture)*

bu·rok·ko·rī ブロッコリー *broccoli*

bu·rū·be·rī ブルーベリー *blueberry*

bu·ta·ni·ku 豚肉 *pork*

bu·ta·ni·ku no shi·o·zu·ke 豚肉の塩漬け *salted pork*

bu·ta no shō·ga·ya·ki 豚の生姜焼き *pork sautéed in ginger & shō·yu*

bu·tsu·ji 仏事 *Buddhist funerary cuisine*

C

chā·han チャーハン *fried rice*

chai·bu チャイブ *chive*

cha·kai·se·ki 茶懐石 *tea kai·se·ki*

cham·pon チャンポン *noodle soup*

chan·ko·na·be ちゃんこ鍋 *sumo wrestler's stew of meat & vegetables*

cha no yu 茶の湯 *tea ceremony*

chā·shū·men チャーシュー麺 rā·men *topped with sliced roast pork*

cha·sō·men 茶そうめん *noodles containing green tea*

cha·wan·mu·shi 茶碗蒸 *savoury steamed custard containing fish stock, chicken & gingko nuts*

che·rī·to·ma·to チェリートマト *cherry tomatoes • plum tomatoes*

chi·dai チダイ *'blood tai' fish (smaller than the* ma·dai)

chi·kin チキン *chicken*

chi·ko·rī チコリー *chicory*

chi·ku·wa ちくわ *sausage-shaped minced fish meat*

chi·ku·zen·ni 筑前煮 *chicken, taro, carrots,* go·bō, *lotus root,* kon·nya·ku, *dried* shi·ta·ke *mushroom & snow peas stewed in a stock made of sugar,* shō·yu & mi·rin

chi·ma·ki ちまき *nonglutinous-rice cake wrapped in large leaves*

chim·pi 陳皮 *citrus zest*

chin·gen·sai チンゲンサイ *bok choy*

chip·pu チップ *chips (crisps)*

chi·ra·shi·zu·shi ちらしずし su·shi·me·shi *topped with raw fish,* a·bu·ra·a·ge *& vegetables*

chi·ri(·na·be) ちり（鍋） *hotpot with white fish & vegetables*

chi·ri·sō·su チリソース *chilli sauce*

chī·zu チーズ *cheese*

chō·ji チョウジ *clove*

cho·ko·rē·to チョコレート *chocolate*

chō·mi·ryō 調味料 *seasoning*

chop·pu チョップ *chops*

chow·dā チャウダー *chowder*

chō·za·me チョウザメ *sturgeon*

chū·go·ku·cha 中国茶 *Chinese tea*

chū·hai 酎ハイ shō·chū *served with various nonalcoholic mixers*

chū·ka·so·ba 中華そば *an old-fashioned term for* rā·men – *now suggests* rā·men *in a lighter, predominantly* shō·yu*-based* da·shi

D

da·ga·shi 駄菓子 *'no good' sweets – cheap and OK but a bit junky*

dai·fu·ku·mo·chi 大福もち *rice cake with* an·ko *inside*

dai·gin·jō·shu 大吟醸酒 *highest grade* sa·ke – *fruitier than* gin·jō·shu

dai·kon 大根 *Chinese radish (giant white radish)*

dai·kon·o·ro·shi 大根おろし *grated* dai·kon

dai·ō ダイオウ *rhubarb*

dai·to·ku·ji·nat·tō 大徳寺納豆 *soy beans fermented with yeast*

dai·zu 大豆 *soy bean*

dan·go だんご *round balls made from rice & flour*

dan·sha·ku·i·mo 男爵芋 *type of potato, especially found on the island of Hokkaidō*

da·ru·ma·ka·re·i ダルマカレイ *turbot (type of fish)*

da·shi だし *stock, usually made from* ka·tsu·o·bu·shi *or* kom·bu

da·shi·ji·ru だし汁 *broth*

da·te·ma·ki だて巻 *sweetened rolled omelette, often served at New Year*

de·be·ra でべら *dried cinnamon flounder (Hiroshima Prefecture)*

de·ka·fe no kō·cha デカフェの紅茶 *decaffeinated tea*

dem·bu でんぶ *boiled & roasted snapper or cod flavoured with sugar & shō·yu & made into pink flakes that are used in su·shi rolls*

den·ga·ku 田楽 *dishes where grilled fish, vegetables & tō·fu are topped with mi·so sauce*

…·don …丼 *rice with savoury topping*

do·jō ドジョウ *loach • oriental weatherfish (type of fish)*

do·rai·bī·ru ドライビール *'dry beer' – it has a higher alcohol content & is more aerated than standard beer*

do·rai·fu·rū·tsu ドライフルーツ *dried fruit*

do·ra·ya·ki どら焼き *sweet a·zu·ki bean paste between two pancakes*

do·te·na·be 土手鍋 *hotpot with mi·so paste stock to which vegetables & seafood are added*

E

e·bi エビ *general term for prawn, shrimp, lobster & crayfish*

e·bi·fu·rai エビフライ *battered prawn*

e·bi·sō·men エビそうめん *shrimp sō·men*

e·da·ma·me 枝豆 *young soy bean – a favourite snack with beer*

e·do·mi·so 江戸味噌 *dark, fiery red & slightly sweet mi·so from Tokyo*

e·i エイ *ray*

e·i·hi·re エイヒレ *dried stingray fin served grilled as a snack with sa·ke*

e·ki·ben 駅弁 *station lunchbox*

en·dai·bu エンダイブ *endive*

en·dō エンドウ *field pea (type of green pea)*

en·ga·wa えんがわ *base of the dorsal fin of flounder & sole*

e·no·ki·da·ke えのきだけ *velvet shank mushroom • winter mushroom*

e·ra えら *gill*

ē·ru エール *ale*

F

fen·ne·ru フェンネル *fennel*

fu 麩 *shapes made from gluten flour used in clear soup*

fu·cha·ryō·ri 普茶料理 *Chinese Zen cuisine*

fu·e·dai フエダイ *snapper*

fu·gu フグ *puffer(fish) • globefish Famous fish that contains the deadly nerve toxin tetrodotoxin – its flesh is eaten as u·su·zu·ku·ri or in fu·gu·chi·ri & the milt (ie the testes of the fish) is regarded as a delicacy*

fu·gu·chi·ri フグチリ *hotpot with fu·gu*

fu·gu·shi·ra·ko フグ白子 *milt (ie the testes of the fish) of the fu·gu*

fu·ka·ga·wa·na·be 深川鍋 *hotpot with baby clam & spring onion*

fu·ka·hi·re フカヒレ *shark fin*

fu·ki フキ *Japanese butterbur (vegetable)*

fu·ki·no·tō フキノトウ *bud of fu·ki plant symbolising the beginning of spring*

fu·ku·ro·ta·ke ふくろたけ *paddy straw mushroom*

fu·na フナ *crucian carp – eaten as kan·ro·ni, tsu·ku·da·ni or a·rai*

fu·na·zu·shi フナずし *female crucian carp with eggs that are salted then pickled whole in fermented cooked rice (Shiga Prefecture)*

fu·rū·tsu·jū·su フルーツジュース *fruit juice*

fu·rū·tsu·kē·ki フルーツケーキ *fruit cake*

fu·rū·tsu·pan·chi フルーツパンチ *fruit punch*

fu·su·ma ふすま *bran*

fu·to·ma·ki 太巻き *various ingredients rolled in no·ri seaweed (large su·shi rolls)*

G

ga·chō ガチョウ *goose*

gai·mai 外米 *foreign-produced rice*

gam·mo·do·ki がんもどき *minced tō·fu fried with finely chopped vegetables & seaweed – used in hotpots* gan ガン goose

ga·ri がり pickled pinkish-red ginger usually served as an accompaniment for su·shi

gek·kê·ju 月桂樹 bay

gem·mai 玄米 brown rice

gem·mai·cha 玄米茶 roasted tea with roasted & popped rice

ge·so げそ squid tentacles

gi ギー ghee

gin·jō 吟醸 sa·ke made of rice ground back to 60% of its weight before soaking and steaming

gin·jō·shu 吟醸酒 a type of sa·ke with a clean, fruity taste

gin·nan ぎんなん gingko nut

go·bo ごぼう burdock root

go·bu·zu·ki 五分づき mix of half white & half brown rice

go·ham·mo·no ご飯もの rice dishes

go·han ご飯 cooked rice · general term for 'a meal'

go·ma ごま sesame seeds

go·ma·a·bu·ra ごま油 sesame oil

go·ma·a·e ごま和え dishes mixed with sesame, salt & sugar sauce

go·ma·da·re ごまだれ sesame sauce

go·ma·dō·fu ごま豆腐 tō·fu-like food made of ground white sesame & starch

go·ma·me ゴマメ a small sardine cooked in shō·yu & sugar

go·mo·ku·so·ba 五目そば rā·men topped with vegetables, seafood & meat

go·ri·ryō·ri カジカ refers to dishes using ka·ji·ka (a type of fish) – a speciality of Kanazawa Prefecture

gu 具 filling · topping

gu·a·va グア ヴァ guava

gu·ji ぐじ see a·ma·dai

gu·rap·pa グラッパ grappa (type of spirit)

gu·rê·pu·fu·rū·tsu グレープフルーツ grapefruit

gu·rin·o·rī·bu グリーンオリーブ green olive

gu·ru·ta·min·san·sō·da グルタミン酸ソーダ MSG

gyo·ku·ro 玉露 highest-quality Japanese green tea

gyō·nyū 凝乳 curd

gyo·shō 魚醤 fish sauce

gyō·za ギョウザ Chinese-style dumplings, normally made from minced pork, cabbage, garlic, ginger & garlic chives

gyū·don 牛丼 thinly sliced beef simmered in sweetened shō·yu & served on rice

gyū·ni·ku 牛肉 beef

gyū·nyū 牛乳 milk

gyū·tan 牛タン beef tongue

H

ha 葉 leaf

hā·bu·tī ハーブティー herbal tea

ha·dok·ku ハドック haddock

hak·ka ハッカ mint · peppermint

ha·ku·mai 白米 plain, white rice

ha·ku·sai 白菜 Chinese cabbage

ha·ma·chi ハマチ yellowtail · amberjack (see bu·ri)

ha·ma·gu·ri ハマグリ clam

ha·mo ハモ conger · daggertooth (type of eel)

ham·pen はんぺん sponge-like fish cake made of ground shark meat mixed with grated yam & rice flour

ha·mu ハム ham

ha·na·dai·kon ハナダイコン rocket

ha·na·ma·me 花豆 flower bean

ha·na·sa·ki·ga·ni 花咲ガニ type of king crab · 'flower opening' crab that opens up when dipped into hot water

hap·pa 葉っぱ leaf

hap·pō·sai 八宝菜 stir-fry with assorted vegetables, meat & seafood, & thickened with a Chinese-style sauce

ha·ra·pe·nyo ハラペニョ jalapeño chilli

ha·ra·wa·ta はらわた gizzards · offal

ha·ru·sa·me はるさめ bean-starch vermicelli

ha·sa·mi はさみ crab claws

ha·ta ハタ grouper (type of fish)

ha·ta·ha·ta ハタハタ sailfin sandfish used to make fermented fish sauce called shot·tsu·ru (Akita Prefecture)

ha·ta·ha·ta·zu·shi ハタハタずし pickled ha·ta·ha·ta

hat·chō·mi·so 八丁味噌 a dark mi·so originally created in Okazaki ha·to 鳩 pigeon

ha·ya·shi·rai·su ハヤシライス stewed meat & vegetables with rice

ha·ya·to·u·ri ハヤトウリ chayote (fruit of a particular tropical climbing plant)

ha·ze ハゼ goby fish

hē·ku ヘイク hake

hē·ze·ru·nat·tsu ヘーゼルナッツ hazelnut

hi·bo·shi·to·ma·to 日干しトマト sun-dried tomatoes

hi·da·ra 干ダラ dried cod

hi·ga·shi 干菓子 dried sweets eaten during the tea ceremony

hi·ji·ki ひじき a type of seaweed

hi·ji·ki no ni·mo·no ひじきの煮物 hi·ji·ki simmered with shō·yu, sugar, fried tō·fu & boiled soy beans

hi·ki·ni·ku ひき肉 mince

hi·ki·wa·ri·mu·gi 挽き割り麦 cracked wheat

hi·ki·wa·ri·tō·mo·ro·ko·shi 挽き割りトウモロコシ hominy (boiled ground maize)

hi·ku·do·ri 肥育鶏 capon (castrated cock fowl fattened for eating)

hi·me·ma·su ヒメマス see ka·wa·ma·su

hi·mo·no 干物 dried fish

hi·ra·ki ひらき fully open ma·tsu·ta·ke mushroom

hi·ra·ma·sa ヒラマサ yellowtail · amberjack · kingfish

hi·ra·me ヒラメ bastard halibut · brill · flatfish · flounder · plaice · turbot

hi·ra·ta·ke ヒラタケ oyster mushroom

hi·re·ka·tsu ヒレカツ fried pork fillet

hi·to·ku·chi·to·ma·to 一口トマト cherry tomatoes · plum tomatoes

hi·tsu·ji 羊 sheep · lamb

hi·ya·mu·gi 冷麦 cold noodles dipped in cold sauce

hi·ya·shi·chū·ka 冷やし中華 cold noodles in sweet & sour soup with cucumber, chicken & egg on top

hi·ya·shi·u·don 冷やしうどん simple cold u·don

hi·ya·yak·ko 冷奴 cold tō·fu

hi·yo·ko·ma·me ヒヨコマメ chickpeas

hi·za·ni·ku ひざ肉 knuckle

hō·bō ホウボウ gurnard · bluefin · sea robin (types of fish)

hō·ji·cha ほうじ茶 parched ban·cha

hok·kai·dō·ryō·ri 北海道料理 Hokkaidō cuisine

hok·ke ホッケ atka mackerel

hok·ki·gai ホッキ貝 hen clam (also known as u·ba·gai)

ho·ko·ri·ta·ke ホコリタケ puffball (fungus)

hom·mi·rin 本みりん good quality mi·rin

hon·jō·zō·shu 本醸造酒 Japanese rice wine, ground back to 70% of its original size, & blended with alcohol & water

hon·shi·me·ji 本しめじ type of mushroom

hō·ren·sō ホウレンソウ spinach

ho·shi·en·dō 干しエンドウ green split pea

ho·shi·ga·ki 干し柿 dried persimmon

ho·so·ma·ki 細まき thin su·shi roll

ho·ta·ru·i·ka ホタルイカ firefly squid

ho·ta·te(·gai) ホタテ (貝) scallop

ho·ta·te·ryō·ri ホタテ料理 scallop cuisine

ho·wai·to·pu·din·gu ホワイトプディング white pudding

ho·ya ホヤ sea squirt mixed with cucumber & vinegar & eaten raw

ho·zon·ryō 保存料 preservative

hya·ku·hi·ro 百尋 boiled whale intestine (Hakata City)

I

i·chi·go イチゴ strawberry

i·chi·ji·ku イチジク fig

ī·da·ko いいだこ 'rice octopus' – a small octopus with lots of eggs inside which look like rice

i·gai 貽貝 mussel (also known as mū·ru·gai)

i·ka イカ squid · cuttlefish

i·ki·zu·ku·ri 活き作り a method of presentation of fish & lobster, where the fish is served alive

i·ku·ra イクラ salted salmon eggs

i·na·go イナゴ rice locust – a type of rice-eating grasshopper, often eaten as tsu·ku·da·ni

i·na·ka·ryō·ri 田舎料理 rustic cuisine

i·na·man·jū いな饅頭 *cleaned mullet stuffed with* mi·so *paste (Nagoya Prefecture) – also see* bo·ra

i·na·ri·zu·shi 稲荷ずし *vinegared rice in a fried* tō·fu *pouch*

in·gem·ma·me インゲンマメ *kidney bean*

i·non·do イノンド *dill*

i·no·shi·shi いのしし *wild boar*

i·ri·do·ri 煎り鳥 *stirfried chicken, dried* shi·ta·ke, go·bo, ta·ro, kon·nya·ku, *lotus root, carrots & bamboo shoots stewed in* shō·yu & mi·rin

i·ri·ko いりこ *sea cucumber • dried trepang (sea cucumber) • dried sardine*

i·se·e·bi イセエビ *Japanese spiny lobster • crayfish*

i·shi·ka·ri·na·be 石狩鍋 *Hokkaidō salmon & vegetable hotpot*

i·so·be·ma·ki 磯辺巻き *grilled rice cakes dipped in* shō·yu & *wrapped in* no·ri

… i·ta·me …炒め *stir-fried …*

i·ta·me·mo·no 炒め物 *stir-fried dishes*

i·ta·ya·gai いたや貝 *a small scallop (also known as* sha·ku·shi·gai)

i·to·kon·nya·ku 糸こんにゃく *thinly sliced* kon·nya·ku

i·to·na 糸菜 *a pot-herb mustard, used as a leafy green vegetable*

i·to·sō·men 糸そうめん *thinnest type of* sō·men

i·wa·na イワナ *char (trout-like fish)*

i·wa·shi いわし *pilchard • sardine*

J

jā·gā·ba·ta ジャガバター *baked potatoes with butter*

ja·ga·i·mo ジャガイモ *potatoes*

ja·po·ni·ka·mai ジャポニカ米 *short-grain rice*

jin·jā ジンジャー *ginger*

…ji·ru …汁 *… juice • … soup*

ji·za·ke 地酒 *local* sa·ke

jō·ryū·shu 蒸留酒 *spirits*

jū·bu·zu·ki 十分づき *plain white rice*

jum·mai·shu 純米酒 *Japanese rice wine made by grinding rice back to 70% of its original weight*

jun·sai じゅんさい *water shield (small water plant)*

ka·ba·ya·ki 蒲焼 *grilled fish or eel dipped in* shō·yu·*based sauce, eg,* u·na·gi no ka·ba·ya·ki

ka·bo·cha かぼちゃ *Japanese pumpkin*

ka·bu かぶ *turnip*

ka·bu·na·me·ko かぶなめこ *wild, slightly larger variety of* na·me·ko *mushroom*

ka·bu·to·mu·shi かぶと蒸し *steamed head of large fish varieties*

ka·bu·to·ni かぶと煮 *stewed head of large fish varieties*

ka·e·ru カエル *frog*

ka·e·ru no a·shi カエルの足 *frog legs*

kai(·ru·i) 貝(類) *shellfish*

kai·sam·bu·tsu 海産物 *seafood*

kai·se·ki 懐石 *see* kai·se·ki·ryō·ri

kai·se·ki·ryō·ri 懐石料理 *multicourse set meal including many small dishes – also known as* kai·se·ki

kai·sō 海藻 *generic term for edible seaweed and sea vegetables*

kai·wa·re·dai·kon 貝割れ大根 *spicy salad sprout from the mustard family*

kai·zo·ku·ryō·ri 海賊料理 *'pirate food' – live seafood put on the BBQ (Tokushima Prefecture)*

ka·ji·ka カジカ *similar to goby (freshwater fish) – dishes cooked in* ka·ji·ka *are called* go·ri·ryō·ri & *are a speciality of Kanazawa Prefecture*

ka·ji·ki カジキ *marlin*

ka·ke·so·ba かけそば *buckwheat noodles in broth*

ka·ke·u·don かけうどん *wheat flour noodles in broth*

ka·ki 柿 *persimmon*

ka·ki カキ *oyster*

ka·ki·a·ge かき揚げ *finely chopped seafood & vegetables fried in* tem·pu·ra *batter*

ka·ki·me·shi かき飯 *oyster rice*

ka·ki·mo·chi かきもち *see* a·ra·re

ka·ki·na·be カキ鍋 *oyster hotpot (Hiroshima Prefecture)*

ka·ma·bo·ko かまぼこ *minced white-fish meat that's steamed & sold in blocks*

ka·ma·su カマス *barracuda • sea pike*

ka·mi·re·ru·cha カミレル茶 chamomile tea

ka·mo 鴨 duck

kam·pa·chi カンパチ amberjack (type of fish best eaten in summer)

kam·pyō かんぴょう dried fruit of bottle gourd, flavoured with shō·yu

kam·pyō·ma·ki かんぴょう巻き su·shi rolls made using kam·pyō

ka·ni カニ crab

ka·ni·ba·sa·mi カニばさみ see ha·sa·mi

ka·ni·mi·so カニ味噌 crab reproductive organs, often eaten as an hors d'oeuvre

kan·ki·tsu·ru·i 柑橘類 citrus

kan·ko·ku·ryō·ri 韓国料理 Korean cuisine

kan·zō カンゾウ liquorice

kan·ro·ni 甘露煮 small fish boiled in & sweetly flavoured with shō·yu & mi·rin • chestnuts boiled in syrup

kan·to·da·ki かんと炊き the name used for o·den in the Kansai region

kap·pa·ma·ki かっぱ巻き cucumber su·shi rolled in no·ri seaweed

ka·ra 殻 shell

ka·ra·a·ge から揚げ meat or fish dusted in flour & deep-fried

ka·ra·me·ru カラメル caramel (baked sugar)

ka·ra·mi·mo·chi からみもち rice cake with grated dai·kon

ka·ra·shi からし mustard

ka·ra·shi·men·tai·ko 辛子明太子 salted cod roe pickled in chilli (Kyūshū) – also just men·tai·ko

ka·ra·shi·na からし菜 brown mustard

ka·ra·shi·zu·ke からし漬け pickled vegetables flavoured with mustard

ka·ra·su·mi からすみ dried mullet roe (Nagasaki & Kyūshū) – also see bo·ra

ka·rē カレー curry

ka·rei カレイ dab • flatfish • flounder

ka·rē·nam·ban カレー南蛮 buckwheat noodles with chicken or pork curry

ka·rē·rai·su カレーライス Japanese-style curry & rice

ka·rē·u·don カレーうどん u·don noodles with curry roux sauce (ie sauce based on equal amounts of fat and flour)

ka·ri·fu·ra·wā カリフラワー cauliflower

ka·rin かりん Chinese quince

ka·rin·tō かりんとう sweet made of flour & baking powder, deep-fried & coated with brown sugar

ka·ru·da·mon カルダモン cardamom

ka·ru·don カルドン cardoon (thistle-like plant with edible stalks)

ka·ru·kan かるかん a confection made from ya·ma·i·mo, rice powder & sugar (Kagoshima)

ka·shi·wa·mo·chi 柏もち rice cake wrapped in oak leaf – eaten on 5 May (Children's Day)

ka·su 粕 lees (sediment) from sa·ke

ka·su·ji·ru 粕汁 thick soup flavoured with lees (sediment) from sa·ke

ka·su·te·ra カステラ yellow sponge cake (Nagasaki Prefecture)

ka·su·zu·ke 粕漬け vegetables pickled in lees (sediment) from sa·ke

ka·ta·ku·chi·i·wa·shi カタクチイワシ anchovy • Japanese anchovy

ka·ta·ku·ri·ko 片栗粉 arrowroot flour

ka·ta·ya·ki·so·ba 固焼きそば crunchy fried noodles topped with vegetables

ka·ta·yu·de·ta·ma·go 固ゆで卵 hard-boiled egg

ka·tsu カツ cutlets

ka·tsu·don カツ丼 fried pork cutlet & egg on rice

ka·tsu·o カツオ bonito • skipjack (fish)

ka·tsu·o·bu·shi カツオ節 dried bonito (fish) flakes

ka·wa·ha·gi カワハギ leatherjacket • filefish

ka·wa·hi·me·ma·su カワヒメマス grayling (salmonoid fish)

ka·wa·ma·su 川マス freshwater red salmon • pike

ka·wa·za·ka·na 川魚 river fish • lake fish

ka·zu·no·ko かずのこ dried herring roe (also see o·se·chi·ryō·ri)

ke·chap·pu ケチャップ (tomato) ketchup

ke·ga·ni 毛がに bristly crab • horsehair crab (best in winter)

kē·ki ケーキ cake(s)

ke·shi no mi ケシの実 poppy seed

kē·sho·ku 軽食 snacks

ki·dai キダイ yellowish tai, a cheap fish served as shi·o·ya·ki

ki·en·dō 黄エンドウ *yellow split pea*

ki·ha·da キハダ *yellowfin tuna*

ki·i·chi·go キイチゴ *raspberry*

ki·ji 雉 *pheasant*

ki·ku·i·mo キクイモ *Jerusalem artichoke*

ki·ku·ko きくこ *cod milt (fish testes) used in hotpot*

ki·ku·ra·ge きくらげ *Jew's ear · Judas' ear · woody ear tree fungus*

ki·mi·sō·men 黄身そうめん *noodles with egg yolk*

kim·ma キンマ *betel (plant with edible leaves and nuts)*

kim·me(·dai) キンメ（ダイ）*redfish*

ki·na·ko きなこ *soy bean flour*

ki·na·ko·mo·chi きなこもち *rice cake covered with sweetened soy bean flour*

kin·kan キンカン *kumquat*

ki no mi 木の実 *berries*

kim·me(·dai) キンメ（ダイ）*redfish · alfonsino*

kim·pi·ra·go·bō きんぴらごぼう *thinly cut go·bō, normally eaten flavoured with shō·yu*

ki·no·ko きのこ *mushroom*

kin·to·ki 金時 *large red bean*

ki·nu·go·shi·dō·fu 絹ごし豆腐 *smooth, soft tō·fu (see also mo·men·dō·fu)*

ki·ri·mi 切り身 *fish or meat fillet*

ki·shi·men きしめん *flat noodles (Nagoya)*

ki·su キス *whiting*

ki·tsu·ne·so·ba きつねそば *buckwheat noodles with fried tō·fu*

ki·tsu·ne·u·don きつねうどん *wheat flour noodles with fried tō·fu*

ki·yu·zu 黄ゆず *yellow yu·zu*

kō·be·gyū 神戸牛 *beef from Kobe renowned as marble beef*

ko·bu·cha 昆布茶 *tea made of kom·bu seaweed (also called kom·bu·cha)*

ko·bu·da·shi 昆布だし *kelp stock*

ko·bu·ma·ki 昆布巻き *small fish or go·bō wrapped in kom·bu & boiled*

kō·cha 紅茶 *(black) tea*

ko·chi·jan コチジャン *a Korean sweet, spicy, pepper-mi·so paste*

ko·e·bi 小エビ *shrimp*

ko·en·do·ro コエンドロ *cilantro (also called Chinese parsley and coriander)*

ko·ha·da こはだ *threadfin shad · gizzard shad (herring-like types of fish also known as ko no shi ro)*

kō·hi コーヒー *coffee*

ko·hi·tsu·ji 子羊 *lamb*

ko·ko·a ココア *cocoa*

ko·ko·na·tsu ココナツ *coconut*

ko·ma·tsu·na 小松菜 *mustard spinach (green leafy vegetable)*

kom·bu 昆布 *kelp (seaweed)*

kom·bu·cha 昆布茶 *see ko·bu·cha*

ko·me 米 *uncooked rice*

ko·me·mi·so 米味噌 *mi·so made from rice*

kōm·mi·ru コーンミール *cornmeal*

ko·mu·gi 小麦 *wheat*

ko·mu·gi·ba·ku·ga 小麦麦芽 *wheat germ*

kō·na·go こうなご *sand eel*

ko·na·za·tō 粉砂糖 *icing sugar*

kon·nya·ku こんにゃく *devil's tongue – a tuber used to make a gelatinous paste which is used in hotpots & stewed foods (Gunma, Tochigi & Fukushima Prefectures)*

ko·no·ko このこ *dried trepang roe eaten as a snack with sa·ke (Ishikawa Prefecture)*

kō no mo no 香の物 *pickled vegetables, served during a cha·ka·se·ki*

ko·no·shi·ro コノシロ *see ko·ha·da*

ko no wa·ta コノワタ *salted trepang (sea cucumber) intestine*

kon·sai 根菜 *root vegetables*

kō·ri·an·da コリアンダ *coriander*

kō·ri·dō·fu 凍り豆腐 *freeze-dried tō·fu used in stewed dishes*

kō ri mi zu 氷水 *ice water*

ko·ro ころ *young, fully closed ma·tsu·ta·ke*

ko·ro·ha コロハ *fenugreek*

ko·rok·ke コロッケ *croquette*

ko·ro·mo ころも *coating of deep-fried food · batter*

kō·ryō·kyō コウリョウキョウ *galangal*

ko·shi·ni·ku 腰肉 *loin*

kō·shin·ryō 香辛料 *condiments*

ko·shō 胡椒 *pepper*

ko·shō·sō コショウソウ *cress*

ko·tsu·zu·i 骨髄 *marrow*

kot·te·ri こってり *general term for rich or thick (see also as·sa·ri)*

ko·u·shi no ni·ku 仔牛の肉 *veal*

culinary reader

koy コイ *carp used for* mi·so *soup or* a·rai

kō·ya·dō·fu こうや豆腐 *see* kō·ri·dō·fu

koy·cha 濃茶 *thick tea*

koy·ku·chi·shō·yu 濃い口しょう油 *dark* shō·yu

ku·chi·ko クチコ *salted trepang roe*

ku·da·mo·no くだもの *fruit*

ku·ji·ra くじら *whale*

ku·mi·a·ge·dō·fu くみ上げ豆腐 *freshly made* tō·fu

ku·min クミン *cumin*

kun·sē 燻製 *smoked*

kun·sē·sa·ke 燻製サケ *kipper*

ku·ra·ge クラゲ *jellyfish*

ku·rak·kā クラッカー *cracker*

ku·ram·be·rī クランベリー *cranberry*

ku·ram·be·rī·sō·su クランベリーソース *cranberry sauce*

ku·res クレス *cress*

ku·re·son クレソン *watercress*

ku·ri 栗 *chestnut*

ku·ri·jō·chū 栗焼酎 shō·chū *made from chestnuts*

ku·ri·kin·ton 栗きんとん *chestnuts boiled in syrup & covered with mashed sweet potatoes*

ku·ro·a·na·go クロアナゴ *black conger eel*

ku·ro·bī·ru 黒ビール *stout (beer)*

ku·rō·bu クローブ *clove*

ku·ro·dai クロダイ *black bream or porgy*

ku·ro·go·ma 黒ごま *black sesame seed*

ku·ro·ma·gu·ro クロマグロ *bluefin tuna*

ku·ro·ma·me 黒豆 *black soy bean*

ku·ro·o·rī·bu 黒オリーブ *black olive*

ku·ro·was·san クロワッサン *croissant*

ku·ru·ma·ba·sō クルマバソウ *sweet woodruff (plant whose leaves are used to flavour wine and liqueurs)*

ku·ru·ma·e·bi 車えび *kuruma prawn • tiger prawn • scampi*

ku·ru·mi クルミ *walnut*

ku·ru·zet·to クルゼット *courgette • zucchini*

ku·sa·mo·chi 草もち *green rice cake mixed with mugwort (a herbal plant)*

ku·sa·ya くさや *strong-smelling dried fish (island of Niijima & Izu archipelago)*

kū·sū 古酒 *or* クースー *aged* a·wa·mo·ri *alcohol*

ku·wai クワイ *arrowhead (water plant)*

ku·wa no mi くわの実 *mulberry*

ku·zu 葛 *the starch extracted from the root of the kudzu vine*

ku·zu·ki·ri 葛きり *thin, vermicelli-like noodles made from* ku·zu

kya·be·tsu キャベツ *(white) cabbage*

kya·bya キャビア *caviar*

kya·ra·me·ru キャラメル *caramel (lolly)*

kya·ra·wē キャラウェー *caraway seed*

kyō·do·ryō·ri 郷土料理 *regionalside speciality cuisine*

kyō·na 京菜 *a pot-herb mustard plant, used as leafy green vegetable*

kyō·ri·ki·ko 強力粉 *strong wheat flour*

kyō·ryō·ri 京料理 *Kyoto specialist cuisine*

kyō·to·shi·ro·mi·so 京都白味噌 *a delicate, sweet, white* mi·so *used in* kyo·ryō·ri

kyū·ri キュウリ *cucumber*

kyū·ri·mo·mi キュウリもみ *thinly sliced cucumber mixed & softened with salt*

kyū·ri no pi·ku·ru·su キュウリのピクルス *gherkin*

kyū·shū·ryō·ri 九州料理 *cuisine of the island of Kyūshū*

kyū·tē·ryō·ri 宮廷料理 *palace cuisine*

M

ma·a·ji マアジ *horse mackerel • jack mackerel • scad (type of fish)*

ma·a·na·go マアナゴ *conger eel*

ma·dai マダイ *red sea bream • silver sea bream • snapper*

ma·ga·mo マガモ *mallard (a duck)*

ma·gu·ro マグロ *tuna – caught mostly outside Japan*

mai·ta·ke まいたけ *hen-of-the-woods mushroom*

ma·i·wa·shi まいわし *sardine • pilchard*

ma·ki·zu·shi 巻きずし *general term for nori-rolled* su·shi

ma·me 豆 *beans, including pea & soy beans*

ma·me·mi·so 豆味噌 mi·so *made from soy beans*

ma·me·ru·i 豆類 *legume*

man·gō マンゴー *mango*

man·jū 饅頭 *steamed bun filled with sweet* a·zu·ki *beans*

ma·ri·ne マリネ *marinade*

ma·ru·me·ro マルメロ *quince*

mas·shu·po·te·to マッシュポテト
mashed potatoes

mas·tā·do マスタード *mustard*

ma·su マス *pink salmon • generic term
for trout*

mat·cha 抹茶 *powdered green tea*

mat·cha·ai·su 抹茶アイス
green tea ice cream

mat·cha·shi·o 抹茶塩 *salt & powdered
green tea, used for dipping* tem·pu·ra

ma·tō·dai マトウダイ *John Dory (fish)*

ma·ton マトン *mutton*

ma·tsu·ka·wa·zu·ku·ri 松皮づくり *a type
of* sa·shi·mi *made from unskinned tai –
the skin is tasty & looks like pine bark*

ma·tsu no mi 松の実 *pine nut*

ma·tsu·ta·ke マツタケ *expensive & highly
fragrant mushroom variety*

ma·yo·nē·zu マヨネーズ *mayonnaise*

me·ba·chi メバチ *bigeye tuna*

me·ba·ru メバル *brown rockfish*

me·bō·ki メボウキ *sweet basil*

me·da·ma·ya·ki 目玉焼き *fried egg*

men 麺 *noodles*

men·chi·ka·tsu メンチカツ *crumbed &
fried mince meat patties*

men·ru·i 麺類 *generic term for noodles*

men·tai·ko 明太子
see ka·ra·shi·men·tai·ko

me·ron メロン *melon • cantaloupe*

mēs メース *mace (a spice)*

mi 身 *generic term for flesh (of fish or
shellfish)*

mi·ga·ki·ni·shin 身欠きにしん
dried herring

mi·kan みかん *mandarin orange*

mi·na·mi·ma·gu·ro ミナミマグロ
southern bluefin tuna

min·to ミント *mint*

mi·rin みりん *sweet rice wine used for
cooking*

mi·ru·gai みる貝 *otter shell*

mi·ru·ku ミルク *milk*

mi·ru·ku·tī ミルクティー *milk tea*

mi·so 味噌 *fermented soy bean paste – can
also be made from rice or barley*

mi·so·ni 味噌煮 *fish simmered in* mi·so
stock

mi·so·rā·men 味噌ラーメン rā·men *with*
mi·so-*flavoured broth*

mi·so·shi·ru 味噌汁 *soup made from*
mi·so *paste with fish stock – often
includes vegetables,* tō·fu & wa·ka·me

mi·so·zu·ke 味噌漬 *meat, fish & vegetables pickled In* mi·so

mi·tsu·ba みつば *Japanese wild
chervil, used to add flavour to hotpots,*
cha·wan·mu·shi & o·ya·ko·don

mi·tsu·ma·me みつまめ *Japanese dessert
made from boiled red peas, diced
Japanese gelatine (agar-agar) & fruit
topped with syrup – similar to* am·mi·tsu,
but does not include an·ko

mi·zu 水 *water*

mi·zu·na ミズナ *a pot-herb mustard
plant, used as leafy green vegetable*

mi·zu·ta·ki 水炊き *hotpot with
chicken & vegetables boiled in their own
stock – eaten with dipping sauce made
from* shō·yu & pon·zu

mi·zu·yō·kan 水羊羹 *mild, sweet* yō·kan
jelly

mo·chi もち *rice cake made from
glutinous rice*

mo·chi·go·me もち米 *glutinous rice, used
to make* mo·chi

mo·dan·ya·ki モダン焼き *Japanese-style
savoury pancake with noodles*

mo·men·dō·fu 木綿豆腐 *rough, firm* tō·fu
(see also ki·nu·go·shi·dō·fu*)*

mo·mi·ji·o·ro·shi もみじおろし *relish
from grated* dai·kon & *chilli*

mo·mo 桃 *peach*

mo·na·ka 最中 *a sweet made of* an·ko
inside a thin wafer shell

mo·ri·so·ba もりそば *cold buckwheat
noodles served in a bamboo steamer &
dipped into a cold sauce before eating*

mo·tsu モツ *chicken, pork, or beef offal*

mo·tsu·na·be モツ鍋 *hotpot made of
chicken, pork or beef offal*

mo·tsu·ni モツ煮 *simmered chicken, pork
or beef offal*

mo·ya·shi モヤシ *bean sprouts*

mo·zu·ku モズク *type of seaweed served
mixed with vinegar*

mo·zu·ku·ga·ni モズクガニ
small freshwater crab

mu·gi 麦 general term for wheat, oat, barley & rye

mu·gi·cha 麦茶 cold tea made of roasted barley

mu·gi·jō·chū 麦焼酎 shō·chū made from wheat (Oita Prefecture)

mu·gi·mi·so 麦味噌 barley mi·so popular on the island of Kyūshū

mu·gi·to·ro 麦とろ cooked rice & wheat with grated yam on top

mu·ne·ni·ku 胸肉 brisket (meat from the breast of a four-legged animal, especially beef)

mu·ni·e·ru ムニエル meunière (describes a dish fried lightly in butter)

mū·ru·gai ムール貝 mussel (also known as i·gai)

mu·shi·gyō·za 蒸しギョウザ steamed gyō·za dumpling

mu·shi·mo·no 蒸し物 steamed dishes

mu·tsu·go·rō ムツゴロウ a kind of goby · mud skipper

myō·ga ミョウガ Japanese ginger

myū·zu·rī ミューズリー muesli

N

na 菜 leaf vegetables (also see nap·pa)

…·na·be …鍋 hotpot made of …

na·be(·mo·no) 鍋(物) general term for hotpot – the diner selects the raw ingredients & cooks them in the na·be pot

na·be·ya·ki·u·don 鍋焼きうどん u·don noodles, seafood, meat, & vegetables cooked in a small pot

na·ma·ga·shi 生菓子 uncooked sweet paste confections filled with red an

na·ma·ko ナマコ trepang (sea cucumber)

na·ma·su なます thinly cut, raw seafood or uncooked vegetables steeped in vinegar

na·ma·ta·ma·go 生卵 raw egg

na·ma·za·ke 生酒 sa·ke that has not been pasteurised

na·ma·zu ナマズ catfish

na·me·ko なめこ a small, golden-brown mushroom related to the ma·tsu·ta·ke

nam·ban·zu·ke 南蛮漬け fried fish marinated in vinegar with sliced onions & chilli

na·no·ha·na·zu·ke 菜の花漬け rape shoot pickle (Kyoto)

nap·pa 菜っ葉 leaf vegetables (also see na)

na·re·zu·shi なれずし salted a·yu pickled in vinegar & cooked rice

na·ru·to·ma·ki なると巻き thinly sliced fish cakes served in noodles, such as rā·men & u·don – contains the same ingredients as ka·ma·bo·ko

na·shi ナシ Japanese pear

na·su ナス eggplant · aubergine

na·ta·ne 菜種 rape seed

na·ta·ne·fu·gu 菜種フグ end-of-season fu·gu, at its tastiest & most poisonous

na·tsu·me なつめ date

na·tsu·me·gu ナツメグ nutmeg

na·tsu·me·ya·shi ナツメヤシ date (fruit)

nat·tō 納豆 sticky, fermented soy beans

ne·gi ねぎ spring onion · scallion · welsh onion

ne·gi·ma ねぎま tuna & spring onion stewed in a hotpot (Tokyo) · grilled spring onion & chicken meat on skewers served in ya·ki·to·ri restaurants

ne·ku·ta·rin ネクタリン nectarine

ni·bo·shi 煮干 dried anchovies used to make stock

ni·ga·u·ri にがうり balsam pear · bitter melon

ni·gi·ri·zu·shi にぎりずし hand-pressed su·shi

ni·go·ri·za·ke にごり酒 cloudy sa·ke

ni·hon·cha 日本茶 Japanese tea

ni·hon·ryō·ri 日本料理 Japanese cuisine

ni·hon·shu 日本酒 another word for sa·ke

ni·ji·ma·su ニジマス see ka·wa·ma·su

ni·ki·ri·mi·rin 煮きりみりん mi·rin with alcohol that is burned off prior to use

nik·kē 肉桂 see nik·ki

nik·ki ニッキ cinnamon

nik·ko·ro·ga·shi 煮っころがし potatoes or ta·ro stewed in shō·yu-based stock

ni·ku 肉 meat

ni·ku·dan·go 肉団子 meatball

ni·ku·ja·ga 肉じゃが potato & meat stew

ni·ku·ji·ru 肉汁 gravy

ni·ku·zu·ku ニクズク nutmeg

ni·mai·gai 二枚貝 clam

ni·mo·no 煮物 simmered dishes

nin·jin ニンジン carrot

nin·ni·ku ニンニク garlic

ni·ra にら Chinese chives · garlic chives

ni·shin にしん herring (best in spring)

ni·tsu·ke 煮つけ fish or vegetables simmered in savoury stock until almost all the liquid evaporates

ni·wa·to·ri にわとり chicken

no·bu·ta 野豚 wild boar

no·mi·ya 飲み屋 Japanese-style bar

no·ri 海苔 sea laver (particular type of seaweed) · type of seaweed formed into sheets & used to wrap su·shi

no·ri·ma·ki 海苔巻 su·shi rolled in seaweed

no·shi·i·ka のしいか dried, hand-rolled squid

no·u·sa·gi 野ウサギ hare

nu·ka 糠 (rice) bran

nu·ka·mi·so 糠味噌 fermented rice bran used as a base to make pickles

nu·ka·zu·ke 糠漬け vegetables pickled in nu·ka·mi·so

nu·ta ぬた clam or tuna with spring onion covered in vinegared mi·so

nyū·men にゅうめん sō·men noodles in hot soup

O

o·a·ge おあげ thinly sliced, thick tō·fu fried in sesame oil

o·ben·tō お弁当 see ben·tō

o·cha お茶 Japanese green tea

o·cha·zu·ke お茶漬け white rice with green tea poured onto it

o·den おでん hotpot with tō·fu, kon·nya·ku, fish-cake meatballs & potato stewed in stock

o·do·ri·gu·i おどり食い shrimps or small fish eaten live & dipped in vinegar or shō·yu

o·gi·gai 扇貝 scallop

o·ha·gi おはぎ see bo·ta·mo·chi

o·hi·ta·shi おひたし boiled green-leaf vegetables served cold with shō·yu

o·kan お燗 warm sa·ke

o·ka·ra おから lees (sediment) from soy milk eaten mixed with finely chopped boiled vegetables

o·ka·shi お菓子 sweets · lollies

o·ka·shi·ra·tsu·ki 尾頭付き dish consisting of a whole fish

o·ka·yu おかゆ rice porridge · congee (gruel of boiled rice and water)

o·ka·zu おかず a (side) dish accompanying rice, mi·so, soup & pickles

o·ko·no·mi·ya·ki お好み焼き Japanese-style savoury pancake

o·ku·ra オクラ okra

ō·mu·gi 大麦 barley

o·mu·rai·su オムライス omelette & rice

o·mu·re·tsu オムレツ omelette

o·ni·ga·ra·ya·ki 鬼殻焼き prawns in the shell, grilled over hot coals

o·ni·gi·ri おにぎり rice ball

on·sen·ta·ma·go 温泉たまご egg boiled in a natural hot spring

o·re·ga·no オレガノ oregano

o·ren·ji オレンジ orange

o·ri·bu オリーブ olive

o·ri·bu·oy·ru オリーブオイル olive oil

…o·ro·shi …おろし grated …

o·ro·shi·shō·ga おろししょうが grated ginger

ō·ru·spais オールスパイス allspice

o·se·chi·ryō·ri おせち料理 various preserved dishes stored in layered lacquerware dishes & served at New Year festivals

o·sa·ke お酒 Japanese wine (also see sa·ke)

o·shi·ru·ko お汁粉 grilled rice cake served with sweet, stewed a·zu·ki bean

o·shi·zus·hi 押しずし su·shi made by pressing vinegared rice into a square box & layering su·shi ingredients on top (Kansai region)

ō·to·mi·ru オートミール oatmeal

o·ya·ko·don 親子丼 chicken & egg on rice

P

pā·chi パーチ perch

pai パイ pie

pai·nap·pu·ru パイナップル pineapple

pan パン bread · bread roll

pan·ga·ta パン型 loaf

pan·ko パン粉 breadcrumbs

pa·pa·i·ya パパイヤ papaya

pa·pu·ri·ka パプリカ paprika

pa·se·ri パセリ parsley

pās·nip·pu パースニップ parsnip

pas·ta パスタ pasta

pas·to·ra·mi パストラミ *pastrami*

pe·kan ペカン *pecan*

pe·pā·min·to ペパーミント *peppermint*

pe·pā·min·to·tī ペパーミントティー *peppermint tea*

pe·pa·rō·ni ペパローニ *pepperoni*

pes·to·rī ペストリー *pastry*

pī·man ピーマン *capsicum (usually green) • bell pepper*

pi·nats ピーナツ *groundnut • peanut*

pis·ta·chi·o ピスタチオ *pistachio*

pō·chi·do·eg·gu ポーチド・エッグ *poached egg*

pō·ku ポーク *pork (also called bu·ta·ni·ku)*

pō·ku·sō·sē·ji ポークソーセージ *pork sausages*

pō·ku·so·tē ポークソテー *sautéed pork*

pon·kan ポンカン *a large type of citrus fruit*

pon·zu ポン酢 *juice from citrus fruits • a mix of shō·yu, da·shi, citrus juices & sometimes vinegar used as a dipping sauce & in salad dressings*

pop·pu·kōn ポップコーン *popcorn*

po·te·to ポテト *potatoes*

po·te·to·fu·rai ポテトフライ *fried potatoes • French fries*

pō·to·wain ポートワイン *port*

pu·ra·mu·to·ma·to プラムトマト *plum tomatoes*

pu·rūn プルーン *prune*

R

ra·dis·shu ラディッシュ *radish*

rā·do ラード *lard*

ra·gā·bī·ru ラガービール *lager*

rak·kyō ラッキョウ *scallion • baker's garlic*

rā·men ラーメン *yellow wheat noodles*

ra·mu ラム *lamb*

rā·yu ラー油 *chilli oil*

re·ba·sa·shi レバ刺し *liver sa·shi·mi*

re·mon レモン *lemon*

re·mon·tī レモンティー *lemon tea*

ren·kon れんこん *lotus root*

ren·zu·ma·me レンズマメ *lentil*

rē·shi レイシ *lychee*

rē·shu 冷酒 *chilled sa·ke*

re·tas レタス *lettuce*

rē·tō 冷凍 *frozen*

rē·zun レーズン *raisin • sultana*

ri·kyū·ru リキュール *liqueur*

rin·go りんご *apple*

ro·bus·tā ロブスター *lobster*

rō·ru·do·ō·to ロールドオート *rolled oats*

rō·ru·kya·be·tsu ロールキャベツ *cabbage rolls*

rō·ru·pan ロールパン *bread roll*

rōs(·to) ロース(ト) *roast*

rōz·ma·rī ローズマリー *rosemary*

ryō·chō 猟鳥 *game (birds)*

ryō·jū 猟獣 *game (other animals)*

ryo·ku·cha 緑茶 *green tea*

(…) ryō·ri (…)料理 *(…-style) cuisine*

S

sa·ba サバ *chub mackerel • Pacific mackerel*

sa·ba no mi·so·ni サバの味噌煮 *mackerel simmered with mi·so*

sa·ba no ni·tsu·ke サバの煮付け *mackerel simmered with shō·yu*

sa·dō 茶道 *tea ceremony*

sa·fu·ran サフラン *saffron*

sa·go サゴ *sago*

sa·ka·na 魚 *fish*

sa·ka·na no pē·sto 魚のペースト *fish paste*

sa·ka·na no ta·ma·go 魚の卵 *fish roe*

sa·ke 酒 *alcohol made from a fermenting process that uses grain (known in the West as rice wine) • general term for alcoholic drinks (also called o·sa·ke & ni·hon·shu)*

sa·ke 鮭 *salmon • chum salmon • dog salmon (also known as sha·ke)*

sa·ke·a·te 酒あて *accompaniments to sa·ke & beer*

sa·ke·ka·su 酒粕 *lees (sediment) from rice wine*

sa·ku·ra·ma·su 桜マス/琵琶マス *cherry salmon*

sa·ku·ra·mo·chi 桜もち *pink rice cake wrapped in a cherry leaf*

sa·ku·ra·ni·ku さくら肉 *horse meat*

sa·ku·ram·bo さくらんぼ *cherry*

sam·ma さんま *Pacific saury • saury pike (types of fish)*

san·do·rai·to·ma·to サンドライトマト sun-dried tomatoes

san·jin·ryō·ri 山人料理 'mountain man food' (Fukushima Prefecture & Tohoku region)

san·sai 山菜 edible, wild mountain vegetables

san·sai·ryō·ri 山菜料理 mountain vegetable cuisine

san·shō 山椒 Japanese prickly ash pod • Sichuan pepper

sa·ra·shi·ne·gi さらしねぎ Welsh onion, soaked in water, drained & thinly sliced

sā·ro·in サーロイン sirloin

sa·sa·ge ささげ black-eyed peas

sā·shi·mi 刺身 raw fish or meat

sa·tō 砂糖 sugar

sa·to·i·mo サトイモ taro

sa·tsu·ma·a·ge さつま揚げ minced fish meat mixed with finely chopped vegetables, then fried in sesame oil – used in ni·mo·no & o·den

sa·tsu·ma·i·mo サツマイモ sweet potato

sa·wa·chi·ryō·ri 皿鉢料理 celebratory cuisine with vegetables, seafood, ni·mo·no & a·ge·mo·no piled on one large platter (Kochi Prefecture & island of Shikoku)

sa·wa·ga·ni 沢がに freshwater crab, often served deep-fried in ka·ra·a·ge

sa·wā·ku·rī·mu サワークリーム sour cream

sa·wa·ra さわら spotted mackerel • Spanish mackerel

sa·ya·en·dō リヤエンドウ snow pea

sa·ya·in·gen サヤインゲン string beans

sa·yo·ri サヨリ garfish • halfbeak • snipe fish

sa·za·e サザエ whelk (mollusc)

sa·za·e no tsu·bo·ya·ki サザエのつぼ焼き whelk (mollusc) grilled in the shell

sē·ji セージ sage

se·ki·han 赤飯 'red rice' with a·zu·ki beans

sem·bē せんべい rice cracker

sem·mai·zu·ke 千枚漬け large turnips pickled in sweet vinegar (Kyoto)

sen·cha 煎茶 a typical Japanese green tea

sen·dai·mi·so 仙台味噌 salty mi·so (Miyagi Prefecture)

sen·gi·ri 千切 vegetables thinly sliced lengthways • julienne

se·ri せり water dropwort (type of plant) – used in su·ki·ya·ki, soups & salads

se·ro·ri セロリ celery

sē·shu 清酒 sa·ke • generic term for clear rice wine

sha·bu·sha·bu しゃぶしゃぶ thinly sliced beef dipped into a boiling hotpot, then into sesame or pon·zu sauces

sha·ko しゃこ mantis shrimp • squilla (type of mantis shrimp)

sha·ku·shi·gai 杓子貝 see i·ta·ya·gai

sham·pen シャンペン sparkling wine

shan·dī シャンディー shandy

she·rī シェリー sherry

shi·ba·e·bi 芝エビ shiba shrimp • prawn

shi·bō 脂肪 fat

shi·bo·ri·ta·te jū·su しぼりたてジュース fresh juice

shi·chi·bu·zu·ki 七分づき a mixture of 70% white & 30% brown rice

shi·chi·men·chō 七面鳥 turkey

shi·chi·mi·tō·ga·ra·shi 七味唐辛子 a blend of seven spices used as a condiment for noodle dishes & na·be·mo·no

shi·chū シチュー stew

shī·fū·do シーフード seafood

shi·ka 鹿 deer

shi·ka·ni·ku 鹿肉 venison

shi·ki·mi シキミ star anise

shi·ma·a·ji シマアジ crevalle jack (type of fish)

shi·ma·dō·fu しまどうふ hard tō·fu suited to frying (Okinawa Prefecture)

shi·me·ji しめじ a type of mushroom

shi·me·sa·ba しめサバ vinegared mackerel

shi·mo·fu·ri(·gyū·ni·ku) 霜降り(牛肉) marbled (beef)

shi·na·chi·ku シナチク pickled Chinese bamboo sprouts

shi·na·mon シナモン cinnamon

shin·cha 新茶 new-season green tea – usually available in stores in early summer

shin·shū·mi·so 信州味噌 mi·so from Nagano Prefecture

shi·o 塩 salt

shi·o·bo·shi·wa·ka·me 塩干しワカメ wa·ka·me *washed in salt water, then dried*

shi·o·ka·ra 塩辛 *seafood pickled with salt*

shi·o·nu·ki·wa·ka·me 塩抜きワカメ wa·ka·me *washed in plain, unsalted water & dried*

shi·o·ya·ki 塩焼き *salted & grilled food*

shi·o·zu·ke 塩漬け *vegetables, meat or seafood pickled in salt*

ship·po·ku·ryō·ri 卓袱料理 *a refined banquet cuisine from Nagasaki Prefecture*

shi·ra·ko 白子 *milt (testes from fish)*

shi·ra·shi·me·yu 白絞め油 *salad oil, normally rape seed oil*

shi·ra·su シラス *whitebait*

shi·ra·su·bo·shi しらす干し *boiled & dried young anchovies or pilchards*

shi·ra·ta·ki しらたき kon·nya·ku *in noodle form*

shi·ra·u·o しらうお *a type of fish eaten live & known in English as ice goby or icefish (Fukuoka Prefecture)*

shi·ri·ni·ku 尻肉 *rump*

shi·ro·a·e 白和え *vegetables mixed with sauce made from* tō·fu

shi·ro·a·ma·dai 白アマダイ *white* a·ma·dai

shi·ro·go·ma 白ごま *white sesame seed*

shi·ro·ke·shi no mi 白ケシの実 *white poppy seed*

shi·ro·mi·so 白味噌 *white* mi·so

shi·ro·mi·za·ka·na 白身魚 *white-fleshed fish*

shi·ro·wain 白ワイン *white wine*

shi·ro·za·ke 白酒 *white, cloudy rice wine*

shi·rya·ru シリアル *cereal*

shi·sha·mo ししゃも *capelin • longfin smelt • night smelt (types of fish)*

shi·so しそ *beefsteak plant • perilla (a member of the mint family). Used as a condiment, a colouring or as a flavouring for pickles.*

shi·ta 舌 *tongue*

shi·ta·bi·ra·me シタビラメ *sole*

shī·ta·ke しいたけ *shiitake mushroom*

shō·chū 焼酎 *distilled spirit made from sweet potato, rice, millet or lees (sediment) from rice wine*

shō·ga しょうが *ginger*

shō·ga·su しょうが酢 *ginger vinegar*

shō·ga·ya·ki しょうが焼き *grilled meat or fish flavoured with ginger &* shō·yu

shō·ga·yu しょうが湯 *ginger & hot water – a traditional cure*

shō·jin·a·ge 精進揚げ *vegetarian* tem·pu·ra

shō·jin·ryō·ri 精進料理 *traditional vegetarian food*

sho·ku·bu·tsu·yu 植物油 *vegetable oil*

sho·ku·pan 食パン *square-shaped loaf of bread*

sho·ku·ryō 食料 *stock (food)*

shop·pai しょっぱい *salty*

shot·tsu·ru しょっつる *fermented fish sauce made from* ha·ta·ha·ta *(Akita Prefecture)*

shō·yu しょう油 *soy sauce made from fermented soy bean & wheat*

shō·yu·ya·ki しょう油焼き *grilled with* shō·yu

shō·yu·zu·ke しょう油漬け *vegetables pickled in* shō·yu

shū·mai シュウマイ *steamed, round Chinese dumplings*

shun·gi·ku 春菊 *crown daisy • garland chrysanthemum – eaten as* o·hi·ta·shi, a·e·mo·no & na·be

shu·tō 酒盗 *salted & fermented* ka·tsu·o *intestine – a good accompaniment for drinking* sa·ke

skam·pi スカンピ *scampi*

skas·shu スカッシュ *squash*

skā·to スカート *skirt (a cut of beef from the flank)*

snak·ku スナック *snacks*

so·ba そば *buckwheat • noodles made of buckwheat*

so·ba·cha そば茶 *buckwheat tea*

so·ba·ga·ki そばがき *dough made of buckwheat flour mixed with boiled water*

sō·da ソーダ *soda water*

sō·men そうめん *fine wheat noodles eaten cold & dipped in sauce*

so·ra·ma·me そら豆 *broad bean*

sō·sē·ji ソーセージ *sausage*

sō·su ソース *sauce • Worcester sauce*

so·tē ソテー *sauté*

su 酢 *vinegar*

su·ga·ta·mu·shi 姿蒸し
steamed whole fish

su·gu·ki 酢茎 turnip pickle
(Kyoto Prefecture)

su·gu·ri スグリ currant • gooseberry

spair·ri·bu スペアリブ sparerib

spā·ku·rin·gu·wain スパークリングワイン sparkling wine

su·i·ka すいか watermelon

su·i·ku·chi 吸い口 topping for clear soup

su·i·mo·no 吸い物 clear Japanese soup
made of fish stock (also called su·ma·shi
or su·ma·shi·ji·ru)

su·i·to·kōn スウィートコーン
sweetcorn

su·i·to·ba·ji·ru スウィート・バジル
sweet basil

su·i·ton すいとん balls made of wheat
flour & boiled with vegetables in soup

su·ji スジ sinew • tendon of pork or beef
(term used in ya·ki·to·ri restaurants)

su·ji·ko すじこ salted salmon roe

su·ki·ya·ki すき焼き beef, tō·fu,
vegetables & shi·ra·ta·ki cooked in an iron
pan with shō·yu, sugar & sa·ke & served
with raw egg dip

su·ma·shi(·ji·ru) 澄まし (汁)
see su·i·mo·no

su·me·shi 酢飯
vinegared rice used for su·shi

su·mi·bi·ya·ki 炭火焼き
charcoal-grilled fish

su·mi·so 酢味噌 sauce made of
vinegar & mi·so

su·mo·mo スモモ plum

su·ne·ni·ku すね肉 shank

su·no·mo·no 酢の物 vinegared food

sup·pon スッポン snapping turtle

sup·pon·na·be スッポン鍋 hotpot of
sup·pon

sup·pon·ryō·ri スッポン料理 snapping
turtle served as na·be·mo·no, sa·shi·mi,
or deep-fried

sū·pu スープ soup

su·ri·ba·chi すり鉢 mortar (as in
mortar & pestle)

su·ri·go·ma すりごま ground sesame

su·ru·me スルメ dried squid

su·shi すし any food served on or rolled in
vinegared rice

su·shi·da·ne すし種 su·shi topping

su·shi·me·shi すし飯
vinegared rice for su·shi

su·ya·ki 素焼き plainly grilled without salt

su·zu·ke 酢漬け vinegared pickles

su·zu·ki スズキ common sea bass •
Japanese sea perch

su·zu·ki no hō·sho·ya·ki スズキの奉書焼
grilled sea bass served wrapped in
traditional Japanese paper (town of
Matsue & Shimane Prefecture)

su·zu·me すずめ sparrow – served at
ya·ki·to·ri restaurants

T

ta·chi·u·o タチウオ
cutlass fish • hairtail (fish)

tai タイ snapper • bream

tai·mu タイム thyme

tai·ra·gai タイラ貝 fan shell • sea pen
(invertebrate sea creature)

tai·ra·gi タイラギ see tai·ra·gai

tai·ryō·ri 鯛料理 sea bream cuisine

tai·shō·e·bi 大正エビ fleshy prawn

ta·ka·na 高菜 broad-leafed mustard

ta·ka·na·zu·ke 高菜漬 mustard leaf
pickles

ta·ka no tsu·me 鷹の爪 red-hot peppers

ta·ke·no·ko タケノコ bamboo shoots

ta·ki·ko·mi·go·han 炊き込み御飯 rice
cooked together with vegetables &
seasonings

ta·ko タコ octopus

ta·ko·ya·ki タコ焼き balls made of flour
with octopus inside (Osaka)

ta·ku·an たくあん pickled dai·kon

ta·ma·go 卵 egg

ta·ma·go·to·ji 卵とじ cooked vegetables
or meat covered with whisked egg

ta·ma·go·ya·ki 卵焼き Japanese-style
fried egg • omelette

ta·ma·ne·gi たまねぎ onion

ta·ma·ne·gi no su·zu·ke たまねぎの
酢漬け pickling onion

ta·ma·ri·dō·fu たまりどうふ tō·fu
infused with egg

ta·ma·ri·jō·yu たまりじょう油
wheat-free shō·yu

tan タン tongue

ta·ra タラ cod • Pacific cod • grey cod

ta·ra·ba·ga·ni タラバガニ Alaskan crab • king crab

ta·ra·gon タラゴン tarragon

ta·ra·ko タラコ salted cod • collack roe

ta·ra·no·me タラノメ angelica tree sprout (available only in early spring)

ta·re たれ sauce – usually made from shō·yu, mi·rin & sugar

ta·ro·i·mo タロイモ taro

ta·ta·ki たたき minced raw fish flesh • meat or fish seared on the outside & served sliced, with the inside remaining rare

ta·tsu·ta·a·ge 竜田揚げ meat or fish dipped in shō·yu & seasoned flour, then deep-fried

te·ki·ra テキーラ tequila

tek·ka·don 鉄火丼 tuna sa·shi·mi on a large bowl of steamed rice

tek·ka·ma·ki 鉄火巻き tuna su·shi roll

te·ma·ki·zu·shi 手巻きずし do-it-yourself su·shi roll

tem·pu·ra てんぷら seafood, meat & vegetables deep-fried in light batter & eaten dipped in a light sauce with ginger & grated dai·kon

tem·pu·ra·so·ba てんぷらそばん buckwheat noodles in broth with tem·pu·ra pieces on top

tem·pu·ra·u·don てんぷらうどん wheat flour noodles in broth with tem·pu·ra pieces on top

ten·don 天丼 battered prawn on rice

te·ri·ya·ki 照り焼き meat or fish, brushed with marinade made of shō·yu, mi·rin & sugar, & then grilled

tē·sho·ku 定食 set menu

tes·sa てっさ fu·gu sa·shi·mi

te·u·chi·so·ba 手打ちそば traditional, handmade so·ba

to·bi·u·o トビウオ flying fish

tō·fu とうふ soy bean curd (tofu)

to·ga·ra·shi とうがらし red chilli pepper • cayenne

to·ki·shi·ra·zu ときしらず see a·ra·ma·ki·za·ke

to·ma·to トマト tomato

to·ma·to·sō·su トマトソース tomato sauce

tō·mo·ro·ko·shi トウモロコシ corn

ton·ko·tsu とんこつ pork broth

ton·ko·tsu·rā·men とんこつラーメン rā·men with white pork broth

ton·ka·tsu·sō·su とんかつソース sauce to go with ton·ka·tsu (pork cutlet)

to·nik·ku トニック tonic water

tō·nyū 豆乳 soy milk

top·pin·gu トッピング topping

to·ra·fu·gu トラフグ tiger fu·gu

to·rai·pu トライプ tripe

to·ra·ma·me とら豆 tiger beans

to·ri·ni·ku 鶏肉 chicken (meat)

to·ri·ni·ku 鳥肉 poultry

to·ro とろ the fattiest (and also considered the tastiest) meat of tuna fish ma·gu·ro

to·ro·ro とろろ grated yam

to·ro·ro·ji·ru とろろ汁 grated yam mixed with stock

to·ryu·fu トリュフ truffle

to·shō·shi·yu 杜松子油 juniper berry oil

tōs·to トースト toast

tsu·ba·me·u·o ツバメ魚 swallow fish • a type of batfish

tsu·bo·ya·ki つぼ焼き shellfish (normally whelks) grilled in its own shell

tsu·ke·mo·no 漬物 pickles

tsu·ki·mi·so·ba 月見そば buckwheat noodles in broth with a raw egg

tsu·ki·mi·u·don 月見うどん wheat flour noodles in broth with a raw egg

tsu·ku·da·ni 佃煮 seafood or vegetables simmered in a thick sauce made from salt, sugar & shō·yu until all moisture is reduced

tsu·ku·ne つくね minced fish or chicken balls eaten fried or boiled

tsu·ku·ri 造り slices of raw fish, another term for sa·shi·mi

tsu·ma つま garnish

tsu·me·mo·no 詰め物 stuffing

tsu·mi·re つみれ fish-cake balls – used in o·den & stew

tsu·no·ga·rē ツノガレイ plaice

tsu·yu つゆ dipping sauce

tu·ke·a·wa·se 付け合せ garnish • relish

U

u·ba·gai ウバ貝 hen clam

u·do ウド mountain vegetable eaten fresh, stewed or pickled

u·don うどん *thick noodles made of wheat flour*

u·kon ウコン *turmeric*

u·me 梅 *Japanese plum*

u·me·bo·shi 梅干 *dried & pickled Japanese plum*

u·me·zu 梅酢 *sour-plum vinegar*

u·mi·u·o 海魚 *fish from the ocean*

u·na·don うな丼 *grilled eel on rice*

u·na·gi うなぎ *eel*

u·na·gi no ka·ba·ya·ki うなぎの蒲焼 *grilled eel flavoured with soy-based sauce*

u·na·jū うな重 *grilled eel served on rice in a lacquered box*

u·ni ウニ *sea urchin*

u·no·ha·na 卯の花 *see* o·ka·ra

u·ro·ko うろこ *fish scales*

ū·ron·cha 烏龍茶 *oolong tea*

u·ru·chi·mai うるち米 *non-glutinous rice*

u·ru·ka ウルカ *salted innards of* a·yu

u·ru·me·i·wa·shi ウルメイワシ *Japanese sardine*

u·shi no o 牛の尾 *oxtail*

u·shi·o·ji·ru うしお汁 *delicately flavoured clear soup made from fish & shellfish*

u·su·a·ji 薄味 *light-tasting or lightly seasoned*

u·su·cha 薄茶 *thinner tea than* koy·cha

u·su·ku·chi·shō·yu 薄口しょう油 *light* shō·yu

u·su·tā·sō·su ウスターソース *Worcester sauce*

u·su·zu·ku·ri 薄作り *raw, thinly sliced* fu·gu *flesh*

u·zu·ra ウズラ *quail*

u·zu·ra no ta·ma·go ウズラの卵 *quail egg*

W

wa·ga·shi 和菓子 *Japanese sweets*

wa·gyū 和牛 *Japanese beef*

wai·ru·do·rai·su ワイルドライス *wild rice*

wa·ka·me ワカメ *type of seaweed*

wa·ka·sa·gi わかさぎ *pond smelt (a freshwater fish)*

wa·ke·gi ワケギ *shallots*

wa·ni ワニ *shark meat (Chūgoku region) • crocodile*

wan·tan·men ワンタン麺 rā·men *noodles in broth, with meat dumplings*

wa·ra·bi 蕨 *a kind of fern of which the tender young shoots are eaten*

wa·ra·ma·ki·bu·ri 藁巻きブリ *salted & dried* bu·ri, *which is then rolled in straw (Toyama Prefecture)*

wa·ri·shi·ta 割り下 *sauce of* shō·yu, mi·rin & *sugar, used in* su·ki·ya·ki

wa·sa·bi ワサビ *very hot Japanese horseradish*

wa·sa·bi·ma·ki ワサビ巻き su·shi *roll containing* wa·sa·bi

wa·sa·bi·zu·ke ワサビ漬け *vegetables pickled in a* wa·sa·bi *base*

wa·ta わた *see* ha·ra·wa·ta

wa·ta·ri·ga·ni ワタリガニ *blue swimmer crab*

wi·kyō ウイキョウ *fennel*

wi·kyō no mi ウイキョウの実 *fennel seed*

wi·rō ういろう *a steamed sweet made of rice flour & arrowroot (Nagoya)*

Y

...·ya ...屋 *shop* • ... *restaurant, eg* su·shi·ya, sha·bu·sha·bu·ya

ya·e·na·ri ヤエナリ *mung bean*

...·ya·ki/ya·ki ... ...焼き/焼き... *food that is grilled, baked, barbecued or pan fried*

ya·ki·dō·fu 焼き豆腐 *grilled* tō·fu *used for hotpot*

ya·ki·gyō·za 焼きギョウザ *grilled* gyō·za *dumpling*

ya·ki·me·shi 焼き飯 *fried rice*

ya·ki·mo·chi 焼きもち *toasted rice cake*

ya·ki·mo·no 焼きもの *broiled, grilled or pan-fried dishes*

ya·ki·na·su 焼きナス *grilled eggplant*

ya·ki·ni·ku 焼肉 *cook-it-yourself, Korean-style barbecue*

ya·ki·no·ri 焼き海苔 *lightly toasted* no·ri

ya·ki·o·ni·gi·ri 焼きおにぎり *grilled rice ball*

ya·ki·so·ba 焼きそば *fried noodles with vegetables & meat*

ya·ki·to·ri 焼きとり *grilled meat on skewers served with* ta·re *or salt*

ya·ki·za·ka·na 焼き魚 *grilled fish*

ya·ku·mi 薬味 *condiment • relish • seasoning*
ya·ma·i·mo 山芋 *yam*
ya·ma·ka·ke 山かけ *grated yam with seasoning*
ya·ma·ku·ji·ra 山鯨 *'mountain whale' – the renamed* i·no·shi·shi *(wild boar)*
ya·ma·me ヤマメ *freshwater salmon*
ya·ma no mo·no 山のもの *mountain dishes*
ya·na·ga·wa·na·be 柳川鍋 *boiled loach or weatherfish with whisked eggs on top*
ya·sai 野菜 *vegetables*
ya·sai·i·ta·me 野菜炒め *fried vegetables*
ya·se 野生 *wild*
ya·sō 野草 *wild greens*
ya·tsu·ga·shi·ra 八ッ頭 *most-sought after type of taro*
ya·tsu·ha·shi 八橋 *sweet cinnamon-flavoured hard crackers (Kyoto Prefecture)*
yō·kan ようかん *sweet jelly made of ground* a·zu·ki *beans*
yo·mo·gi ヨモギ *mugwort*
yō·na·shi 洋ナシ *pear*
yo·se·na·be 寄せ鍋 *hotpot with seafood, chicken & vegetables in a light stock*
yō·sho·ku 洋食 *Japanese versions of Western dishes*
yu·ba ゆば *thin layers of skin skimmed from boiled soy milk*
yu·de·gyō·za ゆでギョウザ *boiled* gyō·za *dumpling*
yu·de·ta·ma·go ゆで卵 *boiled eggs*
yu·dō·fu 湯豆腐 *tō·fu boiled in a weak* kom·bu *broth*

yū·ga·o ユウガオ *white-flower gourd • bottle gourd*
yū·han 夕飯 *dinner*
yu·shi·dō·fu ゆし豆腐 *a soft variety of* tō·fu *from Okinawa*
yu·zu ゆず *a type of citrus fruit*

Z

zak·ko·ku 雑穀 *millet*
za·ku·ro ざくろ *pomegranate*
za·ru·gai ザルガイ *cockle*
za·ru·so·ba ざるそば *cold buckwheat noodles served with* no·ri, *spring onion &* wa·sa·bi
zem·mai ゼンマイ *osmund • royal fern (mountain vegetable)*
zen·ryū·ko·mu·gi 全粒小麦 *wholewheat*
zen·ryū·ko·mu·gi·ko 全粒小麦粉 *wholewheat flour*
zen·zai ぜんざい *sweet* a·zu·ki *bean soup with rice cakes*
ze·ra·chin ゼラチン *gelatine*
ze·rī ゼリー *jelly*
zo·me·ki·ryō·ri ぞめき料理 *cuisine of local vegetables & seafood from Tokushima Prefecture*
zō·mo·tsu 臓物 *offal • giblets*
zō·ni 雑煮 *rice cake in soup*
zō·su·i 雑炊 *rice gruel • soup with vegetables & seafood flavoured with* mi·so *or* shō·yu
zu·i·ki ずいき *taro stem*
zu·wai·ga·ni ズワイガニ *red crab • snow crab*

emergencies

緊急

Help!	たすけて！	tas·ke·te
Stop!	止まれ！	to·ma·re
Go away!	離れろ！	ha·na·re·ro
Thief!	どろぼう！	do·ro·bo
Fire!	火事だ！	ka·ji da
Watch out!	危ない！	a·bu·nai
Careful!	気をつけて！	ki o tsu·ke·te

signs		
病院	byō·in	**Hospital**
警察	kē·sa·tsu	**Police**
警察署	kē·sa·tsu·sho	**Police Station**
交番	kō·ban	**Police Box**
救急	kyū·kyū	**Emergency Department**

It's an emergency.
緊急です。 kin·kyū des

There's been an accident.
事故です。 ji·ko des

Call the police.
警察を呼んで。 kē·sa·tsu o yon·de

Call a doctor.
医者を呼んで。 i·sha o yon·de

Call an ambulance.
救急車を呼んで。 kyū·kyū·sha o yon·de

Could you please help?
たすけてください。 tas·ke·te ku·da·sai

essentials

195

Can I use your phone?
電話を貸して
くれませんか？

den·wa o ka·shi·te
ku·re·ma·sen ka

I'm lost.
迷いました。

ma·yoy·mash·ta

Where are the toilets?
トイレはどこですか？

toy·re wa do·ko des ka

Is it safe …?	…安全ですか？	… an·zen des ka
at night	夜は	yo·ru wa
for gay people	ゲイにとって	gē ni tot·te
for travellers	旅行者にとって	ryo·kō·sha ni tot·te
for women	女性にとって	jo·sē ni tot·te
on your own	独りで	hi·to·ri de

police

警察

Where's the police station?
警察署はどこですか？

kē·sa·tsu·sho wa do·ko des ka

Where's a police box?
交番はどこですか？

kō·ban wa do·ko des ka

I want to report an offence.
犯罪を報告したいの
ですが。

han·zai o hō·ko·ku shi·tai no
des ga

I have insurance.
保険に賭けてあります。

ho·ken ni ka·ke·te a·ri·mas

I've been …	私は	wa·ta·shi wa
	…ました。	…·mash·ta
assaulted	暴行を受け	bō·kō o u·ke
raped	レイプされ	rē·pu sa·re
robbed	強盗に遭い	gō·tō ni ai

He tried to … me.	彼は私を… しようとしました。	ka·re wa wa·ta·shi o … shi·yō to shi·mash·ta
She tried to … me.	彼女は私を …しようとしました。	ka·no·jo wa wa·ta·shi o … shi·yō to shi·mash·ta
assault	暴行	bō·kō
rape	レイプ	rē·pu
rob	強盗	gō·tō

My … was/ were stolen.	私の…が 盗まれました。	wa·ta·shi no … ga nu·su·ma·re·mash·ta
I've lost my …	…をなくしました。	… o na·ku·shi·mash·ta
backpack	バックパック	bak·ku·pak·ku
bags	バッグ	bag·gu
credit card	クレジットカード	ku·re·jit·to·kā·do
handbag	ハンドバッグ	han·do·bag·gu
jewellery	宝石	hō·se·ki
money	お金	o·ka·ne
papers	書類	sho·ru·i
passport	パスポート	pas·pō·to
travellers cheques	トラベラーズ チェック	to·ra·be·rāz· chek·ku
wallet	財布	sai·fu

It was …	やったのは…です。	yat·ta no wa … des
her	彼女	ka·no·jo
him	彼	ka·re

What am I accused of?
どんな理由で告訴
されるのですか?
don·na ri·yū de ko·ku·so
sa·re·ru no des ka

I'm sorry.
ごめんなさい。
go·men·na·sai

I didn't realise I was doing anything wrong.
違法行為をしているつもり
はありませんでした。
i·hō·kōy o shi·te i·ru tsu·mo·ri
wa a·ri·ma·sen desh·ta

I didn't do it.
私はやっていません。 wa·ta·shi wa yat·te i·ma·sen

Can I pay an on-the-spot fine?
この場で罰金を払う ko·no ba de bak·kin o ha·ra·u
ことができますか? ko·to ga de·ki·mas ka

Can I make a phone call?
電話をかけてもいいですか? den·wa o ka·ke·te mo ī des ka

Can I have a lawyer (who speaks English)?
(英語ができる)弁護士を (ē·go ga de·ki·ru) ben·go·shi o
お願いします。 o·ne·gai shi·mas

I have a prescription for this drug.
この薬の処方箋を ko·no ku·su·ri no sho·hō·sen o
持っています。 mot·te i·mas

I want to contact …に連絡 … ni ren·ra·ku
my ... したいです。 shi·tai des
  consulate 領事館 ryō·ji·kan
  embassy 大使館 tai·shi·kan

the police may say ...		
You're charged with ...	あなたは…で告発されます。	a·na·ta wa … de ko·ku·ha·tsu sa·re·mas
assault	暴行	bō·kō
disturbing the peace	治安妨害	chyan·bō·gai
not having a visa	ビザなし	bi·za·na·si
overstaying your visa	不法滞在	fu·hō·tai·zai
possession (of illegal substances)	(不法物)所持	(fu·hō·bu·tsu·) sho·ji
shoplifting	万引き	mam·bi·ki
theft	盗難	tō·nan
It's a ... fine.	これは…の罰金です。	ko·re wa … no bak·kin des
parking	駐車違反	chū·sha·i·han
speeding	速度違反	so·ku·do·i·han

doctor

医者

Where's the nearest ...?	この近くの…はどこですか?	ko·no chi·ka·ku no ... wa do·ko des ka
(night) chemist	(24時間営業の) 薬局	(ni·jū·yo·ji·kan ē·gyō no) yak·kyo·ku
clinic	クリニック	ku·ri·nik·ku
dentist	歯医者	ha·i·sha
doctor	医者	i·sha
emergency department	救急病院	kyū·kyū·byō·in
hospital	病院	byō·in
medical centre	メディカルセンター	me·di·ka·ru·sen·tā
optometrist	検眼医	ken·gan·i

I need a doctor (who speaks English).
(英語ができる) お医者さんが必要です。 (ē·go ga de·ki·ru) oy·sha·san ga hi·tsu·yō des

Could I see a female doctor?
女性のお医者さんをお願いできますか? jo·sē no oy·sha·san o o·ne·gai de·ki·mas ka

Could the doctor come here?
お医者さんはこちらに来ることができますか? oy·sha·san wa ko·chi·ra ni ku·ru·ko·to ga de·ki·mas ka

Is there an after-hours emergency number?
時間外救急の電話番号はありますか? ji·kan·gai·kyū·kyū no den·wa·ban·gō wa a·ri·mas ka

I've run out of my medication.
薬が切れました。 ku·su·ri ga ki·re·mash·ta

This is my usual medicine.
これがいつも使って
いる薬です。

ko·re ga i·tsu·mo tsu·kat·te
i·ru ku·su·ri des

What's the correct dosage?
正しい薬の量は
何ですか?

ta·da·shī ku·su·ri no ryō wa
nan des ka

I don't want a blood transfusion.
輸血はしたくないです。

yu·ke·tsu wa shi·ta·ku·nai des

Please use a new syringe.
新しい注射器を
使ってください。

a·ta·ra·shī chū·sha·ki o
tsu·kat·te ku·da·sai

I have my own syringe.
自分の注射器が
あります。

ji·bun no chū·sha·ki ga
a·ri·mas

I've been vaccinated against (tetanus).
私は(破傷風)の
予防注射をしました。

wa·ta·shi wa (ha·shō·fū) no
yo·bō·chū·sha o shi·mash·ta

He's been vaccinated against (typhoid).
彼は(チフス)の
予防注射をしました。

ka·re wa (chif·su) no
yo·bō·chū·sha o shi·mash·ta

She's been vaccinated against (hepatitis A/B/C).
彼女は
(A/B/C型肝炎)の
予防注射をしました。

ka·no·jo wa
(ē/bī/shī·ga·ta·kan·en) no
yo·bō·chū·sha o shi·mash·ta

I need new contact lenses.
新しい
コンタクトレンズ
が必要です。

a·ta·ra·shī
kon·ta·ku·to·ren·zu
ga hi·tsu·yō des

I need new glasses.
新しい眼鏡
が必要です。

a·ta·ra·shī me·ga·ne
ga hi·tsu·yō des

I have insurance.
保険に賭けてあります。

ho·ken ni ka·ke·te a·ri·mas

Can I have a receipt for my insurance?
保険のためのレシート
をもらえますか?

ho·ken no ta·me no re·shī·to
o mo·ra·e·mas ka

the doctor may say ...

What's the problem?
どうしましたか？　　　　　　dō shi·mash·ta ka

Where does it hurt?
どこが痛いですか？　　　　　do·ko ga i·tai des ka

Do you have a temperature?
熱がありますか？　　　　　　ne·tsu ga a·ri·mas ka

How long have you been like this?
いつからこのような　　　　　i·tsu ka·ra ko·no yō·na
状態ですか？　　　　　　　　jō·tai des ka

Have you had this before?
前にもなったことが　　　　　ma·e ni mo nat·ta ko·to ga
ありますか？　　　　　　　　a·ri·mas ka

Are you sexually active?
最近、性交渉が　　　　　　　sai·kin sē·kō·shō ga
ありましたか？　　　　　　　a·ri·mash·ta ka

Have you had unprotected sex?
コンドームなしの　　　　　　kon·dō·mu·na·shi no
性交渉がありましたか？　　　sē·kō·shō ga a·ri·mash·ta ka

Do you ...?	…ますか？	…mas ka
drink	お酒を飲み	o·sa·ke o no·mi
smoke	タバコを吸い	ta·ba·ko o su·i
take drugs	麻薬を使用	ma·ya·ku o shi·yō
	してい	shi·te i

Are you allergic to anything?
アレルギーがありますか？　　a·re·ru·gī ga a·ri·mas ka

Are you on medication?
薬を使用していますか？　　　ku·su·ri o shi·yō shi·te i·mas ka

How long are you travelling for?
これからどのくらいの　　　　ko·re·ka·ra do·no ku·rai no
期間、旅行するつもり　　　　ki·kan ryo·kō su·ru tsu·mo·ri
ですか？　　　　　　　　　　des ka

You need to be admitted to hospital.
入院する必要が　　　　　　　nyū·in su·ru hi·tsu·yō ga
あります。　　　　　　　　　a·ri·mas

You should return home for treatment.
治療のために帰国　　　　　　chi·ryō no ta·me ni ki·ko·ku
したほうがいいです。　　　　shi·ta hō ga ī des

symptoms & conditions

I'm sick.
私は病気です。 wa·ta·shi wa byō·ki des

My friend is (very) sick.
友達は(ひどい) to·mo·da·chi wa (hi·doy)
病気です。 byō·ki des

My child is (very) sick.
子供は(ひどい) ko·do·mo wa (hi·doy)
病気です。 byō·ki des

He's having	彼は…を	ka·re·wa … o
a/an ...	起こしています	o·ko·shi·te i·mas
She's having	彼女は…を	ka·no·jo·wa … o
a/an ...	起こしています	o·ko·shi·te i·mas
allergic reaction	アレルギー反応	a·re·ru·gī·han·nō
asthma attack	喘息発作	zen·so·ku·hos·sa
baby	陣痛	jin·tsū
epileptic fit	てんかん発作	ten·kan·hos·sa
heart attack	心臓発作	shin·zō·hos·sa

I feel ...	私は…	wa·ta·shi wa …
anxious	不安です	fu·an des
better	良くなりました	yo·ku na·ri·mash·ta
depressed	憂うつです	yū·tsu des
dizzy	めまいがします	me·mai ga shi·mas
hot and cold	暑くなったり	a·tsu·ku nat·ta·ri
	寒くなったり	sa·mu·ku nat·ta·ri
	します	shi·mas
nauseous	吐き気がします	ha·ki·ke ga shi·mas
shivery	寒気がします	sa·mu·ke ga shi·mas
strange	変な気分です	hen·na ki·bun des
weak	ちからが	chi·ka·ra ga
	ありません	a·ri·ma·sen
worse	悪くなって	wa·ru·ku nat·te
	います	i·mas

I've been ... 私は… wa·ta·shi wa ...
   injured けがをしました ke·ga o shi·te i·mas
   vomiting もどしています mo·do·shi·te i·mas

It hurts here.
ここが痛いです。 ko·ko ga i·tai des

I'm dehydrated.
脱水症状です。 das·su·i·shō·jō des

I can't sleep.
眠れません。 ne·mu·re·ma·sen

I think it's the medication I'm on.
今飲んでいる薬の i·ma non·de i·ru ku·su·ri no
せいだと思います。 sē da to o·moy·mas

I'm on medication for ...
…の薬を飲んでいます。 ... no ku·su·ri o non·de i·mas

I have (a/an) ...
私は…があります。 wa·ta·shi wa ... ga a·ri·mas

He has (a/an) ...
彼は…があります。 ka·re wa ... ga a·ri·mas

She has (a/an) ...
彼女は…があります。 ka·no·jo wa ... ga a·ri·mas

I've recently had (a/an) ...
私は最近…が wa·ta·shi wa sai·kin ... ga
ありました。 a·ri·mash·ta

asthma	喘息	zen·so·ku
cold n	風邪	ka·ze
constipation	便秘	bem·pi
cough n	咳	se·ki
diarrhoea	下痢	ge·ri
fever	熱	ne·tsu
headache	頭痛	zu·tsū
nausea	吐き気	ha·ki·ke
pain	痛み	i·ta·mi
sore throat	のどの痛み	no·do no i·ta·mi

health

203

women's health

女性の健康

(I think) I'm pregnant.
私は妊娠して
い(ると思い)ます。

wa·ta·shi wa nin·shin shi·te
i(·ru to o·moy)·mas

I'm on the Pill.
ピルを飲んでいます。

pi·ru o non·de i·mas

I haven't had my period for (six) weeks.
(6)週間月経が
ありません。

(ro·ku)·shū·kan gek·kē ga
a·ri·ma·sen

I've noticed a lump here.
ここにしこりがあります。

ko·ko ni shi·ko·ri ga a·ri·mas

---

the doctor may say ...

Are you using contraception?
避妊はしていますか?

hi·nin wa shi·te i·mas ka

Are you menstruating?
月経がありますか?

gek·kē ga a·ri·mas ka

Are you pregnant?
妊娠していますか?

nin·shin shi·te i·mas ka

When did you last have your period?
最後に月経があった
のはいつですか?

sai·go ni gek·kē ga at·ta
no wa i·tsu des ka

You're pregnant.
妊娠しています。

nin·shin shi·te i·mas

I need ...	…をお願い します。	… o o·ne·gai shi·mas
contraception	避妊薬	hi·nin·ya·ku
the morning- after pill	モーニング アフターピル	mō·nin·gu- af·tā·pi·ru
a pregnancy test	妊娠テスト	nin·shin·tes·to

allergies

I'm allergic to ...	私は…アレルギーです。	wa·ta·shi wa ... a·re·ru·gī des
He's/She's allergic to ...	…アレルギーです。	... a·re·ru·gī des
antibiotics	抗生物質	kō·sē·bus·shi·tsu
anti-inflammatories	抗炎症薬	kō·en·shō·ya·ku
aspirin	アスピリン	as·pi·rin
bees	蜂	ha·chi
codeine	コデイン	ko·de·in
penicillin	ペニシリン	pe·ni·shi·rin
pollen	花粉	ka·fun

I have a skin allergy.
皮膚アレルギーです。   hi·fu·a·re·ru·gī des

For food-related allergies, see **vegetarian & special meals**, page 174.

non-western treatments

I don't use (Western medicine).
(西洋医療)は使いません。   (sē·yō·i·ryō) wa tsu·kai·ma·sen

Can I see someone who practices ...?	…をする人に診てもらいたいのですが。	... o su·ru hi·to ni mi·te mo·rai·tai no des ga
acupuncture	鍼	ha·ri
aromatherapy	アロマテラピー	a·ro·ma·te·ra·pī
Japanese-style physiotherapy	整体	sē·tai
naturopathy	自然療法	shi·zen·ryō·hō
reflexology	リフレクソロジー	ri·fu·re·ku·so·ro·jī
reiki	霊気	rē·ki
shiatsu	指圧	shi·a·tsu

parts of the body

身体部分

My ... hurts.
…が痛いです。 ... ga i·tai des

I can't move my ...
…を動かせません。 ... o u·go·ka·se·ma·sen

I have a cramp in my ...
…がつりました。 ... ga tsu·ri·mash·ta

My ... is swollen.
…が腫れています。 ... ga ha·re·te i·mas

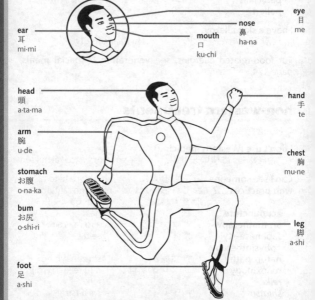

ear
耳
mi·mi

eye
目
me

nose
鼻
ha·na

mouth
口
ku·chi

head
頭
a·ta·ma

hand
手
te

arm
腕
u·de

chest
胸
mu·ne

stomach
お腹
o·na·ka

bum
お尻
o·shi·ri

leg
脚
a·shi

foot
足
a·shi

chemist

薬局

I need something for (a headache).
なにか(頭痛)に
効くものが必要です。
na·nl ka (zu·tsū) ni
ki·ku·mo·no ga hi·tsu·yō des

Do I need a prescription for (antihistamines)?
(抗ヒスタミン剤)の
処方箋が必要
ですか?
(kō·his·ta·min·sai) no
sho·hō·sen ga hi·tsu·yō
des ka

I have a prescription.
処方箋があります。
sho·hō·sen ga a·ri·mas

How many times a day?
1日何回ですか?
i·chi·ni·chi nan·kai des ka

Will it make me drowsy?
眠くなりますか?
ne·mu·ku na·ri·mas ka

antiseptic	消毒液	shō·do·ku·e·ki
contraceptives	避妊具	hi·nin·gu
painkillers	鎮痛剤	chin·tsū·zai
rehydration salts	経口補水塩	kē·kō·ho·su·i·en
thermometer	体温計	tai·on·kē

listen for ...

i·chi·ni·chi ni·kai (sho·ku·ji·do·ki)
1日2回(食事時)。 **Twice a day (with food).**

ko·re o tsu·kat·ta ko·to ga a·ri·mas ka
これを使ったことが
ありますか? **Have you taken this before?**

zem·bu tsu·kai·kit·te ku·da·sai
全部使い切ってください。 **You must complete the course.**

health

207

dentist

歯医者

I have a broken tooth.
歯が折れました。   ha ga o·re·mash·ta

I have a cavity.
虫歯があります。   mu·shi·ba ga a·ri·mas

I have a toothache.
歯が痛いです。   ha ga i·tai des

I've lost a filling.
歯の詰め物が   ha no tsu·me·mo·no ga
とれました。   to·re·mash·ta

My dentures are broken.
入れ歯がこわれました。   i·re·ba ga ko·wa·re·mash·ta

My gums hurt.
歯茎が痛いです。   ha·gu·ki ga i·tai des

I don't want it extracted.
抜かないでください。   nu·ka·nai·de ku·da·sai

Ouch!
痛い！   i·tai

I need a/an ...   …をしてください。   … o shi·te ku·da·sai
  anaesthetic   麻酔   ma·su·i
  filling   詰め物   tsu·me·mo·no

---

listen for ...

ō·ki·ku hi·rai·te
　大きく開いて。   **Open wide.**

i·ta·ku·nai des yo
　痛くないですよ。   **This won't hurt a bit.**

kan·de ku·da·sai
　噛んでください。   **Bite down on this.**

u·gai o shi·te ku·da·sai
　うがいをしてください。   **Rinse.**

ma·da o·wat·te i·ma·sen, ma·ta ki·te ku·da·sai
　まだ終わっていません、   **Come back, I haven't**
　また来てください。   **finished.**

SUSTAINABLE TRAVEL

As the climate change debate heats up, the matter of sustainability becomes an important part of the travel vernacular. In practical terms, this means assessing our impact on the environment and local cultures and economies – and acting to make that impact as positive as possible. Here are some basic phrases to get you on your way …

communication & cultural differences

I'd like to learn some of your local dialects.
方言を習いたいのですが。　hō·gen o na·rai·tai no des ga

Would you like me to teach you some English?
英語を習いたいですか？　ē·go o na·rai·tai des ka

Is this a local or national custom?

これは地元の習慣	ko·re wa ji·mo·to no shū·kan
ですか、それとも	des ka so·re·to·mo
全国的な習慣ですか？	zen·ko·ku·te·ki na shū·kan des ka

I respect your customs.

あなたの習慣を	a·na·ta no shū·kan o
尊重します。	son·chō shi·mas

community benefit & involvement

What sorts of issues is this community facing?

このコミュニティが	ko·no ko·myu·ni·ti ga
抱えている問題は	ka·ka·e·te i·ru mon·dai wa
何ですか？	nan des ka

abnormal weather	異常気象	i·jō·ki·shō
class hierarchy	階級	kaī·kyū
climate change	気候変動	ki·kō·hen·dō
greenhouse effect	温室効果	on·shi·tsu·kō·ka
media control	メディア・	me·di·a
	コントロール	kon·to·rō·ru

I'd like to volunteer my skills.
ボランティアしたいの
ですが。
bo·ran·ti·a shi·tai no
des ga

Are there any volunteer programs available in the area?
この地域にボランティア・
プログラムはありますか？
ko·no chī·ki ni bo·ran·ti·a
pu·ro·gu·ra·mu wa a·ri·mas ka

environment

Where can I recycle this?
これはどこでリサイクル
できますか？
ko·re wa do·ko de ri·sai·ku·ru
de·ki·mas ka

transport

Can we get there by public transport?
そこに公共交通機関で
行けますか？
so·ko ni kō·kyō·kō·tsū·ki·kan de
i·ke·mas ka

Can we get there by bicycle?
そこに自転車で
行けますか？
so·ko ni ji·ten·sha de
i·ke·mas ka

I'd prefer to walk there.
歩いて行きたいです。
a·ru·i·te i·ki·tai des

accommodation

I'd like to stay at a locally run hotel.
地元経営のホテルに
泊まりたいです。
ji·mo·to kē·ē no ho·te·ru ni
to·ma·ri·tai des

Can I turn the air conditioning off and open the window?
エアコンを止めて、
窓を開けてもいいですか？
air·kon o to·me·te
ma·do o a·ke·te mo ī des ka

Are there any ecolodges here?
ここにエコロッジは
ありますか？
ko·ko ni e·ko·roj·ji wa
a·ri·mas ka

There's no need to change my sheets.

シーツを替える必要は
ありません。

shī·tsu o ka·e·ru hi·tsu·yō wa
a·ri·ma·sen

shopping

Where can I buy locally produced goods/souvenirs?

地元産の
製品／お土産は、
どこで買えますか？

ji·mo·to·san no
sē·hin/o·mi·ya·ge wa
do·ko de ka·e·mas ka

Do you sell Fair Trade products?

フェア・トレードの
製品はありますか？

ɸe·a·to·rē·do no
sē·hin wa a·ri·mas ka

food

Do you sell ...?   ... はありますか？   ... wa a·ri·mas ka
  locally   地元産の   ji·mo·to·san no
    produced food   食べ物   ta·be·mo·no
  organic produce   オーガニックの   ō·ga·nik·ku no
                          食べ物   ta·be·mo·no

Can you tell me what traditional foods I should try?

伝統的な食べ物は
どんなものが
おすすめですか？

den·tō·te·ki na ta·be·mo·no wa
don·na mo·no ga
o·su·su·me des ka

sightseeing

Does your company ...?	こちらの会社では...？	ko·chi·ra no kai·sha de wa ...
donate money to charity	慈善事業に募金をしていますか	ji·zen·ji·gyō ni bo·kin o shi·te i·mas ka
hire local guides	地元のガイドを雇っていますか	ji·mo·to no gai·do o ya·tot·te i·mas ka
visit local businesses	地元の産業を訪問しますか	ji·mo·to no san·gyō o hō·mon shi·mas ka

Are cultural tours available?
カルチャー・ツアーが
ありますか？

ka·ru·chā tsu·ā ga
a·ri·mas ka

Does the guide speak local dialects?
ガイドは地元の
方言を話しますか？

gai·do wa ji·mo·to no
hō·gen o ha·na·shi·mas ka

Downtown Tokyo dialect	東京下町言葉	tō·kyō·shi·ta·ma·chi ko·to·ba
Kyoto dialect	京都弁	kyō·to·ben
Kyūshū dialect	九州弁	kyū·shū·ben
Osaka dialect	大阪弁	ō·sa·ka·ben
Tōhoku dialect	東北弁	tō·ho·ku·ben

Verbs in this dictionary are in their ·mas (ます) form (for more information on this, see the **phrasebuilder**, page 25). The symbols ⓝ, ⓐ and ⓥ (indicating noun, adjective and verb) have been added for clarity where an English term could be either. Basic food terms have been included – for a more extensive list of ingredients and dishes, see the **culinary reader**.

A

aboard 乗って not·te
abortion 中絶 chū·ze·tsu
about だいたい dai·tai
above 上に u·e ni
abroad 海外 kai·gai
accident 事故 ji·ko
accommodation 宿泊 shu·ku·ha·ku
(bank) account 口座 kō·za
across 横切っ yo·ko·git·te
actor 俳優 hai·yū
acupuncture 鍼 ha·ri
adaptor アダプター a·da·pu·tā
addiction 中毒 chū·do·ku
address 住所 jū·sho
administration 管理 kan·ri
admission (price) 入場料 nyū·jō·ryō
adult ⓝ 大人 o·to·na
adventure 冒険 bō·ken
advertisement 広告 kō·ko·ku
advice 意見 I·ken
aerobics エアロビクス air·ro·bi·kus
aeroplane 飛行機 hi·kō·ki
Africa アフリカ a·fu·ri·ka
after あと a·to
afternoon 午後 go·go
(this) afternoon (今日の) 午後 (kyō no) go·go
aftershave アフターシェーブ af·tā·shē·bu
again また ma·ta
age ⓝ 年齢 nen·rē
(three days) ago (3日) 前 (mik·ka) ma·e
aggressive 攻撃的な kō·ge·ki·te·ki na
agree 賛成します san·sē shi·mas

agriculture 農業 nō·gyō
ahead 向うに mu·kō ni
AIDS エイズ ē·zu
air 空気 kū·ki
air-conditioned エアコン付きの air·kon·tsu·ki no
air-conditioning エアコン air·kon
airline 航空 kō·kū
airmail 航空便 kō·kū·bin
airplane 飛行機 hi·kō·ki
airport 空港 kū·kō
airport tax 空港税 kū·kō·zē
aisle (eg, on plane) 通路 tsū·ro
alarm clock 目覚し時計 me·za·ma·shi·do·kē
alcohol アルコール a·ru·kō·ru
alcove (in house) 床の間 to·ko·no·ma
all 全部 zem·bu
allergy アレルギー a·re·ru·gī
almond アーモンド ā·mon·do
almost ほとんど ho·ton·do
alone ひとりで hi·to·ri de
already もう mō
also また ma·ta
altar 祭壇 sai·dan
altitude 標高 hyō·kō
always いつも i·tsu·mo
ambassador 大使 tai·shi
ambulance 救急車 kyū·kyū·sha
America アメリカ a·me·ri·ka
amount (money) 総計 sō·kē
anaemia 貧血 hin·ke·tsu
anaesthetic 麻酔 ma·su·i
anchovy アンチョビ・カタクチイワシ an·cho·bi · ka·ta·ku·chi·i·wa·shi
ancient 大昔の ō·mu·ka·shi no

and そして so·shi·te
angry 怒ります o·ko·ri·mas
animal 動物 dō·bu·tsu
ankle 足首 a·shi·ku·bi
annual 年一回の nen·ik·kai no
another もう一つの mō·hi·to·tsu no
answer ⓝ 答 ko·ta·e
ant アリ a·ri
antibiotics 抗生剤 kō·sē·zai
antihistamines 抗ヒスタミン剤
　kō·hi·su·ta·min·zai
antinuclear 反核の han·ka·ku no
antique ⓝ アンティーク an·tī·ku
antiseptic ⓝ 消毒剤 shō·do·ku·zai
any いくらか i·ku·ra·ka
apartment マンション man·shon
apéritif 食前酒 sho·ku·zen·shu
appendix (organ) 盲腸 mō·chō
appetiser 前菜 zen·sai
apple りんご rin·go
appointment 予約 yo·ya·ku
apricot あんず an·zu
archaeological 考古学的な
　kō·ko·ga·ku·te·ki na
architect 建築家 ken·chi·ku·ka
architecture 建築 ken·chi·ku
argue 議論します han·ron shi·mas
arm 腕 u·de
aromatherapy アロマテラピー
　a·ro·ma·te·ra·pī
arrest ⓥ 逮捕します tai·ho shi·mas
arrivals 到着 tō·cha·ku
arrive 到着します tō·cha·ku shi·mas
art 美術 bi·ju·tsu
art gallery 美術館 bi·ju·tsu·kan
artist 芸術家 gē·ju·tsu·ka
ashtray 灰皿 hai·za·ra
Asia アジア a·jya
ask (a question) たずねます ta·zu·ne·mas
ask (for something) たのみます
　ta·no·mi·mas
asparagus アスパラガス as·pa·ra·gas
aspirin アスピリン as·pi·rin
assault 暴行 bō·kō
asthma 喘息 zen·so·ku
at で de
athletics 運動 un·dō
atmosphere 雰囲気 fun·i·ki
aubergine ナス na·su

aunt おばさん o·ba·san
Australia オーストラリア ō·sto·ra·rya
automatic ⓐ オートマチック
　ō·to·ma·chik·ku
automated teller machine (ATM)
　ATM ē·tī·e·mu
autumn 秋 a·ki
avenue 大通り ō·dō·ri
avocado アボガド a·bo·ga·do
awful ひどい hi·doy

B

B&W (film) 白黒（フィルム）
　shi·ro·ku·ro (fi·ru·mu)
baby 赤ちゃん a·ka·chan
baby food 離乳食 ri·nyū·sho·ku
baby powder ベビーパウダー
　be·bī·pow·dā
babysitter ベビーシッター be·bī·shit·tā
back (body part) 背中 se·na·ka
back (position) うしろ u·shi·ro
backpack バックパック bak·ku·pak·ku
bacon ベーコン bē·kon
bad 悪い wa·ru·i
bag (general) かばん ka·ban
bag (shopping) 袋 fu·ku·ro
baggage 手荷物 te·ni·mo·tsu
baggage allowance 手荷物許容量
　te·ni·mo·tsu·kyo·yō·ryō
baggage claim バッゲージクレーム
　bag·gē·ji·ku·rē·mu
bakery パン屋 pan·ya
balance (account) 残高 zan·da·ka
balcony バルコニー ba·ru·ko·nī
ball (sport) ボール bō·ru
ballet バレエ ba·rē
banana バナナ ba·na·na
band (music) バンド ban·do
bandage 包帯 hō·tai
Band-Aids バンドエイド ban·do·ēdo
bank (money) 銀行 gin·kō
bank account 銀行口座 gin·kō·kō·za
banknote 紙幣 shi·hē
bar バー bā
bar fridge ミニバー mi·ni·bā
bar work バーテンダー bā·ten·dā
barber 床屋 to·ko·ya
baseball 野球 ya·kyū

214

basketball バスケット（ボール）
bas·ket·to(·bōru)
bath ⓝ お風呂 o·fu·ro
bath house 銭湯 sen·tō
bathing suit 水着 mi·zu·gi
bathroom 風呂場 fu·ro·ba
batter バター ba·tā
battery (general) 電池 den·chi
battery (for car) バッテリー bat·te·rī
be です des
beach ビーチ bī·chi
beach volleyball ビーチバレー
bī·chi·ba·rē
beans 豆 ma·me
beansprouts もやし mo·ya·shi
bear ⓝ クマ ku·ma
beautiful 美しい u·tsu·ku·shī
beauty salon 美容室 bi·yō·shi·tsu
because だから da·ka·ra
bed ベッド bed·do
bed linen シーツ shī·tsu
bedding 寝具 shin·gu
bedroom 寝室 shin·shi·tsu
bee 蜂 ha·chi
beef 牛肉 gyū·ni·ku
beer ビール bī·ru
beetroot ビートルート bī·to·rū·to
before 前 ma·e
beggar 乞食 ko·ji·ki
behind うしろ u·shi·ro
Belgium ベルギー be·ru·gī
below 下 shi·ta
belt 帯 o·bi
berries 木の実・ベリー ki·no·mi·be·rī
beside 横 yo·ko
best 最高の sai·kō no
bet ⓝ 賭け ka·ke
better より良い yo·ri yoy
between あいだ ai·da
bicycle 自転車 ji·ten·sha
big 大きい ō·kī
bigger より大きい yo·ri ō·kī
biggest いちばん大きい i·chi·ban ō·kī
bike ⓝ 自転車 ji·ten·sha
bike chain 自転車のチェーン
ji·ten·sha no chēn
bike lock 自転車の鍵 ji·ten·sha no ka·gi
bike path 自転車道 ji·ten·sha·dō
bike shop 自転車屋 ji·ten·sha·ya

bill (restaurant etc) ⓝ 勘定 kan·jō
binoculars 双眼鏡 sō·gan·kyō
bird 鳥 to·ri
birth certificate 出生証明書
shus·sē·shō·mē·sho
birthday 誕生日 tan·jō·bi
biscuit ビスケット bis·ket·to
bite (dog) かみ傷 ka·mi·ki·zu
bite (insect) ⓝ 虫刺され mu·shi·sa·sa·re
bitter ⓐ 苦い ni·gai
black 黒い ku·roy
black (coffee) ブラック bu·rak·ku
bladder 膀胱 bō·kō
blanket 毛布 mō·fu
blind 目が見えない me ga mi·e·nai
blister 水疱 su·i·hō
blocked つまります tsu·ma·ri·mas
blood 血 chi
blood group 血液型 ke·tsu·e·ki·ga·ta
blood pressure 血圧 ke·tsu·a·tsu
blood test 血液検査 ke·tsu·e·ki·ken·sa
blue 青い a·oy
board (a plane, ship etc) ⓥ 乗ります
no·ri·mas
boarding house 下宿屋 ge·shu·ku·ya
boarding pass 搭乗券 tō·jō·ken
boat ⓝ 船 fu·ne
boat-trip ボートツアー bō·to·tsu·ā
bok choy チンゲンサイ chin·gen·sai
body 体 ka·ra·da
boil (in hot water) ゆでます yu·de·mas
boil (in stock) 煮ます ni·mas
bone 骨 ho·ne
book ⓝ 本 hon
book (make a booking) ⓥ 予約します
yo·ya·ku shi·mas
booked out 満席 man·se·ki
bookshop 本屋 hon·ya
boots (footwear) ブーツ bū·tsu
border ⓝ 境界 kyō·kai
boring 退屈な tai·ku·tsu na
borrow 借ります ka·ri·mas
botanic garden 植物園 sho·ku·bu·tsu·en
both 両方 ryō·hō
bottle ビン bin
bottle opener 栓抜き sen·nu·ki
bottle shop 酒屋 sa·ka·ya
bottom (body) お尻 o·shi·ri
bottom (position) 最後 sai·go

bowl ⓝ ボール bō·ru
　rice bowl 茶碗 cha·wan
　soup bowl お椀 o·wan
box 箱 ha·ko
boxing ⓝ ボクシング bo·ku·shin·gu
boy 男の子 o·to·ko no ko
boyfriend ボーイフレンド bōy·fu·ren·do
bra ブラジャー bu·ra·jā
Braille ブレール式点字
　bu·rē·ru·shi·ki·ten·ji
brakes ブレーキ bu·rē·ki
brandy ブランデー bu·ran·dē
brave 勇敢な yū·kan na
bread パン pan
bread rolls ロールパン rō·ru·pan
break ⓥ 壊します ko·wa·shi·mas
break down ⓥ 壊れます ko·wa·re·mas
breakfast 朝食・朝ごはん
　chō·sho·ku・a·sa·go·han
breast (body) 乳房 chi·bu·sa
breathe 息をします i·ki o shi·mas
bribe ⓝ わいろ wai·ro
bridge ⓝ 橋 ha·shi
briefcase ブリーフケース bu·rī·fu·kēs
bring 持ってきます mot·te·ki·mas
brochure パンフレット pan·fu·ret·to
broken 壊れた ko·wa·re·ta
broken down 故障した ko·shō·shi·ta
bronchitis 気管支炎 ki·kan·shi·en
broth だし汁 da·shi·ji·ru
brother 兄弟 kyō·dai
brown 茶色い chai·roy
brown rice 玄米 gem·mai
bruise あざ a·za
brush ⓝ ブラシ bu·ra·shi
bucket バケツ ba·ke·tsu
Buddhist ⓝ 仏教徒 buk·kyō·to
budget 予算 yo·san
buffet (meal) ビュッフェ byuf·fe
bug ⓝ 虫 mu·shi
building 建物 ta·te·mo·no
bullet train 新幹線 shin·kan·sen
bum お尻 o·shi·ri
bumbag ウエストポーチ wes·to·pō·chi
burn ⓝ やけど ya·ke·do
burnt 焼けた ya·ke·ta
bus (city) (市)バス (shi·)bas
bus (intercity) (長距離)バス
　(chō·kyo·ri·)bas

bus station バスターミナル
　bas·tā·mi·na·ru
bus stop バス停 bas·tē
business ビジネス bi·ji·nes
business card 名刺 mē·shi
business class ビジネスクラス
　bi·ji·nes·ku·ras
business man サラリーマン sa·ra·rī·man
business person ビジネスマン
　bi·ji·nes·man
business trip 出張 shut·chō
business woman ビジネスウーマン
　bi·ji·nes·ū·man
busker 大道芸人 dai·dō·gē·nin
busy 忙しい i·so·ga·shī
but しかし shi·ka·shi
butcher's shop 肉屋 ni·ku·ya
butter バター ba·tā
butterfly 蝶 chō
button ボタン bo·tan
buy ⓥ 買います kai·mas

cabbage キャベツ kya·be·tsu
cabin 船室 sen·shi·tsu
cable car ケーブルカー kē·bu·ru·kā
café カフェ ka·fe
cake ケーキ kē·ki
cake shop ケーキ屋 kē·ki·ya
calculator 計算機 kē·san·ki
calendar カレンダー ka·ren·dā
call ⓥ 呼びます yo·bi·mas
calligraphy 書道 sho·dō
camera カメラ ka·me·ra
camera shop カメラ屋 ka·me·ra·ya
camp site キャンプ場 kyam·pu·jō
camping store キャンプ用品店
　kyam·pu·yō·hin·ten
can (be able) できます de·ki·mas
can (have permission)
　してもいいです shi·te·mo ī des
can (tin) 缶 kan
can opener 缶切 kan·ki·ri
Canada カナダ ka·na·da
cancel キャンセル kyan·se·ru
cancer (illness) 癌 gan
candle ろうそく rō·so·ku
candy キャンディー kyan·dī
cantaloupe メロン me·ron

capsicum ピーマン pī·man
capsule hotel カプセルホテル
　ka·pu·se·ru·ho·te·ru
car 自動車 ji·dō·sha
car deck 車両甲板 sha·ryō·kam·pan
car hire レンタカー ren·ta·kā
car lights ヘッドライト hed·do·rai·to
car owner's title 自動車所有権
　ji·dō·sha·sho·yū·ken
car park 駐車場 chū·sha·jō
car registration 自動車登録
　ji·dō·sha·tō·ro·ku
caravan キャンピングカー
　kyam·pin·gu·kā
cardiac arrest 心拍停止 shim·pa·ku·tē·shi
cards (playing) トランプ to·ram·pu
care (for someone) ⓥ 面倒を見ます
　men·dō·o mi·mas
carpark 駐車場 chū·sha·jō
carpenter 大工 dai·ku
carrot ニンジン nin·jin
carry 運びます ha·ko·bi·mas
carry-on luggage 機内持込の手荷物
　ki·nai·mo·chi·ko·mi no te·ni·mo·tsu
carton カートン kā·ton
cartoons 漫画 man·ga
cash ⓝ 現金 gen·kin
cash (a cheque) ⓥ 現金化します
　gen·kin·ka shi·mas
cash register レジ re·ji
cashew カシューナッツ ka·shū·nat·tsu
cashier レジ re·ji
casino カジノ ka·ji·no
cassette カセット ka·set·to
castle 城 shi·ro
casual work 臨時の仕事 rin·ji no shi·go·to
cat ネコ ne·ko
cathedral 大聖堂 dai·sē·dō
Catholic ⓝ カトリック ka·to·rik·ku
cauliflower カリフラワー ka·ri·fu·ra·wā
cave 洞窟 dō·ku·tsu
caviar キャビア kya·bya
CD CD shī·dī
celebration お祝い oy·wai
cell phone 携帯電話 kē·tai·den·wa
cemetery 墓地 bo·chi
centimetre センチ sen·chi
central 中央の chū·ō no
centre 中央 chū·ō
ceramics セラミックス se·ra·mik·ku·su

cereal シリアル shi·ri·a·ru
certificate 証明書 shō·mē·sho
chain ⓝ 鎖 ku·sa·ri
chair 椅子 i·su
chair (legless) 座椅子 za·i·su
chairlift (skiing) リフト ri·fu·to
champagne シャンペン sham·pen
championships 選手権 sen·shu·ken
change ⓝ 変化 hen·ka
change (coins) ⓐ 小銭 ko·ze·ni
change (money) ⓥ 換金します
　kan·kin shi·mas
changing room (in shop) 試着室
　shi·cha·ku·shi·tsu
changing room (for sport) 更衣室
　kōy·shi·tsu
charming チャーミングな chā·min·gu·na
cheap 安い ya·su·i
cheat ⓝ ずる zu·ru
check (banking) ⓝ 小切手 ko·git·te
check (bill) ⓝ 確認 ka·ku·nin
check ⓥ 点検します ten·ken shi·mas
check-in (desk) ⓝ チェックイン
　chek·ku·in
checkpoint チェックポイント
　chek·ku·poyn·to
cheese チーズ chī·zu
chef シェフ she·fu
chemist (shop) 薬局 yak·kyo·ku
chemist (person) 薬剤師 ya·ku·zai·shi
cheque (banking) 小切手 ko·git·te
cheque (bill) 手形 te·ga·ta
cherry さくらんぼ sa·ku·ram·bo
cherry blossom 桜 sa·ku·ra
chess (Japanese) 将棋 shō·gi
chess (Western) チェス ches
chest (body) 胸 mu·ne
chestnut 栗 ku·ri
chewing gum チューインガム
　chū·in·ga·mu
chicken (animal) にわとり ni·wa·to·ri
chicken (meat) 鶏肉 to·ri·ni·ku
chicken pox 水ぼうそう mi·zu·bō·sō
chickpeas ヒヨコマメ hi·yo·ko·ma·me
child 子供 ko·do·mo
child seat チャイルドシート
　chai·ru·do·shī·to
childminding 子守り ko·mo·ri
children 子供 ko·do·mo

chilli 唐辛子 tō·ga·ra·shi
chilli oil ラー油 rā·yu
chilli sauce チリソース chi·ri·sō·su
China 中国 chū·go·ku
Chinese ⓐ 中国の chū·go·ku no
Chinese cabbage 白菜 ha·ku·sai
Chinese food 中華料理 chū·ka·ryō·ri
Chinese radish 大根 dai·kon
Chinese tea 中国茶 chū·go·ku·cha
chips チップ chip·pu
chiropractor カイロプラクター
　kai·ro·pu·ra·ku·tā
chocolate チョコレート cho·ko·rē·to
choose 選びます e·ra·bi·mas
chopping board まな板 ma·nai·ta
chopping knife 包丁 hō·chō
chopsticks はし ha·shi
chopsticks (disposable) 割り箸
　wa·ri·ba·shi
chopstick holder はし置き ha·shi·o·ki
Christian ⓝ キリスト教徒
　ki·ri·su·to·kyō·to
Christian name 洗礼名 sen·rē·mē
Christmas クリスマス ku·ri·su·mas
church 教会 kyō·kai
cider サイダー sai·dā
cigar 葉巻 ha·ma·ki
cigarette タバコ ta·ba·ko
cigarette lighter ライター rai·tā
cinema 映画館 ê·ga·kan
circus サーカス sā·kas
citizenship 市民権 shi·min·ken
city 市 shi
city centre 市の中心 shi no chū·shin
civil rights 公民権 kō·min·ken
class (category) 種類 shu·ru·i
class system 階級 kai·kyū
classical クラシックの ku·ra·shik·ku no
classical art 古典芸術 ko·ten·gê·ju·tsu
classical music クラシック音楽
　ku·ra·shik·ku·on·ga·ku
classical theatre 古典演劇 ko·ten·en·ge·ki
clean ⓐ きれいな ki·rê na
clean ⓥ 掃除をします sō·ji o shi·mas
cleaning ⓝ クリーニング ku·rī·nin·gu
client 顧客 ko·kya·ku
cliff がけ ga·ke
climb ⓥ 登ります no·bo·ri·mas
cloakroom クローク ku·rō·ku

clock 時計 to·kē
close (nearby) 近く chi·ka·ku
close ⓥ 閉めます shi·me·mas
closed ⓐ 閉店した hē·ten·shi·ta
cloth フキン fu·kin
clothes 衣類 i·ru·i
clothesline 物干し mo·no·ho·shi
clothing 衣類 i·ru·i
clothing store 衣料店 i·ryō·ten
cloud 雲 ku·mo
cloudy 曇りの ku·mo·ri·no
clutch (car) クラッチ ku·rat·chi
coach (bus) バス bas
coach (sport) コーチ kō·chi
coast 海岸 kai·gan
coat コート kō·to
cocaine コカイン ko·kain
cockroach ゴキブリ go·ki·bu·ri
cocktail カクテル ka·ku·te·ru
cocoa ココア ko·ko·a
coconut ココナツ ko·ko·na·tsu
coffee コーヒー kō·hī
coins コイン ko·in
cold ⓝ 風邪 ka·ze
　have a cold 風邪を引いています
　ka·ze o hī·te i·mas
cold (atmosphere) ⓐ 寒い sa·mu·i
cold (to the touch) ⓐ 冷たい tsu·me·ta·i
colleague 同僚 dō·ryō
collect call コレクトコール
　ko·re·ku·to·kō·ru
college カレッジ ka·rej·ji
colour 色 i·ro
comb くし ku·shi
come 来ます ki·mas
comedy コメディ ko·me·dī
comfortable 心地よい ko·ko·chi·yoy
comics 漫画 man·ga
commission 手数料 te·sū·ryō
communist ⓝ 共産主義者
　kyō·san·shu·gi·sha
companion コンパニオン kom·pa·ni·on
company (firm) 会社 kai·sha
compass 方位磁石 hōy·ji·sha·ku
complaint 苦情 ku·jō
complimentary (free) 無料の mu·ryō no
computer コンピュータ kom·pyū·ta
computer game コンピュータゲーム
　kom·pyū·ta·gê·mu

concert コンサート kon·sā·to
concussion 脳しんとう nō·shin·tō
conditioner (hair) コンディショナー kon·di·sho·nā
condom コンドーム kon·dō·mu
conference (big) コンファレンス kon·fa·ren·su
conference (small) ミーティング mī·tin·gu
confirm (a booking) コンファーム kon·fā·mu
conjunctivitis 結膜炎 ke·tsu·ma·ku·en
conservative ⓝ 保守 ho·shu
constipation 便秘 bem·pi
consulate 領事館 ryō·ji·kan
contact lens solution コンタクトレンズの洗浄液 kon·ta·ku·to·ren·zu no sen·jō·e·ki
contact lenses コンタクトレンズ kon·ta·ku·to·ren·zu
contraceptives (devices) 避妊具 hi·nin·gu
contraceptives (medicine) 避妊薬 hi·nin·ya·ku
contract 契約 kē·ya·ku
convenience store コンビニ kom·bi·ni
cook ⓝ コック kok·ku
cook ⓥ 料理します ryō·ri shi·mas
cooked 火が通った hi ga tōt·ta
cookie クッキー kuk·kī
cooking ⓝ 料理 ryō·ri
cool (temperature) 涼しい su·zu·shī
corkscrew コークスクリュー kō·ku·su·kryū
corn とうもろこし tō·mo·ro·ko·shi
corner 角 ka·do
cornflakes コーンフレーク kōn·fu·rē·ku
corrupt 腐敗した fu·hai shi·ta
cost ⓥ 費用がかかります hi·yō ga ka·ka·ri·mas
cotton 綿 men
cotton balls 脱脂綿 das·shi·men
cotton buds 綿棒 mem·bō
cough ⓥ せきが出ます se·ki ga de·mas
cough medicine せき止め se·ki·do·me
count ⓥ かぞえます ka·zo·e·mas
counter (at bar) カウンター ka·un·tā
country (nation) 国 ku·ni
countryside 田舎 i·na·ka

coupon クーポン kū·pon
courgette クルゼット ku·ru·zet·to
course (class) コース kōs
court (legal) 裁判所 sai·ban·sho
court (tennis) コート kō·to
cover charge カバーチャージ ka·bā·chā·ji
cow 牛 u·shi
crab カニ ka·ni
cracker クラッカー ku·rak·kā
crafts 工芸品 kō·gē·hin
crash ⓝ 衝突 shō·to·tsu
crazy きちがいの ki·chi·gai no
cream クリーム ku·rī·mu
crèche 託児所 ta·ku·ji·sho
credit 預金 yo·kin
credit card クレジットカード ku·re·jit·to·kā·do
cricket (sport) クリケット ku·ri·ket·to
crime 犯罪 han·zai
crowded 混雑している kon·za·tsu shi·te i·ru
cucumber キュウリ kyū·ri
cup カップ kap·pu
cupboard 食器棚 shok·ki·da·na
currency exchange 為替 ka·wa·se
current (electricity) 電流 den·ryū
current affairs 時事問題 ji·ji·mon·dai
curry カレー ka·rē
cushion 座布団 za·bu·ton
custom 習慣 shū·kan
customs 税関 zē·kan
cut (wound) ⓝ 切り傷 ki·ri·ki·zu
cut ⓥ 切りま ki·ri·mas
cutlery ナイフとフォーク nai·fu to fō·ku
CV 履歴書 rī·re·kī·sho
cycling ⓝ サイクリング sai·ku·rin·gu
cyclist サイクリスト sai·ku·ris·to
cystitis ぼうこう炎 bō·kō·en

D

dad お父さん o·tō·san
daily 毎日 mai·ni·chi
dairy 乳製品 nyū·sē·hin
damage 被害 hi·gai
dance ⓥ 踊ります o·do·ri·mas
dancing ⓝ ダンス dan·su
dangerous 危ない a·bu·nai
dark 暗い ku·rai

date (appointment) 予約 yo·ya·ku
date (day) ⓝ 日付 hi·zu·ke
date (fruit) ⓐ ナツメヤシ na·tsu·me·ya·shi
date (with a person) ⓝ デート dē·to
date (a person) ⓥ デートします
　dē·to shi·mas
date of birth 誕生日 tan·jō·bi
daughter 娘 mu·su·me
dawn 夜明け yo·a·ke
day 日中 nit·chū
(the) day after tomorrow あさって a·sat·te
(the) day before yesterday おととい
　o·to·toy
day trip 1日観光 i·chi·ni·chi kan·kō
dead 死んでいる shin·de iru
deaf 耳が聞こえない
　mi·mi ga ki·ko·e·nai
decaffeinated デカフェ de·ka·fe
deck (ship) 甲板 kam·pan
decide 決めます ki·me·mas
deep 深い fu·kai
deep-fried 揚げて a·ge·te
deforestation 森林伐採 shin·rin·bas·sai
degrees (temperature) 度 do
delay 遅れ o·ku·re
delicatessen デリカテッセン
　de·ri·ka·tes·sen
deliver 配達します hai·ta·tsu shi·mas
democracy 民主主義 min·shu·shu·gi
demonstration (protest) デモ de·mo
Denmark デンマーク dem·mā·ku
dental floss デンタルフロス
　den·ta·ru·fu·ros
dentist 歯医者 ha·i·sha
deodorant 消臭剤 shō·shū·zai
depart (leave) 出発します
　shup·pa·tsu shi·mas
department store デパート de·pā·to
departure 出発 shup·pa·tsu
departure gate 出発ゲート
　shup·pa·tsu·gē·to
deposit (bank) 預金 yo·kin
deposit (refundable) 預かり金
　a·zu·ka·ri·kin
desert 砂漠 sa·ba·ku
design ⓝ デザイン de·za·in
dessert デザート de·zā·to
destination 目的地 mo·ku·te·ki·chi
details 詳細 shō·sai

diabetes 糖尿病 tō·nyō·byō
dial tone ダイアルトーン dai·a·ru·tōn
diaper オムツ o·mu·tsu
diaphragm 腹膜 fu·ku·ma·ku
diarrhoea 下痢 ge·ri
diary 日記 nik·ki
dictionary 辞書 ji·sho
die ⓥ 死にます shi·ni·mas
diesel ディーゼル dī·ze·ru
diet ダイエット dai·et·to
different 違う chi·ga·u
difficult 難しい mu·zu·ka·shī
digital デジタルの de·ji·ta·ru no
dining car 食堂車 sho·ku·dō·sha
dinner 夕食・晩ごはん
　yū·sho·ku・ban·go·han
direct 直接に cho·ku·se·tsu ni
direct-dial ⓐ 直通 cho·ku·tsū
direction 方向 hō·kō
director ディレクター di·re·ku·tā
dirty 汚い ki·ta·nai
disabled ⓐ 障害をもつ shō·gai o mo·tsu
discount ⓝ 割引 wa·ri·bi·ki
discrimination 差別 sa·be·tsu
disease 病気 byō·ki
dish (food) 皿 sa·ra
disk (CD-ROM) CD-ROM shī·dī·ro·mu
disk (floppy) フロッピー fu·rop·pī
disposable 使い捨ての tsu·kai·su·te no
disposable chopsticks 割り箸 wa·ri·ba·shi
diving ダイビング dai·bin·gu
diving equipment ダイビング用具
　dai·bin·gu·yō·gu
divorced 離婚した ri·kon shi·ta
dizzy めまいがする me·mai ga su·ru
do します shi·mas
doctor 医者 i·sha
documentary ドキュメンタリー
　do·kyu·men·ta·rī
dog 犬 i·nu
dole 失業手当 shi·tsu·gyō·te·a·te
doll 人形 nin·gyō
dollar ドル do·ru
domestic 国内 ko·ku·nai
door ドア do·a
door (Japanese-style) ふすま fu·su·ma
dope (drugs) マリファナ ma·ri·fa·na
double 2倍の ni·bai no
double bed ダブルベッド
　da·bu·ru·bed·do

double room ダブルルーム
da·bu·ru·rū·mu
down 下へ shi·ta e
downhill 下り坂の ku·da·ri·za·ka no
dozen ダース dās
drama ドラマ do·ra·ma
dream ⓝ 夢 yu·me
dress ⓝ ドレス do·res
dried 乾いた ka·wai·ta
dried fruit ドライフルーツ
do·rai·fu·rū·tsu
drink ⓝ 飲み物 no·mi·mo·no
drink (alcoholic) ⓝ 酒・アルコール
sa·ke・a·ru·kō·ru
drink ⓥ 飲みます no·mi·mas
drive ⓥ 運転しよう un·ten shi·mas
driver 運転手 un·ten·shu
drivers licence 運転免許証
un·ten·men·kyo·shō
drug (medicine) 薬 ku·su·ri
drug (narcotic) 麻薬 ma·ya·ku
drug addiction 麻薬中毒
ma·ya·ku·chū·do·ku
drug dealer 麻薬の密売人
ma·ya·ku no mi·tsu·bai·nin
drug trafficking 麻薬の輸送
ma·ya·ku no yu·sō
drug user 麻薬使用者 ma·ya·ku·shi·yō·sha
drum (music) ⓝ ドラム do·ra·mu
drunk ⓐ 酔った yot·ta
dry ⓐ 乾いた ka·wai·ta
dry ⓥ 乾きます ka·wa·ki·mas
dry (clothes) ⓥ 乾かします
ka·wa·ka·shi·mas
duck アヒル a·hi·ru
dummy (pacifier) おしゃぶり o·sha·bu·ri
dumplings ギョウザ gyō·za
during あいだ ai·da
duty-free 免税店 men·zē·ten
DVD DVD dī·bui·dī

E

each それぞれ so·re·zo·re
ear 耳 mi·mi
early 早く ha·ya·ku
earn 稼ぎます ka·se·gi·mas
earplugs 耳栓 mi·mi·sen
earrings イヤリング i·ya·rin·gu

earthquake 地震 ji·shin
east 東 hi·ga·shi
Easter イースター ī·stā
easy 簡単な kan·tan na
eat 食べます ta·be·mas
economy class エコノミークラス
e·ko·no·mī·ku·ras
ecstacy (drug) エクスタシー e·kus·ta·shī
eczema 湿疹 shis·shin
education 教育 kyōy·ku
eel うなぎ u·na·gi
egg 卵 ta·ma·go
  boiled egg ゆで卵 yu·de·ta·ma·go
  fried egg 目玉焼き me·da·ma·ya·ki
  hard-boiled egg 固ゆで卵
  ka·ta·yu·de·ta·ma·go
  poached egg ポーチドエッグ
  pō·chi·do·eg·gu
  scrambled egg 卵焼き ta·ma·go·ya·ki
  raw egg 生卵 na·ma·ta·ma·go
eggplant ナス na·su
election 選挙 sen·kyo
electrical store 電化製品店 den·ka·sē·hin
electrician 電気技師 den·ki·gi·shi
electricity 電気 den·ki
elevator エレベータ e·re·bē·ta
email Eメール ī·mē·ru
embarrassed 恥ずかしい ha·zu·ka·shī
embassy 大使館 tai·shi·kan
emergency 救急 kyū·kyū
emotional 感情的な kan·jō·te·ki na
Emperor (Japanese) 天皇 ten·nō
Emperor (non-Japanese) 皇帝 kō·tē
Empress 皇后 kō·gō
employee 従業員 jū·gyo·in
employer 雇用者 ko·yō·sha
empty 空の ka·ra no
end ⓝ おわり o·wa·ri
endangered species 絶滅に瀕した生物
ze·tsu·me·tsu ni hin shi·ta sē·bu·tsu
engaged (phone) お話中 o·ha·na·shi·chū
engaged (to be married) 婚約した
kon·ya·ku shi·ta
entrée アントレー an·to·rē
engine エンジン en·jin
engineer 技術者 gi·ju·tsu·sha
engineering 工学 kō·ga·ku
England イギリス i·gi·ri·su
English 英語 ē·go

enjoy (oneself) 楽しみます
ta·no·shi·mi·mas
enough 充分な jū·bun na
enter 入ります hai·ri·mas
entertainment guide エンターテイメ
ントガイド en·tā·tē·men·to·gai·do
entry 入場 nyū·jō
envelope 封筒 fū·tō
environment 環境 kan·kyō
epilepsy てんかん ten·kan
equality 平等 byō·dō
equipment 道具 dō·gu
escalator エスカレータ es·ka·rē·ta
estate agency 不動産屋 fu·dō·san·ya
euro ユーロ yū·ro
Europe ヨーロッパ yō·rop·pa
euthanasia 安楽死 an·ra·ku·shi
evening 晩 ban
every 毎 mai
everyone みんな min·na
everything 全部 zem·bu
exactly ちょうど chō·do
example 例 rē
excellent 素晴らしい su·ba·ra·shī
excess (baggage) 超過 chō·ka
exchange ⓥ 交換 kō·kan
exchange ⓥ 交換します kō·kan shi·mas
exchange rate 為替レート ka·wa·se·rē·to
excluded 抜きで nu·ki de
exhaust (car) 排気 hai·ki
exhibition 展覧会 ten·ran·kai
exit ⓝ 出口 de·gu·chi
expensive 高い ta·kai
experience 経験 kē·ken
exploitation 開発 kai·ha·tsu
express ⓐ 明白な mē·ha·ku na
express (mail) 速達 so·ku·ta·tsu
express train 急行 kyū·kō
extension (visa) 延長 en·chō
eye 目 me
eye drops 目薬 me·gu·su·ri

F

fabric 布 nu·no
face 顔 ka·o
face cloth 洗面タオル sen·men·tow·ru
factory 工場 kō·jō
factory worker 工員 kō·in

fall (autumn) ⓝ 秋 a·ki
fall (down) ⓥ 倒れます tow·re·mas
family 家族 ka·zo·ku
family name 名字 myō·ji
family ticket 家族チケット
ka·zo·ku·chi·ket·to
famous 有名な yū·mē·na
fan (machine) 扇風機 sem·pū·ki
fan (made of paper) 扇子 sen·su
fan (sport, etc) ファン fan
fanbelt ファンベルト fan·be·ru·to
far 遠い tōy
fare 料金 ryō·kin
farm 農場 nō·jō
farmer 農民 nō·min
fashion ファッション fas·shon
fast ⓐ 速い ha·yai
fat ⓐ 太った fu·tot·ta
father お父さん o·tō·san
father-in-law 義理のお父さん
gi·ri no o·tō·san
faucet 蛇口 ja·gu·chi
fault (someone's) 間違い ma·chi·gai
faulty 欠点のある ket·ten no a·ru
favourite 好きな su·ki na
fax (document) ⓝ ファックス fak·kus
fax (machine) ⓝ ファックス fak·kus
fee 料金 ryō·kin
feed ⓥ 餌をやります e·sa o ya·ri·mas
feeling (physical) 感触 kan·sho·ku
feelings 感情 kan·jō
female 女性 jo·sē
fence フェンス fen·su
fencing (sport) ⓝ フェンシング
fen·sin·gu
ferry フェリー fe·rī
festival 祭 ma·tsu·ri
fever 熱 ne·tsu
few (2 or 3) 2、3の ni, san no
few (more than 2 or 3) いくつかの
i·ku·tsu·ka no
fiancé(e) 婚約者 kon·ya·ku·sha
fiction フィクション fik·shon
fig イチジク i·chi·ji·ku
fight ⓝ 戦い ta·ta·kai
fill いっぱいにします ip·pai ni shi·mas
fillet ⓝ フィレ fi·re
film (cinema) ⓝ 映画 ē·ga
film (for camera) ⓝ フィルム fi·ru·mu
film speed フィルムの感度
fi·ru·mu no kan·do

filtered フィルターを通した fi·ru·tā o tō·shi·ta
find ⓥ 見つけます mi·tsu·ke·mas
fine (penalty) ⓝ 罰金 bak·kin
fine ⓐ 元気な gen·ki na
finger 指 yu·bi
finish ⓝ 終わり o·wa·ri
finish ⓥ 終わります o·wa·ri·mas
Finland フィンランド fin·ran·do
fire 火 hi
firewood 薪 ma·ki
first 最初の sai·sho no
first-aid kit 救急箱 kyū·kyū·ba·ko
first class ファーストクラス fā·sto·ku·ras
first name 名前 na·ma·e
first name (Christian only) 洗礼名 sen·rē·mē
fish ⓝ 魚 sa·ka·na
fish paste 魚のペースト sa·ka·na no pē·sto
fish sauce 魚醤 gyo·shō
fish shop 魚屋 sa·ka·na·ya
fishing ⓝ 釣り tsu·ri
flag ⓝ 旗 ha·ta
flannel フランネル fu·ran·ne·ru
flashlight (torch) 懐中電灯 kai·chū·den·tō
flat (apartment) フラット fu·rat·to
flat ⓐ 平らな tai·ra na
flea 蚤 no·mi
fleamarket フリーマーケット fu·rī·mā·ket·to
flight 航空便 kō·kū·bin
flood ⓝ 洪水 kō·zu·i
floor (ground) 床 yu·ka
floor (storey) 階 kai
florist 花屋 ha·na·ya
flour 小麦粉 ko·mu·gi·ko
flower 花 ha·na
flower arranging 生け花 i·ke·ba·na
flu インフルエンザ in·fu·ru·en·za
fly ⓝ ハエ ha·e
fly ⓥ 飛びます to·bi·mas
foggy 霧がかかった ki·ri ga ka·kat·ta
follow ついていきます tsu·i·te i·ki·mas
food 食べ物 ta·be·mo·no
food poisoning 食中毒 sho·ku·chū·do·ku
food supplies 食料 sho·ku·ryō
foot 足 a·shi
football (soccer) サッカー sak·kā

footpath 歩道 ho·dō
foreign 外国の gai·ko·ku no
forest 森 mo·ri
forever 永遠に ēn ni
forget 忘れます wa·su·re·mas
forgive 許します yu·ru·shi·mas
fork フォーク fō·ku
fortnight 2週間 ni·shū·kan
foul ⓝ ファウル fow·ru
foyer ロビー ro·bī
fragile 壊れやすい ko·wa·re·ya·su·i
France フランス fu·ran·su
free (gratis) 無料の mu·ryō no
free (not bound) 自由に ji·yū ni
freeze 凍ります kō·ri·mas
fresh 新鮮な shin·sen na
fridge 冷蔵庫 rē·zō·ko
fried 揚げた a·ge·ta
fried noodles 焼きそば ya·ki·so·ba
fried rice チャーハン・焼き飯 chā·han · ya·ki·me·shi
fried vegetables 野菜炒め ya·sai·i·ta·me
friend 友達 to·mo·da·chi
fries チップ chip·pu
frog カエル ka·e·ru
from から ka·ra
frost 霜 shi·mo
frozen 凍った kōt·ta
fruit 果物 ku·da·mo·no
fruit juice フルーツジュース fu·rū·tsu·jū·su
fry 揚げます a·ge·mas
frying pan フライパン fu·rai·pan
full いっぱいの ip·pai no
full-time work 正社員の仕事 sē·shain no shi·go·to
fun ⓐ 楽しい ta·no·shī
have fun 楽しみます ta·no·shi·mi·mas
funeral 葬式 sō·shi·ki
funny おかしい o·ka·shī
furniture 家具 ka·gu
futon ふとん fu·ton
future ⓝ 未来 mi·rai

G

game (computer) ゲーム gē·mu
game (sport) 試合 shi·ai
garage ガレージ ga·rē·ji
garbage ごみ go·mi

garbage can ごみ箱 go·mi·ba·ko
garden 庭 ni·wa
gardening ⓝ 庭仕事 ni·wa·shi·go·to
garlic ニンニク nin·ni·ku
gas (for cooking) ガス gas
gas (petrol) ガソリン ga·so·rin
gas cartridge ガスカートリッジ
　　gas·kā·to·rij·ji
gastroenteritis 胃腸炎 i·chō·en
gate (airport, etc) ゲート gē·to
gauze ガーゼ gā·ze
gay (homosexual) ⓐ ゲイの gē no
gears (bicycle) ギア gya
geisha 芸者 gē·sha
Germany ドイツ doy·tsu
get 手に入れます te ni i·re·mas
get off (a train, etc) 降ります o·ri·mas
geyser 間欠泉 kan·kets·sen
gift 贈物 o·ku·ri·mo·no
gig ギグ gi·gu
gin ジン jin
ginger しょうが・ジンジャー
　　shō·ga・jin·jā
girl 女の子 on·na no ko
girlfriend ガールフレンド gā·ru·fu·ren·do
give あげます a·ge·mas
given name 名前 na·ma·e
given name (Christian only) 洗礼名
　　sen·rē·mē
glandular fever 腺熱 sen·ne·tsu
glass (drinking) グラス gu·ra·su
glasses (spectacles) 眼鏡 me·ga·ne
gloves 手袋 te·bu·ku·ro
glue 糊 no·ri
go 行きます i·ki·mas
go out 出かけます de·ka·ke·mas
go out with 付き合います tsu·ki·ai·mas
goal ゴール gō·ru
goalkeeper ゴールキーパー gō·ru·kī·pā
goat ヤギ ya·gi
god (general) 神 ka·mi
goggles (skiing) ゴーグル gō·gu·ru
goggles (swimming) 水中眼鏡
　　su·i·chū·me·ga·ne
gold 金 kin
golf ball ゴルフボール go·ru·fu·bō·ru
golf course ゴルフコース go·ru·fu·kō·su
good いい ī
government 政府 sē·fu

gram グラム gu·ra·mu
grandchild 孫 ma·go
grandfather おじいさん o·jī·san
grandmother おばあさん o·bā·san
grapefruit グレープフルーツ
　　gu·rē·pu·fu·rū·tsu
grapes ブドウ bu·dō
grass 草 ku·sa
grateful 感謝している kan·sha·shi·te i·ru
grave 墓 ha·ka
gray 灰色の haī·ro no
great (fantastic) 素晴らしい su·ba·ra·shī
green 緑の mi·do·ri no
greengrocer 八百屋 ya·o·ya
greens 野菜 ya·sai
grey 灰色の haī·ro no
grilled グリルして gu·ri·ru shi·te
grocery 食料品 sho·ku·ryō·hin
groundnut ピーナツ pī·na·tsu
group グループ gu·rū·pu
grow 育ちます so·da·chi·mas
guaranteed 保証された ho·shō sa·re·ta
guess ⓥ 言い当てます ī·a·te·mas
guesthouse ゲストハウス ges·to·how·su
guide (audio) ⓝ 案内 an·nai
guide (person) ⓝ ガイド gai·do
guidebook ガイドブック gai·do·buk·ku
guide dog 盲導犬 mō·dō·ken
guided tour ガイド付きツアー
　　gai·do·tsu·ki·tsu·ā
guilty 有罪の yū·zai no
guitar ギター gi·tā
gum (chewing) ガム ga·mu
gums (of mouth) 歯茎 ha·gu·ki
gun 銃 jū
gym (place) ジム ji·mu
gymnastics 体操 tai·sō
gynaecologist 婦人科医 fu·jin·ka·i

H

hair 毛 ke
hairbrush ヘアブラシ hair·bu·ra·shi
haircut ヘアカット hair·kat·to
hairdresser 美容師 bi·yō·shi
halal ハラルの ha·ra·ru no
half ⓝ 半分 ham·bun
hallucination 幻覚 gen·ka·ku
ham ハム ha·mu

hammer ハンマー ham·mā
hammock ハンモック ham·mok·ku
hand 手 te
handbag ハンドバッグ han·do·bag·gu
handball ハンドボール han·do·bō·ru
handicrafts 手芸品 shu·gē·hin
handkerchief ハンカチ han·ka·chi
handlebars ハンドル han·do·ru
handmade 手作りの te·zu·ku·ri no
handsome ハンサムな han·sa·mu na
happy 幸せな shi·a·wa·se na
harassment いやがらせ i·ya·ga·ra·se
harbour 港 mi·na·to
hard (not soft) かたい ka·tai
hard (not easy) たいへんな tai·hen na
hard-boiled 固ゆでの ka·ta·yu·de no
hardware store ホームセンター
    hō·mu·sen·tā
hash こま切れ ko·ma·gi·re·ni·ku
hat 帽子 bō·shi
have 持っています mot·te i·mas
have a cold 風邪を引いています
    ka·ze o hī·te i·mas
have fun 楽しみます ta·no·shi·mi·mas
hay fever 花粉症 ka·fun·shō
hazelnut ヘーゼルナッツ hē·ze·ru·nat·tsu
he 彼は ka·re wa
head 頭 a·ta·ma
headache 頭痛 zu·tsū
headlights ヘッドライト hed·do·rai·to
health 健康 ken·kō
hear 聞きます ki·ki·mas
hearing aid 補聴器 ho·chō·ki
heart 心臓 shin·zō
heart attack 心臓麻痺 shin·zō·ma·hi
heart condition 心臓病 shin·zō·byo
heat 熱 ne·tsu
heated 熱くなった a·tsu·ku·nat·ta
heater ヒーター hī·tā
heavy 重い o·moy
helmet ヘルメット he·ru·met·to
help ⓝ たすけ tas·ke
help ⓥ たすけます tas·ke·mas
hepatitis 肝炎 kan·en
her (ownership) 彼女の ka·no·jo no
her (object of sentence) 彼女を ka·no·jo o
herb ハーブ hā·bu
herbalist ハーバリスト hā·ba·ris·to
here ここで ko·ko de

heroin ヘロイン he·royn
high 高い ta·kai
high school 高校 kō·kō
highchair ベビーチェア be·bī·che·a
highway 幹線道路 kan·sen·dō·ro
hike ⓥ ハイキングをします
    hai·kin·gu o shi·mas
hiking ⓝ ハイキング hai·kin·gu
hiking boots ハイキングブーツ
    hai·kin·gu·bū·tsu
hiking route ハイキングルート
    hai·kin·gu·rū·to
hill 丘 o·ka
him 彼を ka·re o
Hindu ⓝ ヒンズー教 hin·zū·kyō
hire ⓥ 賃貸します chin·tai·shi·mas
his 彼の ka·re no
historical 歴史的な re·ki·shi·te·ki na
history 歴史 re·ki·shi
hitchhike ヒッチハイク hit·chi·hai·ku
HIV HIV et·chi·ai·vī
hobby 趣味 shu·mi
hockey ホッケー hok·kē
holiday 休日 kyū·ji·tsu
holidays 休暇 kyū·ka
home ⓝ うち u·chi
homeless ホームレス hō·mu·res
homemaker (female) 主婦 shu·fu
homemaker (male) 主夫 shu·fu
homeopathy ホメオパシー
    ho·me·o·pa·shī
homosexual ⓝ ホモ ho·mo
honey 蜂蜜 ha·chi·mi·tsu
honeymoon ハネムーン ha·ne·mūn
horoscope 星占い ho·shi·u·ra·nai
horse 馬 u·ma
horseradish わさび wa·sa·bi
horse riding 乗馬 jō·ba
hospital 病院 byō·in
hospitality もてなし mo·te·na·shi
hot 熱い a·tsu·i
hot pot 鍋・鍋もの
    na·be · na·be·mo·no
hot water お湯 o·yu
hotel ホテル ho·te·ru
hour 時間 ji·kan
house 家 i·e
housework 家事 ka·ji
how どのように do·no yō ni

how much どのくらい do·no ku·rai
how much (money) いくら i·ku·ra
hug ⓥ 抱きます da·ki·mas
huge 巨大な kyo·dai na
human resources 人的資源 jin·te·ki·shi·gen
human rights 人権 jin·ken
humanities 人文科学 jim·bun·ka·ga·ku
hundred 百 hya·ku
hungry (to be) ⓐ お腹がすいた o·na·ka ga su·i·ta
hunting ⓝ 猟 ryō
hurt ⓥ 傷つけます ki·zu·tsu·ke·mas
(to be in a) hurry ⓥ 急ぎます i·so·gi·mas
husband 夫 ot·to

I

I 私は wa·ta·shi wa
ice 氷 kō·ri
ice axe ピッケル pik·ke·ru
ice cream アイスクリーム ais·ku·rī·mu
ice hockey アイスホッケー ais·hok·kē
identification 身分証明 mi·bun·shō·mē
identification card (ID) 身分証明書 mi·bun·shō·mē·sho
idiot ばか ba·ka
if もし mo·shi
ill 病気の byō·ki no
illegal 違法の i·hō no
immigration 移民 i·min
important 大切 tai·se·tsu na
impossible 不可能な fu·ka·nō na
in なか na·ka
in a hurry 急いで i·soy de
in front of 前 ma·e
incense 香 kō
included 含んで fu·kun·de
income tax 所得税 sho·to·ku·zē
India インド in·do
indicator 標識 hyō·shi·ki
indigestion 消化不良 shō·ka·fu·ryō
indoor 室内の shi·tsu·nai no
industry 産業 san·gyō
infection 感染 kan·sen
inflammation 発火 hak·ka
influenza インフルエンザ in·fu·ru·en·za
information 情報 jō·hō
information office 案内所 an·nai·jo
ingredient 成分 sē·bun
inhaler 吸入器 kyū·nyū·ki

injection 注射 chū·sha
injury けが ke·ga
inn (traditional Japanese) 旅館 ryo·kan
inner tube チューブ chū·bu
innocent 潔白な kep·pa·ku na
insect 虫 mu·shi
inside 内部 nai·bu
instructor インストラクター in·sto·rak·tā
insurance 保険 ho·ken
interesting おもしろい o·mo·shi·roy
intermission 中止 chū·shi
international 国際的な ko·ku·sai·te·ki na
Internet インターネット in·tā·net·to
Internet cafe インターネットカフェ in·tā·net·to·ka·fe
interpreter 通訳 tsū·ya·ku
intersection 交差点 kō·sa·ten
interview 面接 men·se·tsu
invite 招待します shō·tai shi·mas
Ireland アイルランド ai·ru·ran·do
iron (for clothes) ⓝ アイロン ai·ron
island 島 shi·ma
Israel イスラエル i·su·ra·e·ru
it それ so·re
IT IT ai·tī
Italy イタリア i·ta·rya
itch かゆみ ka·yu·mi
itemised 箇条書きの ka·jō·ga·ki no
itinerary 旅行日程 ryo·kō·nit·tē
IUD 子宮内リング shi·kyū·nai·rin·gu

J

jacket ジャケット ja·ket·to
jail 牢屋 rō·ya
jam ジャム ja·mu
Japan 日本 ni·hon • nip·pon
Japanese ⓐ 日本の ni·hon no
Japanese doll 日本人形 ni·hon·nin·gyō
Japanese food 和食 wa·sho·ku
Japanese garden 日本庭園 ni·hon·tēn
jar ジャー jā
jaw あご a·go
jealous 嫉妬深い shit·to·bu·kai
jeans ジーンズ jīn·zu
jeep ジープ jī·pu
jet lag 時差ぼけ ji·sa·bo·ke
jewellery 宝石 hō·se·ki
Jewish ユダヤ教の yu·da·ya·kyō no
job 仕事 shi·go·to
jogging ⓝ ジョギング jo·gin·gu

joke 冗談 jō·dan
journalist ジャーナリスト jā·na·ris·to
journey 旅 ta·bi
judge ⓝ 裁判官 sai·ban·kan
judo 柔道 jū·dō
juice ジュース jū·su
jumper (sweater) セーター sē·ta
jumper leads ブースターケーブル
bū·stā·kē·bu·ru

K

kelp 昆布 kom·bu
ketchup ケチャップ ke·chap·pu
key 鍵 ka·gi
keyboard キーボード kī bō do
kick ⓥ けります ke·ri·mas
kill 殺します ko·ro·shi·mas
kidney 腎臓 Jin·zō
kilo(gram) キロ (グラム) ki·ro·(·gu·ra·mu)
kilometre キロメートル ki·ro·mē·to·ru
kimono (bath robe) 浴衣 yu·ka·ta
kind (nice) 親切 shin·se·tsu na
kindergarten 幼稚園 yō·chi·en
king 王 ō
kiosk キヨスク ki·yos·ku
kiss ⓝ キス kis
kiss ⓥ キスします kis shi·mas
kitchen 台所 dai·do·ko·ro
kiwifruit キウィ ki·wi
knee ひざ hi·za
knife ナイフ nai·fu
know 知っています shit·te i·mas
kosher コーシャー kō·shā

L

labourer 労働者 rō·dō·sha
lake 湖 mi·zū·mi
lamb 子羊 ko·hi·tsu·ji
land 陸 ri·ku
landlady 女主人 on·na·shu·jin
landlord 地主 ji·nu·shi
language 言語 gen·go
laptop ラップトップ rap·pu·top·pu
laquerware 漆器 shik ki
large 大きい ō·kī
last (final) 最後の sai·go no
last (previous) 前の ma·e no
last (week) 先 (週) sen·(·shū)

late 遅い o·soy
later あとで a·to de
laugh ⓥ 笑います wa·rai·mas
launderette コインランドリー
ko·in·ran·do·rī
laundry (clothes) 洗濯物 sen·ta·ku·mo·no
laundry (place) 洗濯場 sen·ta·ku·ba
laundry (room) 洗濯室 sen·ta·ku·shi·tsu
law 法律 hō·ri·tsu
law (study, professsion) 法学 hō·ga·ku
lawyer 弁護士 ben·go·shi
laxative 下剤 ge·zai
lazy 怠け者の na·ma·ke·mo·no no
leader リーダー rī·dā
leaf 葉 ha
learn 習います na·rai·mas
leather 皮 ka·wa
ledge 岩礁 gan·shō
leek リーキ rī·ki
left (direction) ⓐ 左 hi·da·ri
left luggage (office) 手荷物預かり所
te·ni·mo·tsu·a·zu·ka·ri·sho
left-wing 左翼 の sa·yo·ku no
leg (body part) 脚 a·shi
legal 法的な hō·te·ki na
legume 豆類 ma·me·ru·i
lemon レモン re·mon
lemonade レモネード re·mo·nē·do
lens レンズ ren·zu
lentil レンズマメ ren·zu·ma·me
lesbian ⓝ レズ re·zu
less 少ない su·ku·nai
letter (mail) 手紙 te·ga·mi
lettuce レタス re·tas
liar うそつき u·so·tsu·ki
library 図書館 to·sho·kan
lice 虱 shi·ra·mi
licence ライセンス rai·sen·su
license plate number ナンバープレート
nam·bā·pu·rē·to
lie (not stand) 横になります
yo·ko ni na·ri·mas
life 命 i·no·chi
life boat 救命艇 kyū·mē·tē
life jacket 救命胴衣 kyū·mē·dōy
lift (elevator) エレベータ e·re·bē·ta
light ⓝ 電気 den·ki
light (not heavy) 軽い ka·ru·i
light (of colour) 明るい a·ka·ru·i
light bulb 電球 den·kyū
light meter 照度計 shō·do·kē

lighter (cigarette) ライター rai·tā
lights (on car) ヘッドライト hed·do·rai·to
like ⓥ 好きです su·ki des
lime ライム rai·mu
linen (material) リンネル rin·ne·ru
linen (sheets etc) リネン ri·nen
lip balm リップクリーム rip·pu·ku·rī·mu
lips 唇 ku·chi·bi·ru
lipstick 口紅 ku·chi·be·ni
liquor store 酒屋 sa·ka·ya
list ⓝ リスト ris·to
listen (to) 聴きます ki·ki·mas
litre リットル rit·to·ru
little (not much) ⓐ 少し su·ko·shi
little ⓐ 小さい chī·sai
live (somewhere) 住みます su·mi·mas
liver 肝臓 kan·zō
lizard トカゲ to·ka·ge
lobster ロブスター ro·bus·tā
local ⓐ 地元 ji·mo·to
local train 各駅停車 ka·ku·e·ki·tē·sha
lock ⓝ 錠 jō
lock ⓥ 鍵をかけます ka·gi o ka·ke·mas
locked 鍵をかけた ka·gi o ka·ke·ta
lollies キャンデー kyan·dē
long 長い na·gai
look ⓥ 見ます mi·mas
look after 面倒を見ます men·dō o mi·mas
look for 探します sa·ga·shi·mas
lookout 見晴台 mi·ha·ra·shi·dai
loose 緩んだ yu·run·da
loose change 小銭 ko·ze·ni
lost なくした na·ku·shi·ta
lost property office 遺失物取扱所
　i·shi·tsu·bu·tsu·to·ri·a·tsu·kai·jo
(a) lot たくさん tak·san
loud うるさい u·ru·sai
love ⓝ 愛 ai
love ⓥ 愛します ai shi·mas
love hotel ラブホテル ra·bu·ho·te·ru
lover 恋人 koy·bi·to
low 低い hi·ku·i
lubricant 潤滑油 jun·ka·tsu·yu
lucky 幸運な kō·un na
luggage 手荷物 te·ni·mo·tsu
luggage lockers ロッカー rok·kā
luggage tag 手荷物札 te·ni·mo·tsu·fu·da
lump こぶ ko·bu
lunch 昼食・昼ごはん
　chū·sho·ku・hi·ru·go·han

lung 肺 hai
luxury ⓐ 豪華な gō·ka na
lychee レイシ rē·shi

M

machine ⓝ 機械 ki·kai
made of (cotton) (コットン) 製の
　(kot·ton)·sē no
Mafia マフィア ma·fya
Mafia (Japanese) ヤクザ ya·ku·za
magazine 雑誌 zas·shi
mail (letters) 郵送 yū·sō
mail (postal system) 郵便 yū·bin
mailbox 郵便ポスト yū·bin·pos·to
main 主な o·mo·na
main course メインコース mēn·kō·su
main road 幹線道路 kan·sen·dō·ro
make ⓥ 作ります tsu·ku·ri·mas
make-up メーキャップ mē·kyap·pu
mammogram マンモグラム
　mam·mo·gu·ra·mu
man (human) 人 hi·to
man (male) 男の人 o·to·ko no hi·to
manager (company) 支配人 shi·hai·nin
manager (restaurant, hotel)
　マネージャー ma·nē·jā
mandarin マンダリン man·da·rin
mango マンゴー man·gō
monorail モノレール mo·no·rē·ru
manual マニュアルの ma·nyu·a·ru no
manual worker 肉体労働者
　ni·ku·tai·rō·dō·sha
many たくさんの ta·ku·san no
map 地図 chi·zu
marble 大理石 dai·ri·se·ki
margarine マーガリン ma·ga·rin
marijuana マリファナ ma·ri·fa·na
marital status 配偶関係 hai·gū·kan·kē
market ⓝ 市場 i·chi·ba
marmalade マーマレード mā·ma·rē·do
married 既婚 ki·kon
marry 結婚します kek·kon shi·mas
martial arts 武道 bu·dō
mass (Catholic) ミサ mi·sa
massage マッサージ mas·sā·ji
masseur マッサージ師 mas·sā·ji·shi
masseuse マッサージ師 mas·sā·ji·shi
mat マット mat·to
mat (reed) たたみ ta·ta·mi

match (sports) 試合 shi·ai
matches (for lighting) マッチ mat·chi
mattress マットレス mat·to·res
maybe たぶん ta·bun
mayonnaise マヨネーズ ma·yo·nē·zu
me 私を wa·ta·shi o
meal 食事 sho·ku·ji
measles はしか ha·shi·ka
meat 肉 ni·ku
mechanic 機械工 ki·kai·kō
media メディア me·dya
medicine (medication) 薬 ku·su·ri
medicine (study, profession) 医学 i·ga·ku
meditation 瞑想 mē·sō
meet 会います ai·mas
meeting ミーティング mī·tin·gu
melon メロン me·ron
member メンバー mem·bā
menstruation 月経 gek·ke
menu メニュー me·nyū
message 伝言 den·gon
metal ⓝ 金属 kin·zo·ku
metre メートル mē·to·ru
meter (in taxi) メーター mē·tā
metro (train) 地下鉄 chi·ka·te·tsu
metro station 地下鉄の駅
    chi·ka·te·tsu no e·ki
microwave (oven) 電子レンジ
    den·shi·ren·ji
midday 正午 shō·go
midnight 真夜中 ma·yo·na·ka
migraine 偏頭痛 hen·zu·tsū
military ⓝ 軍 gun
military service 軍役 gun·e·ki
milk ミルク mi·ru·ku
millimetre ミリ (メートル)
    mi·ri (·mē·to·ru)
million 百万 hya·ku·man
mince ⓝ ひき肉 hi·ki·ni·ku
mineral hot-spring spa 温泉 on·sen
mineral water ミネラルウォーター
    mi·ne·ra·ru·wō·tā
mini-bar ミニバー mi·ni·bā
minute 分 fun
mirror ⓝ 鏡 ka·ga·mi
miscarriage 流産 ryū·zan
miso-soup 味噌汁 mi·so·shi·ru
miso-soup bowl お椀 o·wan
miss (feel absence of) ⓥ 懐かしがります
    na·tsu·ka·shi·ga·ri·mas

mistake 間違い ma·chi·gai
mix ⓥ 混ぜます ma·ze·mas
mobile phone 携帯電話 kē·tai·den·wa
modem モデム mo·de·mu
modern モダンな mo·dan na
moisturiser 保湿剤 ho·shi·tsu·zai
monastery 修道院 shū·dō·in
money お金 o·ka·ne
monk 僧 sō
month 月 ga·tsu
monument 記念碑 ki·nen·hi
moon 月 tsu·ki
more もっと mot·to
morning 朝 a·sa
morning sickness つわり tsu·wa·ri
mosque モスク mos·ku
mosquito 蚊 ka
mosquito coil 蚊取り線香 ka·to·ri·sen·kō
mosquito net 蚊帳 ka·ya
motel モーテル mō·te·ru
mother お母さん o·kā·san
mother-in-law 義理のお母さん
    gi·ri no o·kā·san
motorbike オートバイ ō·to·bai
motorboat モーターボート mō·tā·bō·to
motorcycle オートバイ ō·to·bai
motorway (tollway) 高速道路
    kō·so·ku·dō·ro
mountain 山 ya·ma
mountain bike マウンテンバイク
    ma·un·ten·bai·ku
mountain path 登山道 to·zan·dō
mountain range 山脈 san·mya·ku
mountaineering 登山 to·zan
mouse ネズミ ne·zu·mi
mouth 口 ku·chi
movie 映画 ē·ga
Mr/Mrs/Ms/Miss さん ·san
MSG グルタミン酸ソーダ
    gu·ru·ta·min·san·sō·da
mud 泥 do·ro
muesli ミューズリー myū·zu·rī
mum お母さん o·kā·san
mumps おたふく風邪 o·ta·fu·ku·ka·ze
murder ⓝ 殺人 sa·tsu·jin
muscle 筋肉 kin·ni·ku
museum 博物館 ha·ku·bu·tsu·kan
mushroom キノコ ki·no·ko
music 音楽 on·ga·ku
music shop レコード店 re·kō·do·ten
musician 音楽家 on·gak·ka

Muslim ⓝ イスラム教徒 i·su·ra·mu·kyō·to
mussel ムール貝 mū·ru·gai
mustard マスタード mas·tā·do
mute ⓐ 口のきけない ku·chi no ki·ke·nai
my 私の wa·ta·shi no

N

nail clippers 爪切 tsu·me·ki·ri
name 名前 na·ma·e
napkin ナプキン na·pu·kin
nappy オムツ o·mu·tsu
nappy rash オムツかぶれ
　o·mu·tsu·ka·bu·re
national 国の ku·ni no
national park 国立公園 ko·ku·ri·tsu·kō·en
nationality 国籍 ko·ku·se·ki
nature 自然 shi·zen
naturopathy 自然療法 shi·zen·ryō·hō
nausea 吐き気 ha·ki·ke
near 近く chi·ka·ku
nearby 近くの chi·ka·ku no
nearest いちばん近くの
　i·chi·ban chi·ka·ku no
necessary 必要な hi·tsu·yō na
neck 首 ku·bi
nectarine ネクタリン ne·ku·ta·rin
need ⓥ 必要があります
　hi·tsu·yō ga a·ri·mas
needle (sewing) 針 ha·ri
needle (syringe) 注射針 chū·sha·ba·ri
negative 否定的な hi·tē·te·ki na
net 網 a·mi
Netherlands オランダ o·ran·da
never 決してない kes·shi·te nai
new 新しい a·ta·ra·shī
New Year's Day 元旦 gan·tan
New Year's Eve 大晦日 ō·mi·so·ka
New Zealand ニュージーランド
　nyū·ji·ran·do
news ニュース nyū·su
news stand 新聞販売店
　shim·bun·ham·bai·ten
newsagency 通信社 tsū·shin·sha
newspaper 新聞 shim·bun
next つぎ tsu·gi
next (month) 来(月) rai·(ge·tsu)
next to となり to·na·ri
nice いい ī
nickname あだ名 a·da·na
night 夜 yo·ru

night out 夜遊び yo·a·so·bi
nightclub ナイトクラブ nai·to·ku·ra·bu
no いいえ ī·e
no vacancy 満室 man·shi·tsu
noisy うるさい u·ru·sai
none なにもない na·ni·mo nai
nonsmoking 禁煙の kin·en no
noodles 麺類 men·ru·i
noon (lunchtime) 昼 hi·ru
noon (midday) 正午 shō·go
north 北 ki·ta
Norway ノルウェー no·ru·wē
nose 鼻 ha·na
not ない nai
notebook ノート nō·to
nothing 何もない na·ni·mo nai
not yet まだ ma·da
now 今 i·ma
nuclear energy 核エネルギー
　ka·ku·e·ne·ru·gī
nuclear testing 核実験 ka·ku·jik·ken
nuclear waste 核廃棄物
　ka·ku·hai·ki·bu·tsu
number 数字 sū·ji
numberplate ナンバープレート
　nam·bā·pu·rē·to
nun 修道女 shū·dō·jo
nurse 看護婦 kan·go·fu
nut ナッツ nat·tsu

O

oats オート麦 ō·to·mu·gi
occupation (work) 職業 sho·ku·gyō
ocean 海 u·mi
octopus タコ ta·ko
off (spoiled) いたんだ i·tan·da
office 事務所 ji·mu·sho
office worker 事務員 ji·mu·in
often しばしば shi·ba·shi·ba
oil (food) 油 a·bu·ra
oil (petrol) 石油 se·ki·yu
old 古い fu·ru·i
olive オリーブ o·rī·bu
olive oil オリーブオイル o·rī·bu·oy·ru
Olympic Games オリンピック
　o·rim·pik·ku
omelette オムレツ o·mu·re·tsu
on 上に u·e ni
on time 時間どおり ji·kan·dō·ri
once 1度 i·chi·do

one 1 i·chi
one-way (ticket) 片道(切符)
　ka·ta·mi·chi(·kip·pu)
onion タマネギ ta·ma·ne·gi
only たったの tat·ta no
open ⓐ 開いている hi·rai·te i·ru
open ⓥ 開きます hi·ra·ki·mas
open-air baths 露天風呂 ro·tem·bu·ro
opening hours 開店時間 kai·ten·ji·kan
opera オペラ o·pe·ra
opera house オペラ劇場 o·pe·ra·ge·ki·jō
operation (medical) 手術 shu·ju·tsu
operator オペレーター o·pe·rē·tā
opinion 意見 i·ken
opposite 反対の han·tai no
optometrist 検眼医 ken·gan·i
or または ma·ta·wa
orange (colour) オレンジ
　o·ren·ji
orange (fruit) オレンジ o·ren·ji
orange juice オレンジジュース
　o·ren·ji·jū·su
orchestra オーケストラ ō·kes·to·ra
order ⓝ 命令 mē·rē
order ⓥ 命令します mē·rē shi·mas
ordinary 普通の fu·tsū no
orgasm オーガズム ō·ga·zu·mu
original オリジナルの o·ri·ji·na·ru no
other ほかの ho·ka no
our 私たちの wa·ta·shi·ta·chi no
out of order 故障中 ko·shō·chū
outside 外側の so·to·ga·wa no
ovarian cyst 卵巣の腫 ran·sō·nō·shu
ovary 卵巣 ran·sō
oven オーブン ō·bun
overcoat オーバー ō·bā
overdose 薬の飲みすぎ ku su ri no
　no mi su gi
overnight 一晩 hi·to·ban
overseas 海外 kai·gai
owe 借りがあります ka·ri ga a·ri·mas
owner 所有者 sho·ji·sha
oxygen 酸素 san·so
oyster カキ ka·ki
ozone layer オゾン層 o·zon·sō

P

pacemaker ペースメーカー pēs·mē·kā
pacifier (dummy) おしゃぶり o·sha·bu·ri
package 包み tsu·tsu·mi

packet (general) 小包 ko·zu·tsu·mi
padlock 南京錠 nan·kin·jō
page ページ pē·ji
pain 痛み i·ta·mi
painkiller 鎮痛剤 chin·tsū·zai
painter 画家 ga·ka
painting (a work) ⓝ 絵 e
painting (the art) ⓝ 絵画 kai·ga
pair ⓝ ペア pair
pair of chopsticks 箸 ha·shi
palace 宮殿 kyū·den
pan 鍋 na·be
pants (trousers) ズボン zu·bon
panty liners 生理用ナプキン
　se·ri·yo·na·pu·kin
pantyhose パンティーストッキング
　pan·tī·stok·kin·gu
pap smear 子宮癌塗抹検査
　shi·kyū·gan·to·ma·tsu·ken·sa
paper 紙 ka·mi
papers (documents) 書類 sho·ru·i
paperwork 事務処理 ji·mu·sho·ri
paraplegic ⓝ 下半身不随
　ka·han·shin·fu·zu·i
parcel 小包 ko·zu·tsu·mi
parents 両親 ryō·shin
park ⓝ 公園 kō·en
park (a car) ⓥ 駐車します chū·sha shi·mas
parliament 国会 kok·kai
part (component) 部分 bu·bun
partner (intimate) パートナー pā·to·nā
part-time アルバイト a·ru·bai·to
party (night out) パーティー pā·tī
party (politics) ⓝ 党 tō
pass (document) 許可証 kyo·ka·shō
pass (mountain) ⓝ 山道 ya·ma·mi·chi
pass (sport) ⓝ パス pas
pass ⓥ 通します tsu·ka shi·mas
passenger 乗客 jō·kya·ku
passionfruit パッションフルーツ
　pas·shon·fu·rū·tsu
passport パスポート pas·pō·to
passport number パスポート番号
　pas·pō·to·ban·gō
past ⓝ 過去 ka·ko
pasta パスタ pas·ta
pastry ペストリー pes·to·rī
path 小道 ko·mi·chi
pay 払います ha·rai·mas
payment 支払い shi·ha·rai

pea 豆 ma·me
peace 平和 hē·wa
peach 桃 mo·mo
peak (mountain) ⓝ 峰 mi·ne
peanut ピーナツ pī·na·tsu
pear 洋ナシ yō·na·shi
pedal ⓝ ペダル pe·da·ru
pedestrian 歩行者 ho·kō·sha
pedestrian crossing 横断歩道
　　ō·dan·ho·dō
pegs (camping) ペグ pe·gu
pen (ballpoint) ペン pen
pencil エンピツ em·pi·tsu
penis ペニス pe·nis
penicillin ペニシリン pe·ni·shi·rin
penknife ペンナイフ pen·nai·fu
pensioner 年金者 nen·kin·sha
people 人びと hi·to·bi·to
pepper コショウ koshō
pepper (bell) ピーマン pī·man
per (eg, day) 毎 mai
per cent パーセント pā·sen·to
perfect 完璧な kam·pe·ki na
performance パフォーマンス
　　pa·fō·man·su
perfume 香水 kō·su·i
period 時代 ji·dai
period (menstruation) 月経 gek·kē
period pain 生理痛 sē·ri·tsū
permanent 永久の ē·kyū no
permission 許可 kyo·ka
permit 許可証 kyo·ka·shō
persimmon 柿 ka·ki
person 人 hi·to
personal 個人的な ko·jin·te·ki na
petition 嘆願書 tan·gan·sho
petrol ガソリン ga·so·rin
petrol station ガソリンスタンド
　　ga·so·rin·stan·do
pharmacy 薬局 yak·kyo·ku
phone book 電話帳 den·wa·chō
phone box 電話ボックス
　　den·wa·bok·kus
phone call 電話 den·wa
phone card テレフォンカード
　　te·re·fon·kā·do
phone number 電話番号 den·wa·ban·gō
photo 写真 sha·shin
photographer 写真家 sha·shin·ka

photography 写真 sha·shin
phrasebook フレーズブック
　　fu·rē·zu·buk·ku
pickaxe つるはし tsu·ru·ha·shi
picnic ピクニック pi·ku·nik·ku
pie パイ pai
piece かけら ka·ke·ra
pig 豚 bu·ta
pigeon 鳩 ha·to
pill 錠剤 jō·zai
the Pill ピル pi·ru
pillow 枕 ma·ku·ra
pillowcase 枕カバー ma·ku·ra·ka·bā
pinball ピンボール pin·bō·ru
pineapple パイナップル pai·nap·pu·ru
pink ピンクの pin·ku no
pistachio ピスタチオ pis·ta·chi·o
place 場所 ba·sho
place of birth 出身地 shus·shin·chi
plane ⓝ 飛行機 hi·kō·ki
planet 惑星 wa·ku·sē
plant ⓝ 植物 sho·ku·bu·tsu
plastic ⓐ プラスチックの
　　pu·ras·chik·ku no
plate (big) 皿 sa·ra
plate (small) 小皿 ko·za·ra
plateau 高原 kō·gen
platform プラットフォーム
　　pu·rat·to·fō·mu
play (cards, game) ⓥ します shi·mas
play (instrument) ⓥ 弾きます hi·ki·mas
play (theatre) ⓝ 劇 ge·ki
playground 遊び場 a·so·bi·ba
plug (bath) 栓 sen
plug (electricity) プラグ pu·ra·gu
plum スモモ su·mo·mo
poached ポーチした pō·chi shi·ta
pocket ポケット po·ket·to
pocket knife ポケットナイフ
　　po·ket·to·nai·fu
poetry 詩 shi
point ⓝ 点 ten
point ⓥ 示します shi·me·shi·mas
poisonous 毒の do·ku no
police 警察 kē·sa·tsu
police box 交番 kō·ban
police officer 警官 kē·kan
police station 警察署 kē·sa·tsu·sho
policy 方針 hō·shin

politician 政治家 sē·ji·ka
politics 政治 sē·ji
pollen 花粉 ka·fun
pollution 公害 kō·gai
pool (game) ビリヤード bi·ri·yā·do
pool (swimming) プール pū·ru
poor 貧しい ma·zu·shī
popular 人気がある nin·ki ga a·ru
pork 豚肉 bu·ta·ni·ku
porridge おかゆ o·ka·yu
port (sea) 港 mi·na·to
positive 積極的な sek·kyo·ku·te·ki na
possible 可能な ka·nō na
portion 部分 bu·bun
postcode 郵便番号 yū·bin·ban·gō
post office 郵便局 yu·bin·kyo·ku
poste restante 局留め kyo·ku·do·me
postage 郵送料 yū·sō·ryō
postcard はがき ha·ga·ki
poster ポスター pos·tā
pot (ceramics) つぼ tsu·bo
pot (dope) マリファナ ma·ri·fa·na
potato ジャガイモ ja·ga·i·mo
pottery 陶器 tō·ki
poultry 鳥肉 to·ri·ni·ku
pound (money, weight) ポンド pon·do
poverty 貧困 hin·kon
powder 粉 ko·na
power 力 chi·ka·ra
prawn エビ e·bi
prayer 祈り i·no·ri
prefer ... …のほうがすきです
   ... no hō ga su·ki·des
pregnancy test kit 妊娠テストキット
   nin·shin·tes·to·kit·to
pregnant 妊娠している nin·shin shi·te i·ru
premenstrual tension 月経前緊張症
   gek·kē·zen·kin·chō·shō
prepare 準備します jum·bi shi·mas
prescription 処方箋 sho·hō·sen
present (gift) ⓝ プレゼント
   pu·re·zen·to
present (time) ⓝ 現在 gen·zai
president 大統領 dai·tō·ryō
pretty かわいい ka·wa·ī
previous 前の ma·e no
price 値段 ne·dan
priest (Christian) 牧師 bo·ku·shi
priest (Shinto) 神主 kan·nu·shi

prime minister 総理大臣 sō·ri·dai·jin
prince 王子 ō·ji
princess 姫 hi·me
printer (computer) プリンタ prin·ta
prison 牢屋 rō·ya
prisoner 囚人 shū·jin
private ⓐ 個人的な ko·jin·te·ki na
produce ⓥ 生産します sē·san shi·mas
profit ⓝ 利益 ri·e·ki
program ⓝ プログラム pu·ro·gu·ra·mu
projector 映写機 ē·sha·ki
promise ⓥ 約束します ya·ku·so·ku shi·mas
prostitute 売春 bai·shun
protect 保護します ho·go shi·mas
protected (species) 保護された（生物）
   ho·go sa·re·ta (sē·bu·tsu)
protest ⓝ 反対 han·tai
provisions 食料 sho·ku·ryō
prune プルーン pu·rūn
pub (bar) パブ pa·bu
public baths 銭湯 sen·tō
public gardens 公園 kō·en
public holiday 祭日 sai·ji·tsu
public telephone 公衆電話
   kō·shū·den·wa
public toilet 公衆トイレ kō·shū·toy·re
pufferfish フグ fu·gu
pull 引きます hi·ki·mas
pump ⓝ ポンプ pom·pu
pumpkin カボチャ ka·bo·cha
puncture パンク pan·ku
puppet 人形 nin·gyō
puppet theatre 人形劇 nin·gyō·ge·ki
pure 純粋な jun·su·i na
purple 紫の mu·ra·sa·ki no
purse 財布 sai·fu
push ⓥ 押します o·shi·mas
put 置きます o·ki·mas

Q

quadriplegic 四肢麻痺 shi·shi·ma·hi
qualifications 資格 shi·ka·ku
quality 品質 hin·shi·tsu
quarantine ⓝ 検疫 ken·e·ki
quarter ⓝ 4分の1 yon·bun no i·chi
queen 女王 jō
question ⓝ 質問 shi·tsu·mon
queue ⓝ 列 re·tsu

quick すばやい su·ba·yai
quiet 静かな shi·zu·ka na
quilt 掛け布団 ka·ke·bu·ton
quit 辞めます ya·me·mas

R

rabbit ウサギ u·sa·gi
race (sport) レース rē·su
racetrack 競走場 kyō·gi·jō
racing bike レーシングバイク
   rē·shin·gu·bai·ku
racism 人種差別 jin·shu·sa·be·tsu
racquet ラケット ra·ket·to
radiator ラジエーター ra·ji·ē·tā
radio ラジオ ra·ji·o
radish ラディッシュ ra·dis·shu
railway station 駅 e·ki
rain 雨 a·me
raincoat レインコート re·in·kō·to
raisin レーズン rē·zun
rally 集会 shū·kai
rape (n) レイプ rē·pu
rapid train 快速 kai·so·ku
rare (food) レアの rair·no
rare (uncommon) 珍しい me·zu·ra·shī
rash 発疹 has·shin
raspberry ラズベリー ra·zu·be·rī
rat ネズミ ne·zu·mi
rave (n) レイブ rē·bu
raw 生の na·ma no
razor 剃刀 ka·mi·so·ri
razor blade 剃刀の刃 ka·mi·so·ri no ha
read 読みます yo·mi·mas
ready 準備ができた jum·bi ga de·ki·ta
real estate agent 不動産屋 fu·dō·san·ya
rear (seat etc) (a) 後ろの u·shi·ro no
reason (n) 理由 ri·yū
receipt レシート re·shī·to
recently 最近 sai·kin
recommend 勧めます su·su·me·mas
record (v) 記録します ki·ro·ku shi·mas
recording (n) レコーディング
   re·kō·din·gu
recyclable リサイクルできる
   ri·sai·ku·ru de·ki·ru
recycle リサイクルします
   ri·sai·ku·ru shi·mas
red 赤い a·kai
red wine 赤ワイン a·ka·wain
referee 審判 shim·pan

reference 参照 san·shō
reflexology リフレクソロジー
   ri·fu·re·ku·so·ro·jī
refrigerator 冷蔵庫 rē·zō·ko
refugee 難民 nam·min
refund (n) 払い戻し ha·rai·mo·do·shi
refuse (v) 拒絶します kyo·ze·tsu shi·mas
regional 地方の chi·hō no
registered mail/post 書留 ka·ki·to·me
regular (a) 通常の tsū·jō no
rehydration salts 経口補水塩
   kē·kō·ho·su·i·en
relationship 関係 kan·kē
relax リラックスします
   ri·rak·ku·su shi·mas
relic 遺物 i·bu·tsu
religion 宗教 shū·kyō
religious 宗教的な shū·kyō·te·ki na
remote 遠い tōy
remote control リモコン ri·mo·kon
rent 貸します ka·shi·mas
repair 修理します shū·ri shi·mas
republic 共和国 kyō·wa·ko·ku
reservation (booking) 予約 yo·ya·ku
rest (v) 休みます ya·su·mi·mas
restaurant レストラン res·to·ran
résumé (CV) (n) 履歴書 ri·re·ki·sho
retired 退職した tai·sho·ku shi·ta
return (come back) (v) もどります
   mo·do·ri·mas
return ticket 往復切符 ō·fu·ku·kip·pu
review 評論 hyō·ron
rhythm リズム ri·zu·mu
rib 肋骨 rok·ko·tsu
rice (cooked) ごはん go·han
rice (uncooked) 米 ko·me
rice bowl 茶碗 cha·wan
rice cake もち mo·chi
rice cooker 炊飯器 su·i·han·ki
rice cracker せんべい sen·bē
rich (wealthy) お金持ちの
   o·ka·ne·mo·chi no
ride (n) 乗ること no·ru ko·to
ride (horse) 乗ります no·ri·mas
right (correct) 正しい ta·da·shī
right (direction) 右 mi·gi
right-wing 右翼 u·yo·ku
ring (on finger) (n) 指 yu·bi·wa
ring (by phone) (v) 電話します
   den·wa shi·mas

rip-off ⓝ ぼられること bo·ra·re·ru ko·to
risk ⓝ リスク ris·ku
river 川 ka·wa
road 道 mi·chi
road map ロードマップ rō·do·map·pu
rob 強盗します gō·tō shi·mas
robbery 強奪 gô·da·tsu
rock ⓝ 岩 i·wa
rock (music) ⓝ ロック rok·ku
rock climbing ロッククライミング rok·ku·ku·rai·min·gu
rock group ロックバンド rok·ku·ban·do
rockmelon メロン me·ron
roll (bread) ロール rōru
rollerblading ⓝ ローラーブレード rō·rā·bu·rē·do
romantic ロマンチックな ro·man·chik·ku na
room 部屋 he·ya
room number ルームナンバー rū·mu·nam·bā
rope ロープ rō·pu
round まるい ma·ru·i
roundabout ロータリー rō·ta·rī
route ルート rū·to
rowing ⓝ ローイング rō·in·gu
rubbish ごみ go·mi
rubella 風疹 fū·shin
rug じゅうたん jū·tan
rugby ラグビー ra·gu·bī
ruins 廃墟 hai·kyo
rum ラム ra·mu
run ⓥ 走ります ha·shi·ri·mas
running (sport) ランニング ran·nin·gu

S

sad 悲しい ka·na·shī
saddle サドル sa·do·ru
safe ⓝ 金庫 kin·ko
safe ⓐ 安全な an·zen na
safe sex セーフセックス sē·fu·sek·kus
saint 聖人 sē·jin
salad サラダ sa·ra·da
salary サラリー sa·ra·rī
sale セール sē·ru
sales tax 消費税 shō·hi·zē
salmon サケ sa·ke
salt 塩 shi·o
same 同じ o·na·ji

sand 砂 su·na
sandal サンダル san·da·ru
sandwich サンドイッチ san·do·it·chi
sanitary napkin 生理用ナプキン sē·ri·yō·na·pu·kin
sardine イワシ i·wa·shi
sauce ソース sō·su
saucepan 鍋 na·be
sauna サウナ sow·na
sausage ソーセージ sō·sē·ji
say ⓥ 言います ī·mas
scallop ホタテ ho·ta·te
scalp 頭皮 tō·hi
scampi スカンピ・クルマエビ skam·pi · ku·ru·ma·e·bi
scarf スカーフ skā·fu
school 学校 gak·kō
science 科学 ka·ga·ku
scientist 科学者 ka·ga·ku·sha
scissors ハサミ ha·sa·mi
score ⓥ 得点します to·ku·ten shi·mas
scoreboard スコアボード sko·a·bō·do
Scotland スコットランド skot·to·ran·do
scrambled かき混ぜた ka·ki·ma·ze·ta
screen (room) ついたて tsu·i·ta·te
screen (sliding) 障子 shō·ji
sculpture 彫刻 chō·ko·ku
sea 海 u·mi
seafood 海産物・シーフード kai·sam·bu·tsu · shī·fū·do
seasick 船酔い fu·na·yoy
seaside 海辺 u·mi·be
season 季節 ki·se·tsu
seat (place) 席 se·ki
seatbelt シートベルト shī·to·be·ru·to
sea urchin ウニ u·ni
sea vegetables 海藻 kai·sō
seaweed 海藻 kai·sō
second ⓝ 秒 byō
second ⓐ 2番目の ni·bam·me no
second class ⓝ セカンドクラス se·kan·do·ku·ras
second-hand 中古の chū·ko no
second-hand shop 中古品店 chū·ko·hin·ten
secretary 秘書 hi·sho
see 見ます mi·mas
self service ⓐ セルフサービスの se·ru·fu·sā·bis no

self-employed 自営業 ji·ê·gyō
sell 売ります u·ri·mas
send 送ります o·ku·ri·mas
sensible 分別のある fum·be·tsu no a·ru
sensual 官能的な kan·nō·te·ki na
separate 別々の be·tsu·be·tsu no
serious まじめな ma·ji·me na
service ⑩ サービス sā·bis
service charge サービス料 sā·bis·ryō
service station ガソリンスタンド
　ga·so·rin·stan·do
serviette ナプキン na·pu·kin
sesame oil ごま油 go·ma·a·bu·ra
sesame seed ごま go·ma
several いくつかの i·ku·tsu·ka no
sew 縫います nu·i·mas
sex セックス sek·kus
sexism 性差別 sē·sa·be·tsu
sexy セクシーな sek·shī na
shade 日陰 hi·ka·ge
shadow 影 ka·ge
shallot (onion) ワケギ wa·ke·gi
shampoo ⑩ シャンプー sham·pū
shape ⑩ 形 ka·ta·chi
share (a dorm etc) ⓥ シェアします
　she·a shi·mas
share (with) ⓥ 分け合います
　wa·ke·ai·mas
shave ⑩ シェービング shē·bin·gu
shaving cream シェービングクリーム
　shē·bin·gu·ku·rī·mu
she 彼女は ka·no·jo wa
sheep 羊 hi·tsu·ji
sheet (bed) シーツ shī·tsu
shelf 棚 ta·na
shellfish 貝 kai
shingles (illness) 帯状疱疹 tai·jō·hō·shin
ship ⑩ 船 fu·ne
shirt シャツ sha·tsu
shoe 靴 ku·tsu
shoe shop 靴屋 ku·tsu·ya
shoot 撃ちます u·chi·mas
shop ⑩ 店 mi·se
shop ⓥ 買い物をします
　kai·mo·no o shi·mas
shopping ⑩ 買い物 kai·mo·no
shopping centre ショッピングセンター
　shop·pin·gu·sen·tā
short (height) 低い hi·ku·i
short (length) 短い mi·ji·kai
shortage 不足 fu·so·ku

short-grain rice ジャポニカ米
　ja·po·ni·ka·mai
shorts 半ズボン han·zu·bon
shoulder 肩 ka·ta
shout ⓥ 怒鳴ります do·na·ri·mas
show ⑩ ショー shō
show ⓥ 見せます mi·se·mas
shower シャワー sha·wā
shrine 神社 jin·ja
shrimp 小エビ ko·e·bi
shut ⓐ 閉まった shi·mat·ta
shy 恥ずかしがり屋の
　ha·zu·ka·shi·ga·ri·ya no
sick 病気の byō·ki no
sick bag 乗り物酔いの袋
　no·ri·mo·no·yoy no fu·ku·ro
side 側 ga·wa
sign ⑩ 標識 hyō·shi·ki
side plate 小皿 ko·za·ra
signature サイン sain
silk ⑩ 絹 ki·nu
silver ⑩ 銀 gin
SIM card SIMカード shi·mu·kā·do
similar よく似た yo·ku ni·ta
simple 単純な tan·jun na
since ... (time) …から ... ka·ra
sing 歌います u·tai·mas
singer 歌手 ka·shu
single (for person) ⓐ 独身 do·ku·shin
single room シングルルーム
　shin·gu·ru·rū·mu
singlet アンダーシャツ an·dā·sha·tsu
sister 姉妹 shi·mai
sit 座ります su·wa·ri·mas
size (general) サイズ sai·zu
skate ⓥ スケート skē·to
skateboarding ⑩ スケートボード
　skē·to·bō·do
ski ⑩ スキー skī
ski ⓥ スキーをします skī o shi·mas
skiing ⑩ スキー skī
skim milk スキムミルク ski·mu·mi·ru·ku
skin 皮膚 hi·fu
skirt スカート skā·to
skull 頭蓋骨 zu·gai·ko·tsu
sky 空 ka·ra
sleep ⓥ 眠ります ne·mu·ri·mas
sleeping bag 寝袋 ne·bu·ku·ro
sleeping berth 寝台 shin·dai
sleeping car 寝台車 shin·dai·sha
sleeping pills 睡眠薬 su·i·min·ya·ku

sleepy 眠い ne·mu·i
slice ⓝ スライス su·rai·su
slide (film) ⓝ スライド su·rai·do
sliding screen 障子 shō·ji
slow ⓐ o·soy
slowly ゆっくり yuk·ku·ri
small 小さい chī·sai
smaller より小さい yo·ri chī·sai
smallest いちばん小さい i·chi·ban chī·sai
smell ⓝ におい ni·oy
smile ⓥ 笑顔 e·ga·o
smoke ⓥ タバコを吸います
　　ta·ba·ko o su·i·mas
smoked (food) ⓐ 燻製 kun·sē
smoking ⓝ 喫煙 kits·en
snack 軽食 kē·sho·ku
snail カタツムリ ka·ta·tsu·mu·ri
snake ヘビ he·bi
snorkelling ⓝ シュノーケリング
　　shu·nō·ke·rin·gu
snow 雪 yu·ki
snowboarding ⓝ スノーボード
　　su·nō·bō·do
snow pea サヤエンドウ sa·ya·en·dō
soap 石鹸 sek·ken
soap opera メロドラマ me·ro·do·ra·ma
soccer サッカー sak·kā
social welfare 社会福祉 sha·kai·fu·ku·shi
socialist 社会主義者 sha·kai·shu·gi·sha
socks 靴下 ku·tsu·shi·ta
soft やわらかい ya·wa·ra·kai
soft drink ソフトドリンク
　　so·fu·to·do·rin·ku
soft-boiled 半熟の han·ju·ku no
soldier 兵士 hē·shi
some いくらかの i·ku·ra ka no
someone 誰か da·re ka
something 何か na·ni ka
sometimes ときどき to·ki·do·ki
son 息子 mu·su·ko
song 歌 u·ta
soon すぐに su·gu ni
sore ⓐ 痛い i·tai
soup スープ sū·pu
soup bowl お椀 o·wan
sour cream サワークリーム
　　sa·wā·ku·rī·mu
south 南 mi·na·mi
souvenir お土産 o·mi·ya·ge
souvenir shop お土産屋 o·mi·ya·ge·ya
soy bean 大豆 dai·zu

soy milk 豆乳 tō·nyū
soy sauce しょう油 shō·yu
space スペース spēs
Spain スペイン spe·in
sparkling wine スパークリングワイン
　　spā·ku·rin·gu·wain
speak 話します ha·na·shi·mas
special ⓐ 特別な to·ku·be·tsu na
specialist 専門家 sem·mon·ka
speed (velocity) ⓝ スピード spī·do
speed limit 制限速度 sē·gen·so·ku·do
spicy スパイシー spai·shī
spider クモ ku·mo
spinach ホウレンソウ hō·ren·sō
spoiled 悪くなった wa·ru·ku nat·ta
spoke スポーク spō·ku
spoon スプーン spūn
sport スポーツ spō·tsu
sports store/shop スポーツ用品店
　　spō·tsu·yō·hin·ten
sportsperson スポーツマン spō·tsu·man
sprain ⓝ 捻挫 nen·za
spring (coil) スプリング sprin·gu
spring (season) 春 ha·ru
spring onion ねぎ ne·gi
square (town) 広場 hi·ro·ba
squid イカ i·ka
stadium スタジアム sta·ji·a·mu
stairway 階段 kai·dan
stale 新鮮じゃない shin·sen ja nai
stamp ⓝ 切手 kit·te
stand-by ticket スタンドバイチケット
　　stan·do·bai·chi·ket·to
star 星 ho·shi
(three-/four-)star (3つ/4つ) 星
　　(mi·tsu/yo·tsu)·bo·shi
start ⓝ スタート stā·to
start ⓥ 始めます ha·ji·me·mas
station 駅 e·ki
stationer's (shop) 文房具 (店)
　　bum·bō·gu(·ten)
statue 像 zō
stay (at a hotel) ⓥ 泊まります
　　to·ma·ri·mas
stay (in one place) ⓥ 滞在します tai·zai
　　shi·mas
steak (beef) ステーキ stē·ki
steal 盗みます nu·su·mi·mas
steamed 蒸して mu·shi·te
steep 急な kyū na
step ⓝ 段 dan

stereo ステレオ ste·re·o
still water 静かな水 shi·zu·ka na mi·zu
stock (food) 食料 sho·ku·ryō
stockings ストッキング stok·kin·gu
stolen 盗まれた nu·su·ma·re·ta
stomach 胃 i
stomachache 腹痛 fu·ku·tsū
stone 石 i·shi
stoned (drugged) ラリった ra·rit·ta
stop (bus, tram, etc) ⑪ 停留所 tē·ryū·jo
stop (cease) ⑪ 止まります to·ma·ri·mas
stop (prevent) ⑪ 止めさせます
　ya·me·sa·se·mas
storm 嵐 a·ra·shi
story 話 ha·na·shi
stove ストーブ stō·bu
straight まっすぐな mas·su·gu na
strange 変な hen na
stranger よそ者 yo·so·mo·no
strawberry イチゴ i·chi·go
stream 流れ na·ga·re
street 道 mi·chi
street market 青空市場 a·o·zo·ra·i·chi·ba
strike ⑪ ストライキ sto·rai·ki
string ひも hi·mo
stroke (health) ⑪ 発作 hos·sa
stroller ベビーカー be·bī·kā
strong 強い tsu·yoy
stubborn 頑固な gan·ko na
student 生徒 sē·to
studio スタジオ sta·ji·o
stupid ばかな ba·ka na
style スタイル stai·ru
subtitles 字幕 ji·ma·ku
suburb 郊外 kō·gai
subway (underpass) 地下道 chi·ka·dō
subway (train) 地下鉄 chi·ka·te·tsu
sugar 砂糖 sa·tō
suitcase スーツケース sūts·kēs
sultana レーズン rē·zun
summer 夏 na·tsu
sun 太陽 tai·yō
sunblock 日焼け止め hi·ya·ke·do·me
sunburn 日焼け hi·ya·ke
sunglasses サングラス san·gu·ras
sunny 晴れた ha·re·ta
sunrise 日の出 hi·no·de
sunscreen 日焼け止め hi·ya·ke·do·me
sunset 日の入り hi·no·i·ri
sunstroke 日射病 nis·sha·byō
supermarket スーパー sū·pā

superstition 迷信 mē·shin
supporter (politics) 支持者 shi·ji·sha
supporter (sport) ファン fan
surf ⑪ サーフィンをします
　sā·fin o shi·mas
surface mail (land) 普通便 fu·tsū·bin
surface mail (sea) 船便 fu·na·bin
surfboard サーフボード sā·fu·bō·do
surfing ⑪ サーフィン sā·fin
surname 名字 myō·ji
surprise 驚き o·do·ro·ki
sushi bar すし屋 su·shi·ya
sweater セーター sē·tā
Sweden スウェーデン swē·den
sweet ⓐ 甘い a·mai
sweets お菓子 o·ka·shi
swelling 腫れ ha·re
swim ⑪ 泳ぎます o·yo·gi·mas
swimming (sport) 水泳 su·i·ē
swimming pool プール pū·ru
swimsuit 水着 mi·zu·gi
Switzerland スイス su·i·su
sword 刀 ka·ta·na
synagogue シナゴーグ shi·na·gō·gu
synthetic 合成の gō·sē no
syringe 注射器 chū·sha·ki

T

table テーブル tē·bu·ru
table (low) ちゃぶ台 cha·bu·dai
table tennis 卓球 tak·kyū
tablecloth テーブルクロス tē·bu·ru·ku·ros
tail 尻尾 ship·po
tailor テーラー tē·rā
take 取ります to·ri·mas
take a photo 写真を撮ります
　sha·shin o to·ri·mas
talk 話します ha·na·shi·mas
tall 高い ta·kai
tampon タンポン tam·pon
tanning lotion 日焼けローション
　hi·ya·ke·rō·shon
tap (music, video) ⑪ テープ tē·pu
tap water 水道水 su·i·dō·su·i
tasty おいしい oy·shī
tatoo 刺青 i·re·zu·mi
tattooing ⑪ 刺青 i·re·zu·mi
tax ⑪ 税金 zē·kin
taxi タクシー tak·shī

taxi stand タクシー乗り場 tak·shi·no·ri·ba
tea (Japanese) お茶 o·cha
tea (Western) 紅茶 kō·cha
tea ceremony 茶道 sa·dō
tea cup 湯飲み茶碗 yu·no·mi·ja·wan
tea garden 茶畑 cha·ba·ta·ke
teacher 教師 kyō·shi
team チーム chī·mu
teapot ティーポット tī·pot·to
teaspoon ティースプーン tī·spūn
technique 技術 gi·ju·tsu
teeth 歯 ha
telegram 電報 dem·pō
telephone ⓝ 電話 den·wa
telephone ⓥ 電話します den·wa shi·mas
telephone box 電話ボックス den·wa·bōk·kus
telephone centre テレフォンセンター te·re·fon·sen·tā
telescope 望遠鏡 bō·en·kyō
television テレビ te·re·bi
tell 言います i·mas
temperature (fever) 体温 tai·on
temperature (weather) 気温 ki·on
temple 寺 te·ra
tennis テニス te·nis
tennis court テニスコート te·nis kō·to
tent テント ten·to
tent peg ペグ pe·gu
terrible ひどい hi·doy
test ⓝ テスト tes·to
thank 感謝します kan·sha shi·mas
that (one) あれ a·re
theatre 劇場 ge·ki·jō
their 彼らの ka·re·ra no
there そこに so·ko ni
thermometer 体温計 tai·on·kē
they 彼らは ka·re·ra wa
thick 厚い a·tsu·i
thief どろぼう do·ro·bō
thin 薄い u·su·i
think 思います o·moy·mas
third 3番の sam·ban no
(to be) thirsty ⓐ のどが渇いた no·do ga ka·wai·ta
this (one) これ ko·re
this month 今月 kon·ge·tsu
this week 今週 kon·shū
this year 今年 ko·to·shi
thread 糸 i·to

throat のど no·do
thrush (health) 口腔カンジダ症 kō·kū kan·ji·da·shō
thunderstorm 嵐 a·ra·shi
ticket 切符 kip·pu
ticket collector 切符回収 kip·pu·kai·shū·ga·ka·ri
ticket machine 切符販売 kip·pu·ham·bai·ki
ticket office 切符売り kip·pu·u·ri·ba
tide 潮 shi·o
tight きつい ki·tsu·i
time 時間 ji·kan
time difference 時差 ji·sa
timetable 時刻表 ji·ko·ku·hyō
tin (can) 缶 kan
tin opener 缶切り kan·ki·ri
tiny とても小さい to·te·mo chī·sai
tip (gratuity) ⓝ チップ chip·pu
tire ⓝ タイヤ tai·ya
tired 疲れた tsu·ka·re·ta
tissues ティッシュ tis·shu
to へ e
toast トースト tōs·to
toaster トースター tōs·tā
tobacco タバコ tabako
tobacconist タバコ屋 ta·ba·ko·ya
tobogganing ⓝ そり so·ri
today 今日 kyō
toe つま先 tsu·ma·sa·ki
tofu 豆腐 tō·fu
together いっしょに is·sho ni
toilet トイレ toy·re
toilet paper トイレットペーパー toy·ret·to·pē·pā
token トークン tō·kun
toll ⓝ 通行料 tsū·kō·ryō
tomato トマト to·ma·to
tomato sauce トマトソース to·ma·to·sō·su
tomorrow 明日 a·shi·ta
tomorrow afternoon 明日の午後 a·shi·ta no go·go
tomorrow evening 明日の夜 a·shi·ta no yo·ru
tomorrow morning 明日の朝 a·shi·ta no a·sa
tonight 今夜 kon·ya
too (expensive etc) すぎる su·gi·ru
too many/much 多すぎます ō·su·gi·mas
tooth 歯 ha
toothache 歯痛 hai·ta

toothbrush 歯ブラシ ha·bu·ra·shi
toothpaste 練り歯磨き ne·ri·ha·mi·ga·ki
toothpick 楊枝 yō·ji
torch (flashlight) 懐中電灯 kai·chū·den·tō
touch ⓥ 触ります sa·wa·ri·mas
tour ⓝ ツアー tsu·ā
tourist 旅行者 ryo·kō·sha
tourist office 観光案内所 kan·kō·an·nai·jo
towel タオル tow·ru
tower 塔 tō
toxic waste 有害廃棄物 yū·gai·hai·ki·bu·tsu
toy shop おもちゃ屋 o·mo·cha·ya
track (path) ⓝ 通路 tsū·ro
track (sport) ⓝ トラック競技
    to·rak·ku·kyō·gi
trade 貿易 bō·e·ki
tradesperson 貿易商 bō·e·ki·shō
traffic 交通 kō·tsū
traffic jam 渋滞 jū·tai
traffic light 信号 shin·gō
trail ⓝ 足跡 a·shi·a·to
train 電車 den·sha
train station 駅 e·ki
tram 市電 shi·den
transfer ⓝ 乗り換え no·ri·ka·e
transit lounge 待合室 ma·chi·ai·shi·tsu
translate 翻訳します hon·ya·ku shi·mas
transport ⓝ 輸送 yu·sō
travel ⓥ 旅行します ryo·kō shi·mas
travel agency 旅行代理店
    ryo·kō·dai·ri·ten
travel sickness 乗り物酔い
    no·ri·mo·no·yoy
travellers cheque トラベラーズチェック
    to·ra·be·rāz·chek·ku
tree 木 ki
trip (journey) 旅 ta·bi
trolley トロリー to·ro·rī
trousers ズボン zu·bon
truck トラック to·rak·ku
true 本当の hon·tō no
try (attempt) ⓥ 試します ta·me·shi·mas
T-shirt Tシャツ tī·sha·tsu
tube (tyre) チューブ chū·bu
tumour 腫瘍 shu·yō
tuna マグロ ma·gu·ro
tune チューン chūn
turkey 七面鳥 shi·chi·men·chō
turn ⓥ 曲がります ma·ga·ri·mas
TV テレビ te·re·bi
tweezers 毛抜き ke·nu·ki

twice 2倍に ni·bai ni
twin beds ツインベッド tsu·in·bed·do
twins 双子 fu·ta·go
two 2 ni
type ⓝ タイプ tai·pu
typical 典型的な ten·kē·te·ki na
typhoon 台風 tai·fū
tyre タイヤ tai·ya

U

ugly みにくい mi·ni·ku·i
ultrasound 超音波 chō·on·pa
umbrella かさ ka·sa
uncomfortable 不安な fu·an na
understand 理解します ri·kai shi·mas
underwear 下着 shi·ta·gi
unemployed 失業した shi·tsu·gyō shi·ta
unfair 不公平な fu·kō·hē na
uniform ⓝ 制服 sē·fu·ku
universe 宇宙 u·chū
university 大学 dai·ga·ku
unleaded 無鉛の mu·en no
unsafe 安全じゃない an·zen ja nai
until (time) まで ma·de
unusual 珍しい me·zu·ra·shī
up 上に u·e ni
uphill 上り坂の no·bo·ri·za·ka no
urgent 緊急の kin·kyū no
urinary infection 尿道炎 nyō·dō·en
USA アメリカ a·me·ri·ka
useful 便利な ben·ri na

V

vacancy 空室の kū·shi·tsu no
    no vacancy 満室 man·shi·tsu
vacant 空いている ai·te i·ru
vacation 休暇 kyū·ka
vaccination 予防注射 yo·bō·chū·sha
vagina ヴァギナ va·gi·na
validate 有効にします yū·kō ni shi·mas
valley 谷 ta·ni
valuable ⓐ 高価な kō·ka na
valuables ⓝ 貴重品 ki·chō·hin
value (price) ⓝ 価値 ka·chi
van バン ban
veal 子牛 ko·u·shi
vegan 厳格な菜食主義者
    gen·ka·ku na sai·sho·ku·shu·gi·sha

vegetable(s) 野菜 ya·sai
vegetables (fried) 野菜炒め
　ya·sai·i·ta·me
vegetarian ベジタリアン be·ji·ta·ri·an
vein 静脈 jō·mya·ku
vending machine 自動販売機
　ji·dō·ham·bai·ki
venereal disease 性病 sē·byō
venue 現場 gem·ba
very とても to·te·mo
video camera ビデオカメラ
　bi·de·o·ka·me·ra
video recorder ビデオレコーダー
　bi·de·o·re·kō·dā
video tape ⓝ ビデオテープ bi·de·o·tē·pu
view ⓝ 眺め na·ga·me
village 村 mu·ra
vinegar 酢 su
vineyard ブドウ畑 bu·dō·ba·ta·ke
virus ウィルス wi·ru·su
visa ビザ bi·za
visit ⓥ 訪問します hō·mon shi·mas
vitamins ビタミン bi·ta·min
vodka ウォッカ wok·ka
voice ⓝ 声 ko·e
volcano 火山 ka·zan
volleyball バレー ba·rē
volume 量 ryō
vote ⓥ 投票します tō·hyō shi·mas

W

wage 賃金 chin·gin
wait (for) ⓥ 待ちます ma·chi·mas
waiter ウェイター wē·tā
waiting room 待合室 ma·chi·ai·shi·tsu
wake (someone) up 起こします
　o·ko·shi·mas
Wales ウェールズ wē·ru·zu
walk 歩きます a·ru·ki·mas
wallet 財布 sai·fu
wall 壁 ka·be
want ⓥ 欲しいです ho·shī des
war 戦争 sen·sō
wardrobe たんす tan·su
warm あたたかい a·ta·ta·kai
warn 警告します kē·ko·ku shi·mas
wash (oneself/something) 洗います
　a·rai·mas

wash cloth (flannel) 洗濯します
　sen·ta·ku shi·mas
washing machine 洗濯機 sen·tak·ki
watch ⓝ 腕時計 u·de·do·kē
watch ⓥ 見ます mi·mas
water 水 mi·zu
water bottle 水筒 su·i·tō
water bottle (hot) ポット pot·to
waterfall 滝 ta·ki
watermelon スイカ su·i·ka
waterproof 防水 bō·su·i
water-skiing ⓝ 水上スキー su·i·jō·skī
wave ⓝ 波 na·mi
way 道 mi·chi
we 私たちは wa·ta·shi·ta·chi wa
weak 弱い yo·wai
wealthy 裕福な yū·fu·ku na
wear 着ます ki·mas
weather 天気 ten·ki
wedding 結婚式 kek·kon·shi·ki
week 週 shū
weekend 週末 shū·ma·tsu
weekly 1週間 is·shū·kan
weight 重さ o·mo·sa
welfare 福祉 fu·ku·shi
well よく yo·ku
west 西 ni·shi
wet ⓐ 濡れている nu·re·te i·ru
whale くじら ku·ji·ra
what なに na·ni
wheel 車輪 sha·rin
wheelchair 車椅子 ku·ru·ma·i·su
when いつ i·tsu
where どこ do·ko
which どちら do·chi·ra
whisky ウィスキー wis·kī
white 白い shi·roy
white (coffee) ホワイト ho·wai·to
white wine 白ワイン shi·ro·wain
who だれ da·re
wholemeal bread ホールミールのパン
　hō·ru·mī·ru no pan
why なぜ na·ze
wide 広く hi·ro·ku
wife 妻 tsu·ma
wild 野生 ya·sē
wild rice ワイルドライス wai·ru·do·rai·su
win ⓥ 勝ちます ka·chi·mas
wind 風 ka·ze

wineglass ワイングラス wain·gu·ra·su
window 窓 ma·do
windscreen フロントガラス
fu·ron·to·ga·ra·su
windsurfing ⓝ ウィンドサーフィン
win·do·sā·fin
wine ワイン wain
wing 翼 tsu·ba·sa
winner 受賞者 ju·shō·sha
winter 冬 fu·yu
with いっしょに is·sho ni
within (an hour) (1時間)内に
(i·chi·ji·kan) nai ni
without なしで na·shi de
wok 中華鍋 chū·ka·na·be
woman 女性 jo·sē
wonderful 素晴らしい su·ba·ra·shī
wood 木 ki
wood-block prints 浮世絵 u·ki·yo·e
wool ウール ū·ru
word 言葉 ko·to·ba
work ⓝ 仕事 shi·go·to
work ⓥ 働きます ha·ta·ra·ki·mas
work experience 職歴 sho·ku·re·ki
work permit 就労許可 shū·rō·kyo·ka
workout ⓝ 練習 ren·shū
world 世界 se·kai
World Cup ワールドカップ
wā·ru·do·kap·pu

worms イモムシ i·mo·mu·shi
worried 心配な shim·pai na
wrist 手首 te·ku·bi
write 書きます ka·ki·mas
writer 作家 sak·ka
wrong 間違った ma·chi·gat·ta

Y

year 年 nen
yellow 黄色い kī·roy
yes はい hai
yesterday きのう ki·nō
yoga ヨガ yo·ga
yogurt ヨーグルト yō·gu·ru·to
you sg あなた a·na·ta
you pl あなたたち a·na·ta·ta·chi
young 若い wa·kai
your あなたの a·na·ta no
youth hostel ユースホステル
yū·su·ho·su·te·ru

Z

zip(per) ジッパー jip·pâ
zodiac 12宮 jū·ni·gū
zoo 動物園 dō·bu·tsu·en
zucchini ズッキーニ zuk·kī·ni

If you're having trouble understanding Japanese, hand over this section to a Japanese-speaking person, show the Japanese text below and they'll be able to look up and show you the English translation.

この日英辞書を使って日本語の言葉の英訳を教えてください。第一列目は五十音順に配列されています。言葉が見つかりましたらこの人に英訳を見せてください。どうもありがとうございます。

The entries in this Japanese–English dictionary are ordered according to the gojūon (or aiueo) system which is widely used in Japan. You won't need to know it for useability, but in case you're interested, the gojūon system converts all terms from Japanese script to our roman script after which they're alphabetised according to the alphabetical order given below. The term gojūon actually means 'fifty-syllabic system' although there are more than 50 different syllables. Once alphabetised, each Japanese word appears in its original script (hiragana, katakana or kanji – for more information see **pronunciation**, page 14), and can easily be looked up by people familiar with the gojūon order.

The order is: **a**-i-u-e-o-**ka**-ga-ki-gi-kya-gya-kyu-gyu-kyo-gyo-ku-gu-ke-ge-ko-go-**sa**-za-shi-ji-sha-ja-shu-ju-sho-jo-su-zu-se-ze-so-zo-**ta**-da-chi-(ji)-cha-chu-cho-tsu-(zu)-te-de-to-do-**na**-ni-nya-nyu-nyo-nu-ne-no-**ha**-ba-pa-hi-bi-pi-hya-bya-pya-hyu-byu-pyu-hyo-byo-pyo-fu-bu-pu-he-be-pe-ho-bo-po-**ma**-mi-mya-myu-myo-mu-me-mo-**ya**-yu-yo-**ra**-ri-rya-ryu-ryo-ru-re-ro-**wa**-n

Verbs in the dictionary are given in their -mas（ます）form (for more information on this, see the **phrasebuilder**, page 25). The symbols ⓝ, ⓐ and ⓥ (indicating noun, adjective and verb) have been added for clarity where an English term could be either.

あ A

愛 ai love ⓝ
愛します ai shi·mas love ⓥ
アイスクリーム ais·ku·rī·mu ice cream
空いている ai·te i·ru vacant
アイルランド ai·ru·ran·do Ireland
アイロン ai·ron iron (for clothes)
青い a·oy blue
青空市場 a·o·zo·ra·i·chi·ba street market
赤い a·kai red
赤ちゃん a·ka·chan baby
明るい a·ka·ru·i light (of colour) ⓐ
赤ワイン a·ka·wain red wine
秋 a·ki autumn • fall
揚げます a·ge·mas fry
朝 a·sa morning

朝ごはん a·sa·go·han breakfast
あさって a·sat·te
　(the) day after tomorrow
足 a·shi foot
脚 a·shi leg (body part)
足首 a·shi·ku·bi ankle
明日 a·shi·ta tomorrow
明日の朝 a·shi·ta no a·sa
　tomorrow morning
明日の午後 a·shi·ta no go·go
　tomorrow afternoon
明日の夜 a·shi·ta no yo·ru
　tomorrow evening
アスピリン as·pi·rin aspirin
あたたかい a·ta·ta·kai warm
頭 a·ta·ma head ⓝ
新しい a·ta·ra·shī new
熱い a·tsu·i hot

熱くなった a·tsu·ku nat·ta **heated**
あと a·to **after**
あとで a·to de **later**
あなた a·na·ta **you** sg
あなたたち a·na·ta·ta·chi **you** pl
危ない a·bu·nai **dangerous**
油 a·bu·ra **oil (food)**
甘い a·mai **sweet** ⓐ
雨 a·me **rain**
アメリカ a·me·ri·ka **USA**
歩きます a·ru·ki·mas **walk**
アルコール a·ru·kō·ru **alcohol**
あれ a·re **that (one)**
アレルギー a·re·ru·gī **allergy**
アントレー an·to·rē **entrée**
案内所 an·nai·jo **information office**
胃 i **stomach**
いい ī **good**
いいえ ī·e **no**
Eメール i·mē·ru **email** ⓝ
医学 i·ga·ku **medicine (study, profession)**
行きます i·ki·mas **go** ⓥ
イギリス i·gi·ri·su **England**
遺失物取扱所 i·shi·tsu·bu·tsu·
　to·ri·a·tsu·kai·jo **lost property office**
医者 i·sha **doctor**
椅子 i·su **chair**
忙しい i·so·ga·shī **busy**
痛み i·ta·mi **pain**
いたんだ i·tan·da **off (spoiled)**
1 i·chi **one**
市場 i·chi·ba **market**
いちばん大きい i·chi·ban ō·kī **biggest**
いちばん小さい i·chi·ban chi·sai **smallest**
いちばん近くの i·chi·ban chi·ka·ku no
　nearest
胃腸炎 i·chō·en **gastroenteritis**
いつ i·tsu **when**
いっしょに is·sho ni **together**
いっぱいの ip·pai no **full**
田舎 i·na·ka **countryside**
犬 i·nu **dog**
今 i·ma **now**
妹 i·mō·to **younger sister**
衣料店 i·ryō·ten **clothing store**
衣類 i·ru·i **clothing**
刺青 i·re·zu·mi **tattoo • tattooing**
色 i·ro **colour**
インターネット in·tā·net·to **Internet**
インターネットカフェ
　in·tā·net·to·ka·fe **Internet café**
インフルエンザ in·fu·ru·en·za
　flu • influenza

ウール ū·ru **wool**
ウェイター wē·tā **waiter**
ウェールズ wē·ru·zu **Wales**
上に u·e ni on • **up**
うしろ u·shi·ro **behind**
後ろの u·shi·ro no **rear (seat etc)** ⓐ
美しい u·tsu·ku·shī **beautiful**
腕 u·de **arm**
腕時計 u·de·do·kē **watch** ⓝ
海 u·mi **sea**
うるさい u·ru·sai **loud • noisy**
運転します un·ten shi·mas **drive**
運転手 un·ten·shu **driver**
運転免許証 un·ten·men·kyo·shō
　drivers licence
絵 e **painting (a work)**
エアコン付きの air·kon·tsu·ki no
　air-conditioned
映画 ē·ga **film (cinema) • movie**
映画館 ē·ga·kan **cinema**
英語 ē·go **English**
ATM ē·ti·e·mu
　automated teller machine (ATM)
駅 e·ki **(train) station**
エコノミークラス e·ko·no·mī·ku·ras
　economy class
エスカレータ es·ka·rē·ta **escalator**
エレベータ e·re·bē·ta **elevator • lift**
エンジン en·jin **engine**
エンターテイメントガイド
　en·tā·tē·men·to·gai·do
　entertainment guide
エンピツ em·pi·tsu **pencil**
おいしい oy·shī **tasty**
往復切符 ō·fu·ku·kip·pu **return ticket**
OL ō·e·ru **female office worker**
大きい ō·kī **big**
オーストラリア ō·sto·ra·rya **Australia**
オートバイ ō·to·bai **motorcycle**
オートマチック ō·to·ma·chik·ku
　automatic ⓐ
大晦日 ō·mi·so·ka **New Year's Eve**
お母さん o·kā·san **mother**
おかしい o·ka·shī **funny**
お金 o·ka·ne **money**
贈物 o·ku·ri·mo·no **gift**
遅れ o·ku·re **delay** ⓝ
起こします o·ko·shi·mas
　wake (someone) up
おじいさん o·jī·san **grandfather**
おしゃぶり o·sha·bu·ri **dummy • pacifier**
遅い o·soy **late**
お茶 o·cha **tea (Japanese)**

為替 ka·wa·se currency exchange
為替レート ka·wa·se·rē·to exchange rate
缶 kan can • tin
缶切り kan·ki·ri can opener • tin opener
換金します kan·kin shi·mas change (money) ⓥ
間欠泉 kan·kets·sen geyser
観光案内所 kan·kō·an·nai·jo tourist office
看護婦 kan·go·fu nurse
感謝している kan·sha shi·te i·ru grateful
勘定 kan·jō bill (restaurant etc) ⓝ
感触 kan·sho·ku feeling (physical)
感染 kan·sen infection
幹線道路 kan·sen dō·ro highway
元旦 gan·tan New Year's Day
黄色い kī·ro·y yellow
気温 ki·on temperature (weather)
聴きます ki·ki·mas listen (to)
既婚 ki·kon married
技術者 gi·ju·tsu·sha engineer
季節 ki·se·tsu season
北 ki·ta north
汚い ki·ta·nai dirty
喫煙 kits·en smoking ⓐ
切って kit·te stamp ⓝ
切符 kip·pu ticket
切符売り kip·pu·u·ri·ba ticket office
切符販売機 kip·pu·ham·bai·ki ticket machine
絹 ki·nu silk ⓝ
きのう ki·nō yesterday
キャンセル kyan·se·ru cancel ⓥ
キャンプ場 kyam·pu·jō camping ground
休暇 kyū·ka holidays • vacation
救急 kyū·kyū emergency
救急車 kyū·kyū·sha ambulance
救急箱 kyū·kyū·ba·ko first-aid kit
宮殿 kyū·den palace
救命胴衣 kyū·me·doy life jacket
今日 kyō today
境界 kyō·kai border
教会 kyō·kai church
教師 kyō·shi teacher
兄弟 kyō·dai brother
キヨスク ki·yos·ku kiosk
義理のお母さん gi·ri no o·kā·san mother-in-law
義理のお父さん gi·ri no o·tō·san father-in-law
切りま ki·ri·mas cut ⓥ
きれいな ki·rē na clean ⓐ
キロ(グラム) ki·ro(·gu·ra·mu) kilo(gram)

キロメートル ki·ro·mē·to·ru kilometre
金 kin gold ⓝ
銀 gin silver ⓝ
禁煙の kin·en no nonsmoking
緊急の kin·kyū no urgent
金庫 kin·ko safe ⓝ
銀行 gin·kō bank (money) ⓝ
銀行口座 gin·kō·za bank account
航空 kō·kū airline
空港 kū·kō airport
空港税 kū·kō·zē airport tax
航空便 kō·kū·bin airmail
空室 kū·shi·tsu vacancy
くし ku·shi comb
苦情 ku·jō complaint
薬 ku·su·ri drug (medicine) • medication
果物 ku·da·mō·no fruit
口 ku·chi mouth
口紅 ku·chi·be·ni lipstick
靴 ku·tsu shoe
靴下 ku·tsu·shi·ta socks
靴屋 ku·tsu·ya shoe shop
首 ku·bi neck
暗い ku·rai dark
クラシックの ku·ra·shik·ku no classical
グラス gu·ra·su glass (for drinking)
グラム gu·ra·mu gram
クリーニング ku·rī·nin·gu cleaning ⓝ
クリーム ku·rī·mu cream
クリスマス ku·ri·su·mas Christmas
車椅子 ku·ru·ma·i·su wheelchair
クレジットカード ku·re·jit·to·kā·do credit card
黒い ku·roy black
クローク ku·rō·ku cloakroom
警官 kē·kan police officer
警察 kē·sa·tsu police
警察署 kē·sa·tsu·sho police station
計算機 kē·san ki calculator
芸術家 gē·ju·tsu·ka artist
軽食 kē·sho·ku snack
携帯電話 kē·tai·den·wa mobile phone
ゲイの gē no gay ⓐ
けが ke·ga injury
劇場 ge·ki·jō play (theatre) ⓝ
劇場 ge·ki·jō theatre
下剤 ge·zai laxative ⓝ
下宿 ge·shu·ku·ya boarding house
ゲストハウス ges·to·how·su guesthouse
血液型 ke·tsu·e·ki·ga·ta blood group
欠点のある ket·ten no a·ru faulty
毛抜き ke·nu·ki tweezers

夫 ot·to husband
お父さん o·tō·san father
弟 o·tō·to younger brother
男の子 o·to·ko no ko boy
おととい o·to·toy
　(the) day before yesterday
踊ります o·do·ri·mas dance
お腹がすいた o·na·ka ga su·i·ta
　(to be) hungry
お兄さん o·nī·san older brother
お姉さん o·nē·san older sister
おばあさん o·bā·san grandmother
おばさん o·ba·san aunt
お話中 o·ha·na·shi·chū engaged (phone)
お風呂 o·fu·ro bath ⓝ
お土産 o·mi·ya·ge souvenir
お土産屋 o·mi·ya·ge·ya souvenir shop
オムツ o·mu·tsu diaper (nappy)
おめでとう o·me·de·tō congratulations
重い o·moy heavy
泳ぎます o·yo·gi·mas swim
オランダ o·ran·da Netherlands
降ります o·ri·mas get off (a train, etc)
オレンジ o·ren·ji orange (fruit)
オレンジ o·ren·ji
　orange (colour)
おわり o·wa·ri end ⓝ
お椀 o·wan miso-soup bowl • soup bowl
音楽 on·ga·ku music
温泉 on·sen mineral hot-spring spa
女の子 on·na no ko girl

か KA

ガールフレンド gā·ru·fu·ren·do
　girlfriend
階 kai floor (storey)
絵画 kai·ga painting (the art)
海外 kai·gai abroad • overseas
外国の gai·ko·ku no foreign
会社 kai·sha company (firm)
快速 kai·so·ku rapid train
階段 kai·dan stairway
懐中電灯 kai·chū·den·tō torch (flashlight)
開店時間 kai·ten·ji·kan opening hours
ガイド gai·do guide (person)
ガイド付きツアー gai·do·tsu·ki·tsu·ā
　guided tour
ガイドブック gai·do·buk·ku guidebook
買います kai·mas buy
買い物をします kai·mo·no o shi·mas
　shop ⓥ

顔 ka·o face
画家 ga·ka painter
科学 ka·ga·ku science
鏡 ka·ga·mi mirror
鍵 ka·gi key
書留 ka·ki·to·me registered mail
書きます ka·ki·mas write
鍵をかけた ka·gi o ka·ke·ta locked
鍵をかけます ka·gi o ka·ke·mas lock ⓥ
家具 ka·gu furniture
カクテル ka·ku·te·ru cocktail
かさ ka·sa umbrella
貸します ka·shi·mas rent ⓥ
ガス gas gas (for cooking)
カセット ka·set·to cassette
家族 ka·zo·ku family
ガソリン ga·so·rin gas • petrol
ガソリンスタンド ga·so·rin·stan·do
　petrol station • service station
肩 ka·ta shoulder
かたい ka·tai hard (not soft)
片道切符 ka·ta·mi·chi·kip·pu
　one-way ticket
月 ga·tsu month
カップ kap·pu cup
カナダ ka·na·da Canada
彼女の ka·no·jo no her (ownership)
彼女は ka·no·jo wa she
彼女を ka·no·jo o her (as object of
　sentence)
カバーチャージ ka·bā·chā·ji cover charge
かばん ka·ban bag
カフェ ka·fe café
カプセルホテル ka·pu·se·ru·ho·te·ru
　capsule hotel
花粉症 ka·fun·shō hay fever
紙 ka·mi paper
剃刀 ka·mi·so·ri razor
剃刀の刃 ka·mi·so·ri no ha razor blade
カメラ ka·me·ra camera
かゆみ ka·yu·mi itch ⓝ
から ka·ra from
空っぽの ka·rap·po no empty
軽い ka·ru·i light (not heavy) ⓐ
彼の ka·re no his
彼は ka·re wa he
彼を ka·re o him
皮 ka·wa leather ⓝ
川 ka·wa river
乾いた ka·wai·ta dry ⓐ
乾かします ka·wa·ka·shi·mas
　dry (clothes) ⓥ

下痢 ge·ri **diarrhoea**
現金 gen·kin **cash**
現金化します gen·kin ka shi·mas
   cash (a cheque) ⓥ
言語 gen·go **language**
建築 ken·chi·ku **architecture**
建築家 ken·chi·ku·ka **architect**
コイン ko·in **coins**
コインランドリー ko·in·ran·do·rī
   launderette
更衣室 kōy·shi·tsu
   changing room (for sport)
公園 kō·en **park** ⓝ
工学 kō·ga·ku **engineering**
高価な kō·ka na **valuable** ⓝ
豪華な gō·ka na **luxury** ⓐ
交換 kō·kan **exchange** ⓝ
交換します kō·kan shi·mas **exchange** ⓥ
航空便 kō·kū·bin **flight**
工芸品 kō·gē·hin **crafts**
公衆電話 kō·shū·den·wa **public telephone**
公衆トイレ kō·shū·toy·re **public toilet**
香水 kō·su·i **perfume**
抗生剤 kō·sē·zai **antibiotics**
高速道路 kō·so·ku·dō·ro
   motorway (tollway)
紅茶 kō·cha **tea (Western)**
交番 kō·ban **police box**
コークスクリュー kō·ku·sku·ryū
   corkscrew
凍った kōt·ta **frozen**
コート kō·to **coat • court (tennis)**
コーヒー kō·hī **coffee**
氷 kō·ri **ice**
小切手 ko·git·te **check (banking)** ⓝ
顧客 ko·kya·ku **client**
午後 go·go **afternoon**
心地よい ko·ko·chi·yoy **comfortable**
ここで ko·ko de **here**
小皿 ko·za·ra **plate (small)**
故障した ko·shō·shi·ta **broken down**
故障中 ko·shō·chū **out of order**
個人的な ko·jin·te·ki na **private**
小銭 ko·ze·ni **change (coins)**
コック kok·ku **cook** ⓝ
小包 ko·zu·tsu·mi
   packet (general) • parcel
子供 ko·do·mo **child • children**
ごはん go·han **rice (cooked)**
小道 ko·mi·chi **path**
ごみ箱 go·mi·ba·ko **garbage can**
米 ko·me **rice (uncooked)**

子守り ko·mo·ri **childminding** ⓝ
ゴルフ go·ru·fu **golf**
ゴルフコース go·ru·fu·kō·su **golf course**
これ ko·re **this (one)**
コレクトコール ko·re·ku·to·kō·ru
   collect call
壊れた ko·wa·re·ta **broken**
壊れやすい ko·wa·re·ya·su·i **fragile**
コンサート kon·sā·to **concert**
コンタクトレンズ kon·ta·ku·to·ren·zu
   contact lenses
コンドーム kon·dō·mu **condom**
コンパニオン kom·pa·ni·on **companion**
コンビニ kom·bi·ni **convenience store**
コンピュータ kom·pyū·ta **computer**
コンファーム kon·fā·mu
   confirm (a booking)
コンファレンス kon·fa·ren·su
   conference (big)
今夜 kon·ya **tonight**
婚約者 kon·ya·ku·sha **fiancé(e)**

さ SA

サーカス sā·kas **circus**
サービス sā·bis **service**
サービス料 sā·bis·ryō **service charge**
最高の sai·kō no **best**
最後の sai·go no **last (final)**
祭日 sai·ji·tsu **public holiday**
(厳格な) 菜食主義者 (gen·ka·ku na)
   sai·sho·ku·shu·gi·sha **vegan**
サイズ sai·zu **size (general)**
財布 sai·fu **purse • wallet**
魚 sa·ka·na **fish**
魚屋 sa·ka·na·ya **fish shop**
酒屋 sa·ka·ya **liquor store**
酒 sa·ke **alcoholic drink • sake**
サッカー sak·kā **football (soccer)**
茶道 sa·dō **tea ceremony**
寒い sa·mu·i **cold (atmosphere)**
皿 sa·ra **dish • plate (big)**
サラリーマン sa·ra·rī·man **business man**
さん ·san **Mr • Mrs • Ms • Miss**
サングラス san·gu·ras **sunglasses**
市 shi **city**
試合 shi·ai **game (sport) • match**
幸せな shi·a·wa·se na **happy**
シーツ shī·tsu **bed linen • sheet (bed)**
シートベルト shī·to·be·ru·to **seatbelt**
ジーンズ jīn·zu **jeans**
シェアします she·a shi·mas

share (a dorm etc) ⓥ
シェービングクリーム
　shē·bin·gu·ku·rī·mu shaving cream
シェフ she·fu chef
時間 ji·kan hour
時間どおり ji·kan·dō·ri on time
事故 ji·ko accident
時刻表 ji·ko·ku·hyō timetable
仕事 shi·go·to job
時差 ji·sa time difference
時差ぼけ ji·sa·bo·ke jet lag
辞書 ji·sho dictionary
静かな shi·zu·ka na quiet
下着 shi·ta·gi underwear
下へ shi·ta e down
試着室 shi·cha·ku·shi·tsu
　changing room (in shop)
失業した shi·tsu·gyō shi·ta unemployed
ジッパー jip·pā zip • zipper
自転車 ji·ten·sha bicycle
自動車 ji·dō·sha car
自動車所有権 ji·dō·sha·sho·yū·ken
　car owner's title
自動車登録 ji·dō·sha·tō·ro·ku
　car registration
自動販売機 ji·dō·ham·bai·ki
　vending machine
市の中心 shi no chū·shin city centre
支払い shi·ha·rai payment
紙幣 shi·hē banknote
島 shi·ma island
姉妹 shi·mai sister
字幕 ji·ma·ku subtitles
閉まった shi·mat·ta shut
ジム ji·mu gym (place)
事務処理 ji·mu·sho·ri paperwork
閉めます shi·me·mas close ⓥ
地元の ji·mo·to local ⓐ
ジャーナリスト jā·na·ris·to journalist
蛇口 ja·gu·chi faucet • tap
ジャケット ja·ket·to jacket
写真 sha·shin photo • photography
写真家 sha·shin·ka photographer
シャツ sha·tsu shirt
シャワー sha·wā shower
シャンペン sham·pen champagne
週 shū week
習慣 shū·kan custom
住所 jū·sho address
充分な jū·bun na enough
週末 shū·ma·tsu weekend
修理します shū·ri shi·mas repair ⓥ

手芸品 shu·gē·hin handicrafts
出張 shut·chō business trip
出発 shup·pa·tsu departure
潤滑油 jun·ka·tsu·yu lubricant
障害をもつ shō·gai o mo·tsu disabled ⓐ
消化不良 shō·ka·fu·ryō indigestion
乗客 jō·kya·ku passenger
正午 shō·go midday • noon
錠剤 jō·zai pill
消臭剤 shō·shū·zai deodorant
消毒剤 shō·do·ku·zai antiseptic ⓝ
乗馬 jō·ba horse riding
情報 jō·hō information
ショー shō show ⓝ
食事 sho·ku·ji meal
食前酒 sho·ku·zen·shu apéritif
食中毒 sho·ku·chū·do·ku food poisoning
食堂車 sho·ku·dō·sha dining car
食料 sho·ku·ryō food supplies
食料品 sho·ku·ryō·hin grocery
女性 jo·sē female • woman
ショッピングセンター
　shop·pin·gu·sen·tā shopping centre
処方箋 sho·hō·sen prescription
書類 sho·ru·i papers (documents)
城 shi·ro castle
白い shi·roy white
白黒 （フィルム）shi·ro·ku·ro (fi·ru·mu)
　B&W (film)
白ワイン shi·ro·wain white wine
新幹線 shin·kan·sen bullet train
シングルルーム shin·gu·ru·rū·mu
　single room
寝室 shin·shi·tsu bedroom
親切 shin·se·tsu na kind (nice)
新鮮な shin·sen na fresh
心臓 shin·zō heart
心臓病 shin·zō·byō heart condition
寝台車 shin·dai·sha sleeping car
新聞 shim·bun newspaper
水筒 su·i·tō water bottle
炊飯器 su·i·han·ki rice cooker
水疱 su·i·hō blister
数字 sū·ji number
スーツケース sūts·kēs suitcase
スーパー sū·pā supermarket
スカート skā·to skirt
スカーフ skā·fu scarf
スキー su·kī skiing ⓥ
好きです su·ki des like ⓥ
すぎる su·gi·ru too (expensive etc)
少ない su·ku·nai less

すぐに su-gu ni **soon**
スコットランド skot-to-ran-do **Scotland**
涼しい su-zu-shī **cool (temperature)**
勧めます su-su-me-mas **recommend** Ⓥ
スタンドバイチケット
　stan-do-bai-chi-ket-to **stand-by ticket**
頭痛 zu-tsū **headache**
ストッキング stok-kin-gu **stockings**
ストライキ sto-rai-ki **strike** Ⓝ
素晴らしい su-ba-ra-shī **great (fantastic)**
スプーン spūn **spoon**
スポーツ用品店 spō-tsu-yō-hin-ten
　sports shop• sports store
ズボン zu-bon **pants • trousers**
スライス su-rai-su **slice**
スライド su-rai-do **slide (film)** Ⓝ
税関 zē-kan **customs**
税金 zē-kin **tax**
制限速度 sē-gen-so-ku-do **speed limit**
生徒 sē-to **student**
生理用ナプキン sē-ri-yō-na-pu-kin
　panty liners • sanitary napkins
セーター sē-tā **jumper • sweater**
セーフセックス sē-fu-sek-kus **safe sex**
セカンドクラス se-kan-do-ku-ras
　second class Ⓝ
席 se-ki **seat (place)**
せきが出ます se-ki ga de-mas **cough** Ⓥ
せき止め se-ki-do-me **cough medicine** Ⓝ
石油 se-ki-yu **oil (petrol)**
セックス sek-kus **sex**
石鹸 sek-ken **soap**
接続 se-tsu-zo-ku **connection (transport)**
背中 se-na-ka **back (body part)**
セルフサービスの se-ru-fu-sā-bis no
　self service
栓 sen **plug (bath)**
前菜 zen-sai **appetiser**
洗濯場 sen-ta-ku-ba **laundry (place)**
洗濯物 sen-ta-ku-mo-no **laundry (clothes)**
洗濯機 sen-tak-ki **washing machine**
センチ sen-chi **centimetre**
銭湯 sen-tō **bath house • public baths**
栓抜き sen-nu-ki **bottle opener**
全部 zem-bu **all • everything**
掃除をします sō-ji o shi-mas **clean** Ⓥ
連速 so-ku-ta-tsu **express (mail)** Ⓝ
そこに so-ko ni **there**
そして so-shi-te **and**
外側の so-to-ga-wa no **outside**
剃ります so-ri-mas **shave** Ⓥ

それぞれ so-re-zo-re **each**

た TA

ダイアルトーン dai-a-ru-tōn **dial tone**
大学 dai-ga-ku **university**
退屈な tai-ku-tsu na **boring**
大使館 tai-shi-kan **embassy**
大聖堂 dai-sē-dō **cathedral**
台所 dai-do-ko-ro **kitchen**
たいへんな tai-hen na **hard (not easy)**
タイヤ tai-ya **tire • tyre**
太陽 tai-yō **sun**
タオル tow-ru **towel**
高い ta-kai **expensive • high**
タクシー tak-shī **taxi**
タクシー乗り場 tak-shī-no-ri-ba **taxi stand**
たすけ tas-ke **help** Ⓥ
たすけます tas-ke-mas **help** Ⓥ
脱脂綿 das-shi-men **cotton balls**
建物 ta-te-mo-no **building**
タバコ ta-ba-ko **cigarette**
タバコを吸います ta-ba-ko o su-i-mas
　smoke Ⓥ
旅 ta-bi **journey**
ダブルベッド da-bu-ru-bed-do
　double bed
ダブルルーム da-bu-ru-rū-mu
　double room
食べます ta-be-mas **eat**
食べ物 ta-be-mo-no **food**
だれ da-re **who**
誕生日 tan-jō-bi **birthday • date of birth**
ダンス dan-su **dancing** Ⓝ
タンポン tam-pon **tampon**
血 chi **blood**
小さい chī-sai **small**
チーズ chī-zu **cheese**
チーム chī-mu **team**
チェックイン chek-ku-in
　check-in (desk)
違う chi-ga-u **different**
近く chi-ka-ku **close • near • nearby**
地下鉄の駅 chi-ka-te-tsu no eki
　metro station
地下道 chi-ka-dō **subway (underpass)**
地図 chi-zu **map**
チップ chip-pu **tip (gratuity)** Ⓝ
チャイルドシート chai-ru-do-shī-to
　child seat

茶色い chai-ro-i **brown** (a)
茶畑 cha-ba-ta-ke **tea garden**
茶碗 cha-wan **rice bowl**
中央 chū-ō **centre**
中止 chū-shi **intermission**
注射 chū-sha **injection**
駐車します chū-sha shi-mas **park (a car)** (v)
駐車場 chū-sha-jō **carpark**
注射針 chū-sha-ba-ri **needle (syringe)**
昼食 chū-sho-ku **lunch**
超過 chō-ka **excess (baggage)**
彫刻 chō-ko-ku **sculpture**
朝食 chō-sho-ku **breakfast**
ちょうど chō-do **exactly**
直接に cho-ku-se-tsu ni **direct**
直通 cho-ku-tsū **direct-dial**
チョコレート cho-ko-rē-to **chocolate**
賃貸します chin-tai shi-mas **hire** (v)
鎮痛剤 chin-tsū-zai **painkiller**
ツアー tsu-ā **tour**
ツインベッド tsu-in-bed-do **twin beds**
通信社 tsū-shin-sha **newsagency**
通訳 tsū-ya-ku **interpreter**
通路 tsū-ro **aisle (on plane)**
疲れた tsu-ka-re-ta **tired**
つぎ tsu-gi **next**
包み tsu-tsu-mi **package**
妻 tsu-ma **wife**
つまります tsu-ma-ri-mas **blocked**
爪切 tsu-me-ki-ri **nail clippers**
冷たい tsu-me-tai **cold (to the touch)** (a)
釣り tsu-ri **fishing** (n)
手 te **hand**
で de **at**
Tシャツ tī-sha-tsu **T-shirt**
ティースプーン tī-spūn **teaspoon**
ティーポット tī-pot-to **teapot**
ティッシュ tis-shu **tissues**
テーラー tē-rā **tailor**
手形 te-ga-ta **check (bill)**
出かけます de-ka-ke-mas **go out**
手紙 te-ga-mi **letter (mail)**
出口 de-gu-chi **exit** (n)
デザート de-zā-to **dessert**
手数料 te-sū-ryō **commission**
手作りの te-zu-ku-ri no **handmade**
テニス te-nis **tennis**
テニスコート te-nis kō-to **tennis court**
手荷物 te-ni-mo-tsu **baggage • luggage**
手荷物預かり所 te-ni-mo-tsu-a-zu-ka-ri-sho

left luggage (office)
手荷物許容量 te-ni-mo-tsu-kyo-yō-ryō
baggage allowance
デパート de-pā-to **department store**
手袋 te-bu-ku-ro **gloves**
寺 te-ra **temple**
デリカテッセン de-ri-ka-tes-sen
delicatessen
テレビ te-re-bi **television**
テレフォンカード te-re-fon-kā-do
phone card
電化製品店 den-ka-sē-hin **electrical store**
電気 den-ki **electricity • light**
電気技師 den-ki-gi-shi **electrician**
伝言 den-gon **message**
電車 den-sha **train**
電子レンジ den-shi-ren-ji
microwave (oven)
電池 den-chi **battery (general)**
電報 dem-pō **telegram**
展覧会 ten-ran-kai **exhibition**
電流 den-ryū **current (electricity)**
電話 den-wa **telephone • phone call** (n)
電話します den-wa shi-mas **telephone** (v)
電話帳 den-wa-chō **phone book**
電話番号 den-wa-ban-gō **phone number**
電話ボックス den-wa-bok-kus **phone box**
ドイツ doy-tsu **Germany**
トイレ toy-re **toilet**
トイレットペーパー toy-ret-to-pē-pā
toilet paper
搭乗券 tō-jō-ken **boarding pass**
到着 tō-cha-ku **arrivals**
糖尿病 tō-nyō-byō **diabetes**
動物園 dō-bu-tsu-en **zoo**
同僚 dō-ryo **colleague**
遠い tôy **far**
トースター tōs-tā **toaster**
トースト tōs-to **toast**
独身 do-ku-shin **single (person)**
毒の do-ku no **poisonous**
どこ do-ko **where**
図書館 to-sho-kan **library**
どちら do-chi-ra **which**
飛びます to-bi-mas **fly** (v)
友達 to-mo-da-chi **friend**
トラベラーズチェック
to-ra-be-rāz-chek-ku **travellers cheque**
鶏肉 to-ri-ni-ku **chicken (meat)**
努力します do-ryo-ku shi-mas **try** (v)

ドル do·ru **dollar**
ドレス do·res **dress**
トロリー to·ro·rī **trolley**

な NA

ナイトクラブ nai·to·ku·ra·bu **nightclub**
ナイフ nai·fu **knife**
ナイフとフォーク nai·fu to fō·ku
    cutlery (lit: knife and fork)
なか na·ka **in**
長い na·gai **long**
眺め na·ga·me **view**
なくした na·ku·shi·ta **lost**
なしで na·shi de **without**
なぜ na·ze **why**
夏 na·tsu **summer**
なに na·ni **what**
何もない na·ni·mo nai **nothing**
ナプキン na·pu·kin **napkin**
名前 na·ma·e **name** ⓝ
南京錠 nan·kin·jō **padlock**
2 ni **two**
におい ni·oy **smell** ⓝ
肉 ni·ku **meat**
肉屋 ni·ku·ya **butcher's shop**
西 ni·shi **west**
2週間 ni·shū·kan **fortnight**
日記 nik·ki **diary**
日中 nit·chū **day**
ニュージーランド nyū·jī·ran·do
    New Zealand
入場 nyū·jō **entry**
入場料 nyū·jō·ryō **admission (price)**
ニュース nyū·su **news**
庭 ni·wa **garden**
妊娠している nin·shin shi·te i·ru **pregnant**
盗まれた nu·su·ma·re·ta **stolen**
値段 ne·dan **price**
熱 ne·tsu **heat • fever**
寝袋 ne·bu·ku·ro **sleeping bag**
眠ります ne·mu·ri·mas **sleep** ⓥ
練り歯磨き ne·ri·ha·mi·ga·ki **toothpaste**
年 nen **year**
年金者 nen·kin·sha **pensioner**
捻挫 nen·za **sprain** ⓝ
脳しんとう nō·shin·tō **concussion**
ノート nō·to **notebook**
乗って not·te **aboard**
のど no·do **throat**

のどが渇い no·do ga ka·wai·ta
    (to be) thirsty
飲みます no·mi·mas **drink** ⓥ
飲み物 no·mi·mo·no **drink** ⓝ
乗り換え no·ri·ka·e **transfer** ⓝ
乗ります no·ri·mas
    board (a plane, ship etc)
乗り物酔い no·ri·mo·no·yoy
    travel sickness

は HA

バー bā **bar**
パーティー pā·tī **party** (night out)
パートナー pā·to·nā **partner** (intimate)
はい hai **yes**
灰色の hai·ro no **grey • grey**
廃墟 hai·kyo **ruins**
ハイキング hai·kin·gu **hiking** ⓝ
灰皿 hai·za·ra **ashtray**
歯医者 ha·i·sha **dentist**
売春 bai·shun **prostitute**
歯痛 hai·ta **toothache**
配達します hai·ta·tsu shi·mas **deliver**
俳優 hai·yū **actor**
入ります hai·ri·mas **enter**
はがき ha·ga·ki **postcard**
吐き気 ha·ki·ke **nausea**
博物館 ha·ku·bu·tsu·kan **museum**
箱 ha·ko **box**
ハサミ ha·sa·mi **scissors**
橋 ha·shi **bridge**
箸 ha·shi **(pair of) chopsticks**
はしけ ha·shi·ke **lighter**
(市)バス (shi·)bas **bus** (city)
(長距離)バス (chō·kyo·ri·)bas
    bus (intercity)
バスターミナル bas·tā·mi·na·ru
    bus station
バス停 bas·tê **bus stop**
パスポート pas·pô·to **passport**
パスポート番号 pas·pô·to·ban·gô
    passport number
罰金 bak·kin **fine (penalty)**
バックパック bak·ku·pak·ku **backpack**
バッゲージクレーム bag·gê·ji·ku·rê·mu
    baggage claim
鼻 ha·na **nose**
話します ha·na·shi·mas **speak**
花屋 ha·na·ya **florist**
ハネムーン ha·ne·mûn **honeymoon**
パブ pa·bu **pub (bar)**

歯ブラシ ha·bu·ra·shi toothbrush
葉巻 ha·ma·ki cigar
速い ha·yai fast
早く ha·ya·ku early
払い戻し ha·rai·mo·do·shi refund ⓝ
針 ha·ri needle (sewing)
春 ha·ru spring (season)
晩 ban evening
パン pan bread
ハンカチ han·ka·chi handkerchief
晩ごはん ban·go·han dinner
半ズボン han·zu·bon shorts
バンド ban·do band (music)
バンドエイド ban·do·ēdo Band-Aids
ハンドバッグ han·do·bag·gu handbag
パンフレット pan·fu·ret·to brochure
半分 ham·bun half
パン屋 pan·ya bakery
ヒーター hī·tā heater
ビーチ bī·chi beach
ビール bī·ru beer
日陰 hi·ka·ge shade
東 hi·ga·shi east
低い hi·ku·i short (height)
ピクニック pi·ku·nik·ku picnic
飛行機 hi·kō·ki aeroplane • airplane
ひざ hi·za knee
ビザ bi·za visa
ビジネス bi·ji·nes business
ビジネスクラス bi·ji·nes·ku·ras
    business class
ビジネスマン bi·ji·nes·man business
    person
美術 bi·ju·tsu art
美術館 bi·ju·tsu·kan art gallery
左 hi·da·ri left (direction)
日付 hi·zu·ke date (day)
ヒッチハイク hit·chi·hai·ku hitchhike
ビデオカメラ bi·de·o·ka·me·ra
    video camera
ビデオテープ bi·de·o·tē·pu video tape
ビデオレコーダー bi·de·o·re·kō·dā
    video recorder
人 hi·to man (human being) • person
ひどい hi·doy awful
一晩 hi·to·ban overnight
ひとりで hi·to·ri de alone
日の入り hi·no·i·ri sunset
日の出 hi·no·de sunrise
日焼け hi·ya·ke sunburn
日焼け止め hi·ya·ke·do·me sunblock
日焼けローション hi·ya·ke·rō·shon

tanning lotion
ビュッフェ byuf·fe buffet
病院 byō·in hospital
費用がかかります hi·yō ga ka·ka·ri·mas
    cost ⓥ
病気の byō·ki no ill • sick
美容師 bi·yō·shi hairdresser
昼ごはん hi·ru·go·han lunch
広場 hi·ro·ba square (town) ⓝ
ビン bin bottle
ピンクの pin·ku no pink
ピンボール pin·bō·ru pinball
ファーストクラス fā·sto·ku·ras
    first class ⓝ
ファックス fak·kus fax • fax machine
不安な fu·an na uncomfortable
フィルム fi·ru·mu film (for camera)
フィルムの感度 fi·ru·mu no kan·do
    film speed
封筒 fū·tō envelope
プール pū·ru swimming pool
フェリー fe·rī ferry ⓝ
フォーク fō·ku fork
不可能な fu·ka·nō na impossible
腹痛 fu·ku·tsū stomachache
含んで fu·kun·de included
普通便 fu·tsū·bin surface mail (land)
不動産屋 fu·dō·san·ya estate agency
太った fu·tot·ta fat ⓐ
ふとん fu·ton futon
船便 fu·na·bin surface mail (sea)
船 fu·ne boat
冬 fu·yu winter
フライパン fu·rai·pan frying pan
プラグ pu·ra·gu plug (electricity)
ブラシ bu·ra·shi brush ⓝ
ブラジャー bu·ra·jā bra
プラットフォーム pu·rat·to·fō·mu
    platform
ブリーフケース bu·rī·fu·kēs briefcase
フリーマーケット fu·rī·mä·ket·to
    fleamarket
プリンタ pu·rin·ta printer (computer)
古い fu·ru·i old
ブレーキ bu·rē·ki brakes
フレーズブック fu·rē·zu·buk·ku
    phrasebook
プレゼント pu·re·zen·to present (gift) ⓝ
フロッピー fu·rop·pī disk (floppy)
風呂場 fu·ro·ba bathroom
分 fun minute

文房具 (店) bum·bō·gu(·ten) stationer's (shop)
へ e to
ヘアカット hair·kat·to haircut
閉店した hē·ten·shi·ta closed
ベジタリアン be·ji·ta·ri·an vegetarian ⓝ
ベッド bed·do bed
ヘッドライト hed·do·rai·to headlights
ペニシリン pe·ni·shi·rin penicillin
ペニス pe·nis penis
ベビーカー be·bī·kā stroller
ベビーシッター be·bi·shit·tā babysitter
部屋 he·ya room
ペン pen pen (ballpoint)
変化 hen·ka change ⓝ
弁護士 ben·go·shi lawyer
ペンナイフ pen·nai·fu penknife
法学 hō·ga·ku law (study, professsion)
方向 hō·kō direction
帽子 bō·shi hat
宝石 hō·se·ki jewellery
包帯 hō·tai bandage
ボーイフレンド bōy·fu·ren·do boyfriend
ボール bō·ru bowl
ほかの ho·ka no other
保険 ho·ken insurance
保証された ho·shō sa·re·ta guaranteed
墓地 bo·chi cemetery
ポット pot·to water bottle (hot)
ホテル ho·te·ru hotel
歩道 ho·dō footpath
ホモ ho·mo homosexual ⓝ
本 hon book ⓝ
ポンド pon·do pound (money, weight)
本屋 hon·ya bookshop
翻訳します hon·ya·ku shi·mas translate

ま MA

毎 mai every
毎 mai per (day etc)
毎日 mai·ni·chi daily
前 ma·e before
前の ma·e no last (previous)
枕 ma·ku·ra pillow
枕カバー ma·ku·ra·ka·bā pillowcase
孫 ma·go grandchild
また ma·ta again
待合室 ma·chi·ai·shi·tsu transit lounge · waiting room
待ちます ma·chi·mas wait (for) ⓥ
マッサージ mas·sā·ji massage

マッチ mat·chi matches (for lighting)
マットレス mat·to·res mattress
まで ma·de until (time)
窓 ma·do window
マネージャー ma·nē·jā manager (restaurant, hotel)
麻薬 ma·ya·ku drug (narcotic)
真夜中 ma·yo·na·ka midnight
マリファナ ma·ri·fa·na dope (drugs)
漫画 man·ga comics
満室 man·shi·tsu no vacancy
マンション man·shon apartment
ミーティング mī·tin·gu conference (small)
右 mi·gi right (direction) ⓐ
短い mi·ji·kai short (length)
水 mi·zu water
湖 mi·zū·mi lake
水着 mi·zu·gi swimsuit
店 mi·se shop ⓝ
見せます mi·se·mas show ⓥ
味噌汁 mi·so·shi·ru miso-soup
道 mi·chi street · road
緑の mi·do·ri no green
南 mi·na·mi south
ミネラルウォーター mi·ne·ra·ru·wō·tā mineral water
身分証明 mi·bun·shō·mē identification
身分証明書 mi·bun·shō·mē·sho identification card (ID)
耳 mi·mi ear
ミリ (メートル) mi·ri(·mē·to·ru) millimetre
ミルク mi·ru·ku milk
みんな min·na everyone
息子 mu·su·ko son
娘 mu·su·me daughter
胸 mu·ne chest (body part)
無料の mu·ryō no free (gratis) · complimentary (free)
目 me eye
名刺 mē·shi business card
メインコース mēn·kō·su main course
メーキャップ mē·kyap·pu make-up
メートル mē·to·ru metre
眼鏡 me·ga·ne glasses (spectacles)
目覚し時計 me·za·ma·shi do·kē alarm clock
珍しい me·zu·ra·shī rare (uncommon)
メニュー me·nyū menu
綿 men cotton
もう一つの mō·hi·to·tsu no another
毛布 mō·fu blanket

モーテル mō·te·ru **motel**
目的地 mo·ku·te·ki·chi **destination**
モダンな mo·dan na **modern**
持っています mot·te i·mas **have**
もっと mot·to **more**
モデム mo·de·mu **modem**
もどります mo·do·ri·mas
　return (come back) ⓥ
森 mo·ri **forest**

や YA

薬剤師 ya·ku·zai·shi **chemist (person)**
野菜 ya·sai **vegetable**
安い ya·su·i **cheap**
薬局 yak·kyo·ku **chemist (shop)・pharmacy**
山 ya·ma **mountain**
有効にします yū·kō ni shi·mas **validate**
夕食 yū·sho·ku **dinner**
ユースホステル yū·su·ho·su·te·ru
　youth hostel
郵送 yū·sō **mail (letters)**
郵便局 yū·bin **mail (postal system)**
郵便局 yū·bin·kyo·ku **post office**
郵便番号 yū·bin·ban·gō **postcode**
郵便ポスト yū·bin·pos·to **mailbox**
ユーロ yū·ro **euro**
雪 yu·ki **snow**
ゆっくり yuk·ku·ri **slowly**
湯飲み茶碗 yu·no·mi·ja·wan **tea cup**
yu·bi **finger**
指 yu·bi·wa **ring (on finger)** ⓝ
夜明け yo·a·ke **dawn**
夜遊び yo·a·so·bi **night out**
ヨーロッパ yō·rop·pa **Europe**
預金 yo·kin **credit・deposit (bank)**
横 yo·ko **beside**
予算 yo·san **budget**
酔った yot·ta **drunk** ⓐ
呼びます yo·bi·mas **call** ⓥ
予防注射 yo·bō·chū·sha **vaccination**
予約 yo·ya·ku **appointment・**
　reservation (booking)
予約します yo·ya·ku shi·mas
　book (make a booking) ⓥ
より大きい yo·ri ō·ki **bigger**
より小さい yo·ri chī·sai **smaller**
より良い yo·ri yoy **better**

夜 yo·ru **night**

ら RA

来(月) rai(·ge·tsu) **next (month)**
ライター rai·tā **cigarette lighter**
ラジオ ra·ji·o **radio**
ラップトップ rap·pu·top·pu **laptop**
離婚した ri·kon shi·ta **divorced**
離乳食 ri·nyū·sho·ku **baby food**
リネン ri·nen **linen (sheets etc)**
リフト ri·fu·to **chairlift (skiing)**
リモコン ri·mo·kon **remote control**
料金 ryō·kin **fare・toll**
領事館 ryō·ji·kan **consulate**
両親 ryō·shin **parents**
両方 ryō·hō **both**
料理します ryō·ri shi·mas **cook** ⓥ
旅館 ryo·kan **traditional Japanese inn**
旅行代理店 ryo·kō·dai·ri·ten
　travel agency
旅行日程 ryo·kō·nit·tē **itinerary**
リンネル rin·ne·ru **linen (material)**
ルームナンバー rū·mu·nam·bā
　room number
冷蔵庫 rē·zō·ko **fridge・refrigerator**
レインコート re·in·kō·to **raincoat**
レコード店 re·kō·do·ten **music shop**
レジ re·ji **cashier・cash register**
レシート re·shī·to **receipt**
レズ re·zu **lesbian**
レストラン res·to·ran **restaurant**
レンズ ren·zu **lens**
レンタカー ren·ta·kā **car hire**
ローカル線 rō·ka·ru·sen
　local train (country)
ロッカー rok·kā **luggage lockers**
ロック rok·ku **rock (music)** ⓝ
露天風呂 ro·tem·bu·ro **open-air baths**
ロマンチックな ro·man·chik·ku na
　romantic
ワイン wain **wine**

わ WA

分け合います wa·ke·ai·mas
　share (with)
私たちの wa·ta·shi·ta·chi no **our**
私の wa·ta·shi no **my**
私は wa·ta·shi wa **I**
私を wa·ta·shi o **me**
割引 wa·ri·bi·ki **discount**
悪い wa·ru·i **bad**

What kind of traveller are you?

A. You're eating chicken for dinner *again* because it's the only word you know.

B. When no one understands what you say, you step closer and shout louder.

C. When the barman doesn't understand your order, you point frantically at the beer.

D. You're surrounded by locals, swapping jokes, email addresses and experiences – other travellers want to borrow your phrasebook or audio guide.

If you answered A, B, or C, you NEED Lonely Planet's language products ...

- **Lonely Planet Phrasebooks** – for every phrase you need in every language you want

- **Lonely Planet Language & Culture** – get behind the scenes of English as it's spoken around the world – learn and laugh

- **Lonely Planet Fast Talk & Fast Talk Audio** – essential phrases for short trips and weekends away – read, listen and talk like a local

- **Lonely Planet Small Talk** – 10 essential languages for city breaks

- **Lonely Planet Real Talk** – downloadable language audio guides from lonelyplanet.com to your MP3 player

... and this is why

- **Talk to everyone everywhere**
  Over 120 languages, more than any other publisher

- **The right words at the right time**
  Quick-reference colour sections, two-way dictionary, easy pronunciation, every possible subject – and audio to support it

Lonely Planet Offices

Australia
90 Maribyrnong St, Footscray,
Victoria 3011
☎ 03 8379 8000
fax 03 8379 8111
✉ talk2us@lonelyplanet.com.au

USA
150 Linden St, Oakland,
CA 94607
☎ 510 250 6400
fax 510 893 8572
✉ info@lonelyplanet.com

UK
2nd floor, 186 City Rd
London EC1V 2NT
☎ 020 7106 2100
fax 020 7106 2101
✉ go@lonelyplanet.co.uk

lonelyplanet.com